IB French B

SL and HL

Marie-Laure Delvallée

About this book:

This book is designed to assist with revision for the various aspects of the new French B course (*first examination May 2013*), at both Standard and Higher Levels. These aspects comprise the Oral, the Text Handling (*Paper 1*), the Written Assignment and the Written Production (*Paper 2*). Within the book, you will find examples of types of texts as well as examples and / or practice exercises or questions for both question papers.

You will also find guidelines and advice on how to approach the Oral examinations, for the Individual Oral and some techniques to help with the Interactive Oral.

Wherever possible, texts and questions are intended to represent as closely as possible the style of material used by the International Baccalaureate Organisation but bear in mind that there is probably no better material to revise and practice than past IB papers themselves; even if they were primarily designed for the old syllabus.

In addition, you will find sections containing grammatical advice, intended to consolidate your own knowledge of French grammar. These are presented in clear, easy to read boxes, with checklists to assist you in your revision. This book won't teach you how to do the exams, but what you will hopefully find are some tips and hints, as well as some techniques which will help to maximise your performance in the exam. There are also practice exercises for you to complete if you wish too! One of the aims of this book is also to help you find out what aspects of the course you need to devote more revision time to.

This guide does not pretend to bring you all the answers. It does not replace the essential hard work that, I am sure, you have put in over the past year and a half. It is only a revision guide and can only go into so much detail.

NB: *This book is intended for SL and HL Levels students alike. Both levels are similar in terms of the main aspects of the programme (Core Topics and options) and in their requirements as far as the format of some of the tasks is concerned. However, a distinction will be made in chapters when requirements and level of tasks differ between the two levels.*

In order to help you navigate your way through this guide better, below are a few hints to explain the symbols used:

More specific to HL students…	*Whenever this box appears at the top of a page, this means that the material covered is only relevant to Higher Level students.*
→	*An arrow at the beginning of a sentence points out that an example is given.*
⚠	*The triangle sign is the "danger" sign. It is designed to attract your attention to a particular point of interest; a grammar exception for example.*
Let's practise !	*To indicate a practice exercise or activity.*
	All the examples of texts are in slightly coloured boxes.

Once again, I hope that you will find this guide helpful and user-friendly. It is meant to be a practical and hands-on guide and there are even a couple of pages for your notes at the end. All the best for the forthcoming exam and... ***Au travail!***

Contents

General Introduction

As this is a revision book only, I expect that you are familiar with the requirements of the French B exam components, their length and their value in terms of marks awarded. However, before we start looking in detail at the different components of the exam, and in case you are picking up this guide at the beginning of your IB adventure, here is a refresher of what it comprises:

Whether you are a **HL** or **SL** student, you need to study at least two aspects of each of the following **Core topics** detailed below along with at least two aspects of **2** of the **Options** also highlighted below:

Relations sociales

- La famille et les amis
- Les discriminations / préjugés
- Le concept d'identité
- L'éducation
- Tabous sociaux

Etc.

Communication et medias

- La presse
- Internet , facebook
- Les téléphones portables
- L'influence des médias
- La censure

Etc.

Questions mondiales

- L'environnement
- La crise alimentaire
- Le trafic d'organes
- Les conflits (*guerre et paix*)
- Le terrorisme

Etc.

OPTIONS

Les Loisirs

- Sports
- Voyages
- Spectacles

Etc.

Coutumes et traditions

- Codes vestimentaires
- Traditions culinaires
- Rites religieux
- Etc.

Sciences et technologie

- Expérimentations
- Ethiques et sciences

Etc.

La santé

- Épidémies
- Chirurgie
- Accoutumances (*drogues / tabac…*)

Etc.

La diversité culturelle

- Diversité linguistique
- Sous-cultures
- Mariages mixtes

Etc.

NB: *It is worth noting that those are only examples of possible topics / sub-topics to explore. The list is endless so don't panic if the topics / themes that you have studied don't appear in the above diagrams. They are still valid and will still come under one of the Core topics or one of the Option topics as appropriate. If you are not sure which one they come under, why not ask your teacher to shed light on it all?*

And…

More specific to HL students…

Littérature

Étude obligatoire de ***2 œuvres*** littéraires.

It may be novels, plays, a collection of short stories or poems. They do not have to be linked between them by a genre, author, period topic etc.

What does studying Literature mean for me as a B HL student? Well; it is not about literary analysis, but it is mainly about:

- understanding the story / plot
- understanding the characters
- understanding / studying themes covered in the book, play, short story etc.
- vocabulary and language acquisition
- being able to produce my own piece of creative writing inspired by an aspect of one of the literary work I have studied

This is only a brief outline of the course requirements with which I am sure you are familiar by now.

Of course, as a true IB learner, you will have been inquisitive, open-minded, etc. all the way through the learning process and within your French B class, you will have encountered and discussed many thought provoking topics and let the Theory of Knowledge in on many occasions.

You must also bear in mind the notion of "***dimension internationale***" (international mindedness). This is not being directly assessed but it is an integral part of Language learning.

What does this mean?
Learning a language goes hand in hand with looking at the culture(s) of the people who speak that language. For French, this means France and French speaking countries too. It means exploring new customs, traditions, different ways of apprehending the world and different ways of thinking. So hopefully, throughout your linguistic journey, you will have been curious and open minded and this will be reflected in some ways in your work.

An overview of the evaluation per level and per component

HL

	CORE	OPTIONS	LITERATURE	*Percentage of final mark*
Paper 1	✓			25% *(mark out of 60)*
Paper 2 Section A		✓		*(Mark out of 25)* 25%
Paper 2 Section B	✓			*(Mark out of 20)*
Written Assignment			✓	20% *(mark out of 25)*
individual oral		✓		20% *(mark out of 20)*
Interactive oral	✓			10% (mark out of 10)

SL

	CORE	OPTIONS	*Percentage of final mark*
Paper 1	✓		25% *(mark out of 45)*
Paper 2		✓	25% *(mark out of 25)*
Written Assignment	✓		20% *(mark out of 25)*
Individual oral		✓	20% *(mark out of 20)*
Interactive oral	✓		10% *(mark out of 10)*

Note that it is essential to familiarise yourself with the assessment criteria and understand what is expected of you in each component / paper and at each level. If you do not have a copy of each specific set of criteria, ask your teacher (***en français***) to provide you with one (exemplaire en français aussi!)!

Chapter 1: **Paper 1 or text handling *(receptive skills)***

At both SL and HL levels, Paper 1 lasts 1h30.
You must make sure that you manage your time efficiently in order to answer ALL the questions. Don't leave any blanks. Try and find an answer even if you are not sure as no marks will be deducted if you get it wrong!

Paper 1 represents 25% of your final mark. You will have 45 questions at SL and 60 at HL.

The texts will be on topics studied as part of the **CORE**.

A) **The texts**

At **Standard Level**, Paper 1 is made up of 4 texts all of a different nature. For example, you might have an article, a film review, a speech and a brochure.

At **Higher Level**, your paper will contain 5 texts and one of these texts will be of a literary nature / a literary text. This can be an extract from a novel, a short story or a play for example. Note that you will not be asked to analyse the text using specific literary terms. However, you will have questions to test both your comprehension of the text and maybe even a few questions on the images in the extract or the tone of the passage.

All the texts will be of a different level of difficulty. Some will be easier than others. Text A is generally the easiest but bear in mind that everyone is different in his or her approach to texts and a text that others may find difficult, you may find easy (and vice versa). So don't panic if you find the first text difficult. Move on and come back to it later. All texts will have some connection with an aspect of Francophone culture (*la francophonie*)

B) **The questions**

In Paper 1, the questions are designed to test your general comprehension of any given text in the target language. You will also have to try and understand the meaning of words and expressions in context and to find very precise and detailed pieces of information. Some questions are designed to see if you have understood the general structure of a text or to check if you understand what type of text you are working on. There will also be a few questions designed to test your understanding of a few grammatical elements in context.

Like the texts, the questions are varied and some will be more difficult than others.
Here are some examples of the types of questions you may encounter in your exam paper so that it gives you an idea of what to expect.

- link titles to paragraphs
- link words or expressions to synonyms
- multiple choice questions
- match beginning of sentences to appropriate endings
- gap filling exercises (*this will mainly be about link words such as "malgré", "bien que", "avant que" etc.)*
- put sentences in the right order according to the text
- match words or expressions to definitions
- true or false statements ***with precise justifications***
- choose sentences which summarise a paragraph
- identify very precise grammar references (*e.g.- line 45, which words does "y" replace*)

etc.

NB: All the questions will be in the target language...

C) The answers

You must aim to answer **ALL** questions. If you are unsure about an answer you might as well try and have a guess as no marks will be deducted for incorrect answers. However, if you leave blanks, you will get no credit.

The answers follow the order of the text, so this should help you find your bearings.

Read **ALL** instructions carefully to avoid getting caught out. Sometimes, one word can have two synonyms in a text but the question will require you to look in a specific part of the text in order to find the "right" one!

Your answers will be marked out of 1 unless otherwise stated in the margin. No half mark will be awarded...*it is all or nothing*!

You do not have to write full sentences and the good news is that as the aim of Paper 1 is not to test your grammar but your comprehension. You will therefore not be penalised for any spelling or grammar mistakes that might accidentally creep up in your answers. **However,** be warned that if your mistakes are such that your answer becomes unclear or ambiguous you will then lose marks as your answer will not be accepted.

Remember also that it is not up to the examiner to choose which answer you think may be the right one for a question. If you initially write several answers down, cross out clearly the ones you are discarding. Equally, if your answer is too long (especially for finding a synonym to an expression in the text type of questions), even if the right answer is amongst what you have written, you may not get the mark.

Do not use a pencil to write your answers. Use a black or blue pen. Make sure that your handwriting is clear, otherwise, if your answer is correct but your examiner is struggling to decipher your hieroglyphs, your answers will not be accepted either. It is only fair after all as your examiner should not have to spend time trying to understand what you wanted to say!

Some tips on how to approach some of the types of questions ...

- *Vrai ou faux?*
  As far as the ***true or false*** questions are concerned, it is ***essential*** to remember that a ***justification*** is required and must be given. If you fail to do so but you have ticked the right box, you will not be awarded any marks at all. Equally, if you provide the right justification but tick the wrong box, you will gain no mark. BOTH need to be provided.
  It is also **important** to remember that the justification must be a **precise** piece of information lifted from the text. There is no need to copy full sentences or even paragraphs (!) when one word or part of a sentence are sufficient to justify the correctness or incorrectness of a given statement. If your justification is too broad and so too vague, you will not be given credit for it even if it contains the correct element. Again, it is not up to your examiner to make up your mind and decide for you.

- *Matching words or expressions to words or expressions of an equivalent meaning*
  You must obviously look at the words and expressions in the context of the text. Do not assume that because you know the word you can match them to words of equivalent meanings without referring back to the original text. ***Words do take different meanings in different contexts!*** Furthermore, don't forget to ***look at the grammar***. This will help you narrow your search and could prove invaluable when stuck on a word or two as it could help you make the right choice in the end. So, if the word is an adjective, it should be linked to another adjective. If it is an adjective in the feminine form, then the equivalent adjective should also show a feminine agreement. If it is a verb, you are looking for another verb and so on. Obviously, it will not always be as straightforward and sometimes you might get really stuck on a word or two but using this technique should prove really helpful.

- *Beginning and end of sentences*

The above advice is also useful for this type of exercise. ***Do look at the grammar***. If the beginning of the sentence does not contain any verb, so you are looking for an ending that contains one. Etc.

- *Fill in the blank with connecting words*

Again, the grammar can help you here too. If you know what should follow each one of the link or connecting words (on top of knowing what they mean and what kind of nuance(s) they bring in a sentence: chronology? Cause? Consequence? etc.) this will help you narrow down choices and / or options.

For example, "***bien que***" is always followed by a verb in the subjunctive form so is there a verb in the subjunctive after a blank in the text? If there is one, will "*bien que*" make sense here or is there another link word in the list given to you that precedes a verb in the subjunctive that would make sense / work?

Here is another example: "***Afin de***" is followed by a verb in the infinitive and expresses an aim. (*Elle a menti à son patron* ***afin de*** *conserver sont travail. S'il avait su la vérité, elle aurait été licenciée.* = She lied to her boss ***so that*** she could keep her job. If he had known the truth, she would have been fired.)

NB: It is obviously up to you to divide your time according to your needs in order to complete the paper, but you must learn to pace yourself.

It is also up to you to find out for yourself what technique works best for you, but I would give you the following pieces of advice:

- Read each text once with a pen in your hand to underline any potential key words or important details before reading the related questions
- Read the questions afterwards
- Then go back to the text

BUT above all you must bear in mind that you always need to refer to the texts and check your answers in relation to the texts. All the questions aim at testing your comprehension and understanding of a text and must be put in context.

Remember to keep cool (*pas de panique*!). It is not always essential to understand every single word in order to make out the general meaning of the text so don't panic and don't get stuck on a word or a question. Leave it but don't forget to come back to it as, remember, you must endeavour to answer ALL the questions.

And a final piece of advice…

Look carefully at any new words that you may encounter and check that it is not formed from a word or the stem of a word that you know and then make sense of it in context. Again, it does not always work but it may help on occasions.

EX:

L'amitié ⟹ ami= friend ⟹ amitié = friendship

nuageux ⟹ nuage = cloud ⟹ nuageux = cloudy

immangeable ⟹ manger = to eat ⟹ immangeable = inedible

renouvelable ⟹ nouveau = new ⟹ renouvelable = renewable

dévisager (*quelqu'un*) ⟹ visage = face ⟹ dévisager = to peer at someone

Let's practise! *(answers to all exercises on pages 182-187)*

Below are a few examples of texts and questions. Read the texts, answer the questions and practise both techniques and vocabulary at the same time! Each text aims at tackling one type of questions. It is not a full paper but it gives you the opportunity to practice each type of question individually and to see more texts, so more vocabulary in context, at the same time.
Bear in mind that in the exam, all the texts will be authentic and not made up. They will also be numbered and the questions will often refer to a specific line or a section of the text. Make sure you read the instructions carefully.

It is also worth saying that it is easy for you to get hold of past papers. So be proactive, ask your teachers and keep practising! And it does not matter if the topic of a given text in a past paper does not refer to a topic studied in the Core part of the programme; you are still practicing the technique for Paper 1, improving your vocabulary and getting ideas and vocabulary for Paper 2!

TRONC COMMUN : *relations sociales*

Vivre au quotidien avec un handicap
Aidez-nous à les aider !

Une maladie, un accident…
Des jours, des semaines voire des mois d'hospitalisation et de rééducation.
Une vie qui bascule du jour au lendemain…
Des gestes quotidiens à réapprendre, une maison à réorganiser, une vie à vivre autrement.

C'est ce à quoi sont confrontées des centaines de personnes touchées par le handicap chaque année à la suite d'une maladie ou d'un accident.
Comme si accepter le handicap et parfois même affronter le regard des autres n'étaient pas suffisants, on oublie trop souvent que le handicap pose aussi des questions d'ordre matériel. En effet, les soins ne sont pas gratuits…

De plus, avez-vous pensé à l'achat du matériel médicalisé comme les fauteuils roulants ?
Et la maison à étages dans laquelle elle habitait depuis plusieurs années ; est-elle encore pratique pour la personne qui se voit contrainte de se déplacer en fauteuil roulant ?
Qui va payer pour un aménagement du logement en équipement spécialisé et adapté aux besoins spécifiques de la personne ou pour un déménagement ?

Et la voiture ? Comment financer l'achat d'un véhicule adapté aux besoins de la personne handicapée et qui pourrait l'aider à retrouver un peu d'autonomie, surtout lorsque le handicap a aussi entraîné l'incapacité de la reprise du travail?

Et si c'était vous ? Pourriez-vous supporter de telles conditions de vie au quotidien ? N'aimeriez-vous pas que l'on vous vienne en aide pour vous aider à retrouver une partie de votre autonomie ainsi que votre place dans la société ?

Le handicap isole.

C'est pourquoi, nous, les membres de l'association ***Aide face au handicap*** *(AFAH)*, nous vous demandons de faire un geste pour aider les personnes qui souffrent d'un handicap.

Un geste, ce n'est rien, mais ça peut vraiment aider leur quotidien.
Soyons, soyez solidaires !
Aidons-les à mieux vivre leur handicap !

Dons à envoyer à l'AFAH – 16 rue de L'espoir- Paris-

1. Le but de ce texte est d' :

   a. inciter les personnes handicapées à demander de l'aide.
   b. informer le public des difficultés rencontrées par les personnes handicapées.
   c. inciter les gens à donner de l'argent à l'association pour aider les handicapés.
   d. informer les personnes handicapées au sujet de l'association et de ses actions.

   ☐

Below is an example of a "***Vrai ou faux***" type of question. Read the text and complete the exercise. Remember that in order to get the mark for this type of question both the justification and the box ticked must be correct.

TRONC COMMUN: Questions mondiales (environnement)

- *La gazette des Ecolos – 12 octobre 2007* –

Les Français et les moyens de transport

De nos jours, la majorité des familles françaises possède une voiture et parfois même deux. Cette augmentation du nombre des véhicules sur les routes est à l'origine de plusieurs problèmes.

Plus de véhicules, plus de circulation

L'augmentation du nombre de véhicules en France ces dernières années a contribué à aggraver le problème déjà existant de la circulation routière, notamment autour des grandes villes. Les bouchons sont de plus en plus fréquents, particulièrement aux heures de pointe. A ce problème vient s'ajouter l'augmentation du nombre des accidents de la route, souvent mortels, qui se produisent chaque année sur nos routes.

Plus de véhicules, plus de pollution

Qui dit augmentation du nombre de voitures, dit aussi augmentation de la pollution, en particulier dans les grandes agglomérations comme l'agglomération parisienne. L'air est devenu irrespirable et le bruit engendré par les turbines du moteur et l'utilisation excessive du klaxon par certains automobilistes nous rendent la vie insupportable.

Des solutions ?

Malheureusement, le concept de covoiturage ne semble pas très populaire et peu nombreuses sont les bonnes consciences qui partagent leur trajet quotidien avec leurs collègues. Quant aux moyens de transport en commun, dont l'utilisation est légèrement à la hausse, beaucoup d'entre vous n'en sont toujours pas satisfaits. Leur fiabilité reste votre plus grand souci. Alors, votre engouement récent pour le *vélib*, ce système de location de vélos par les municipalités telles que Paris ou Lyon, serait-il le seul moyen de lutte efficace ? Affaire à suivre...

Par Xavier Deschamps

VRAI ou FAUX?
Justifiez vos réponses.

	VRAI	FAUX
1) Le nombre de voitures a diminué récemment.	☐	☐
2) Il n'y a pas de problème de circulation.	☐	☐
3) Les accidents de la route peuvent tuer.	☐	☐
4) L'air de Paris est malsain.	☐	☐
5) Le covoiturage est une option très populaire.	☐	☐
6) Les Français pensent qu'ils peuvent compter sur l'efficacité des moyens de transport en commun.	☐	☐

In this simple example, all these people have written to a French magazine to express their problems and share them with others. You need to read each paragraph and then match each person with the appropriate statement. Who is saying what?
This exercise is, I hope, rather easy as they all have different problems. However, bear in mind that you will have longer texts in the exam. So again, Make sure that you check each statement carefully in context to avoid any potential tricks.

TRONC COMMUN : Relations sociales

Bonjour, je m'appelle Antoine et j'ai un problème. Je suis nouveau au lycée et je n'arrive pas à me faire des copains et créer des liens solides et durables. Pourtant je fais des efforts pour aller vers les autres mais j'ai toujours l'impression de gêner. Peux-tu m'aider à résoudre mon problème ?

Salut!
Je m'appelle Aurore et j'ai besoin d'aide. Dans ma classe, il y a un garçon que je trouve super mignon mais je suis trop timide pour oser aller lui parler. J'ai peur qu'il m'ignore ou se moque de moi.
Que puis-je faire ?
Merci à toutes et à tous.

Salut tout le monde!
Moi c'est Arthur et je viens d'entrer en première. Je trouve le rythme de travail très intense et je me sens très stressé. Je suis toujours en retard avec mon travail et mes profs pensent que je suis paresseux. Que puis-je faire pour réussir mon bac et être plus détendu ?

Merci à tous pour vos conseils!

Je m'appelle Hélène et j'ai 16 ans. L'été prochain, j'aimerais partir en vacances avec mes amis mais mes parents refusent. J'ai l'impression qu'ils s'inquiètent et qu'ils ne me font pas confiance. Comment puis-je les convaincre de me laisser partir avec mes amis ?

Salut, moi c'est Xavier. Depuis quelque temps, mon meilleur ami Olivier fréquente un groupe de jeunes peu recommandables. Il a commencé à sortir tous les soirs; il fume et boit de l'alcool régulièrement. Je m'inquiète pour lui et j'ai peur qu'il ne soit tenté par la drogue. Je ne sais pas quoi faire pour l'aider ? En plus, quand j'essaie d'aborder le sujet avec lui, il se braque. Pourriez-vous m'aider ?

Bonjour. Je m'appelle Anaïs et j'ai 17 ans. Je soupçonne mon meilleur ami d'être anorexique mais je n'arrive pas à lui en parler. Il a perdu beaucoup de poids depuis l'été dernier et il trouve toujours une excuse pour ne pas prendre son déjeuner avec moi à la cantine. J'ai essayé de demander conseils à mes parents mais ils pensent que je me fais des idées car, pour eux, l'anorexie est un problème qui ne touche que les filles. Je ne sais pas quoi faire. J'ai peur de perdre l'amitié de mon ami en abordant le sujet avec lui mais j'aimerais l'aider et, pour le moment, je me sens impuissante. Auriez-vous des conseils à me donner ?

1. Antoine	☐	A. À présent, ils ont une fausse image de moi.
2. Aurore	☐	B. Et si lui en parler compromettait notre amitié ?
3. Arthur	☐	C. Il se fâche si je tente de lui en toucher un mot.
4. Hélène	☐	D. L'amitié ne va pas de soi pour moi.
5. Xavier	☐	E. Comment les persuader ?
6. Anaïs	☐	F. Il me plaît mais je n'arrive pas à faire le premier pas.

TRONC COMMUN: Communication et médias

Bonjour à tous,

Je m'appelle Julie et je suis un « Cyber-bourreau ». Ma victime ; elle s'appelait Chloé et c'était ma meilleure amie. Tout à commencé il y a trois ans quand nous étions encore au collège. Chloé était ma meilleure amie depuis la sixième. Nous étions inséparables. Nous n'avions aucun secret l'une pour l'autre et on faisait tout ensemble. Et puis un jour, tout a changé. Chloé est tombée amoureuse du garçon avec qui je sortais... Elle m'a piqué mon petit copain. Je n'ai pas pu supporter cette trahison et j'ai lancé une campagne de haine contre Chloé...sur internet. À mes yeux, Chloé était devenue l'ennemie et j'allais lui faire payer cher sa trahison...trop cher ...
J'ai commencé par lui envoyer des messages d'insultes tous les jours. Ensuite, J'ai dévoilé tous les secrets qu'elle m'avait confiés dans des courriels que j'envoyais régulièrement au reste de la classe.
Non contente d'envoyer des courriels et des remarques déplaisantes sur celle qui était mon amie, J'ai encouragé d'autres copains à poster des commentaires blessants sur Chloé. Nous avions même créé un site et un forum sur lequel nous échangions des vannes aux dépens de Chloé. J'ai ensuite commencé à afficher des photos peu flatteuses (et certaines même révélatrices) de celle qui fut autrefois mon amie et avec qui je partageais tout sans honte. Chloé n'a pas supporté...je suis allée trop loin.
Si j'ai décidé de témoigner aujourd'hui et de partager avec vous le calvaire que j'ai fait endurer à Chloé sans vraiment me rendre compte des conséquences potentielles de mes actions et de la tournure tragique que les événements allaient prendre, c'est pour que ma mauvaise expérience puisse servir d'exemple à tous.
Aujourd'hui Chloé n'est plus là pour raconter le calvaire que je lui ai fait endurer pendant des mois. Elle a décidé de mettre fin à la cyber-intimidation dont elle était la victime en mettant fin à ses jours. Deux ans déjà que tu es partie Chloé. Ton amitié, je ne la méritais pas. Ma méchanceté, tu ne la méritais pas ! Il me faut désormais vivre le reste de ma vie avec ta mort sur ma conscience car moi seule en suis responsable. Mes actions sont impardonnables... irréparables ...
Si l'idée vous vient de poster des photos ou commentaires compromettants ou inappropriés sur le net pour vous venger d'un ami ou d'une amie qui aurait trahi votre confiance ou simplement pour « se marrer » et victimiser quelqu'un que vous n'aimez pas ou que vous avez pris en grippe; souvenez-vous de mon témoignage, rappelez-vous de Chloé et réfléchissez à deux fois avant de cliquer sur la touche « envoi » de votre clavier !

Relie chaque mot de la colonne de gauche à son synonyme dans la colonne de droite.
NB: *Remember...verbs should be matched with verbs, adjectives with adjectives etc...but don't just rush; words can take different meanings according to the context. Always check in context!* Note as well that here you have the exact number of synonyms (*they follow the order of the text*) but that you may have more than the required number in the exam.

1. piqué	☐	A. révélé
2. supporter	☐	B. subir
3. insultes	☐	C. sarcasmes
4. dévoilé	☐	D. volé
5. déplaisantes	☐	E. supplice
6. vannes	☐	F. railleries
7. calvaire	☐	G. désagréables
8. endurer	☐	H. tolérer

The topic of the following text is not linked to the TRONC COMMUN but to one of the options (Health) it therefore would not appear in Paper 1. However, it is still a valid exercise to practice this type of questions. It will also help you revise some more specific vocabulary so it is always helpful. To prepare for Paper 1, you should be using past papers even if they were designed for the old syllabus. That will enable you to practice the techniques that you need to master for Paper 1 and it will also be good for your reading and vocabulary building skills.

Bonjour à tous!

Je m'appelle Elodie et je suis boulimique depuis plus de deux ans maintenant. Je voudrais m'en sortir mais c'est difficile et pour l'instant tous mes efforts ont été vains. Alors j'ai décidé de vous parler de mon problème pour que vous sachiez reconnaître les premiers signes de la boulimie et pour que vous aidiez vos amis qui en ont besoin.

Au début, ce n'était pas très grave. Je ne me sentais pas très bien dans ma peau et j'écoutais toutes mes envies pour me faire plaisir : un morceau de chocolat de temps en temps, quelques biscuits, un deuxième morceau de gâteau à la fin du repas... Mais peu à peu les quantités ont augmenté, voire doublé. J'ai commencé par en prendre un peu plus, toujours un peu plus de gâteau, à me resservir plusieurs fois en frites... Je ne m'en suis pas rendu compte tout de suite. Pourquoi est-ce que je me suis mise à manger autant? Etait-ce pour me faire du bien? Pour combler un vide intérieur? Etait-ce une manière de faire face à mes problèmes et mes angoisses quotidiennes? En général, quand je mange, je n'ai pas vraiment faim. Je mange par gourmandise. Souvent, je n'apprécie même pas ce que je mange...et quand j'ai trop mangé, je me fais vomir...Je crois que je voulais plaire à tout le monde, j'en avais besoin. Maintenant je me déteste et j'ai honte ! Ça me déprime.
La boulimie est une maladie et c'est encore très difficile pour moi d'en parler. Je commence tout juste à accepter ma condition. Alors si vous connaissez quelqu'un qui est boulimique, surtout ne vous moquez pas mais essayez plutôt de comprendre et d'aider.

Elodie, 16 ans (Paris)

1) vains	☐	A) remplir
2) une envie	☐	B) reprendre de quelque chose
3) un morceau de	☐	C) affronter
4) se resservir	☐	D) un désir
5) je m'en suis rendu compte	☐	E) inutiles
6) je me suis mise à	☐	F) j'ai commencé à
7) combler	☐	G) une part de
8) faire face à	☐	H) je m'en suis apercu

Read the text below and answer the related questions.
Note that with the intended audience being teenagers, the language used in the article is mainly familiar (E.g. "sont constamment sur mon dos")

TRONC COMMUN: Relations sociales

- JEUNES MAG - - semaine du 12 au 17 juin 2007 -

La Famille et vous!

Pas toujours facile la vie de famille ! Cette semaine, six jeunes nous donnent leur avis sur la famille. Si vous voulez leur répondre, envoyez-leur vos messages par courrier électronique à l'adresse suivante : larédac@jeunemag.fr

La famille c'est la chose la plus importante pour moi. C'est vrai que les parents peuvent parfois être un peu vieux jeu et strictes et que mes petits frères peuvent être trop collants, mais on n'a qu'une seule famille. Je pense qu'il faut apprendre à être tolérant...après tout, nous non plus nous ne sommes pas toujours faciles à vivre !

Olivia, Paris- 17 ans

Ma famille me tape sur les nerfs!! Mes parents sont constamment sur mon dos ! J'ai l'impression qu'ils me surveillent tout le temps. Je ne peux rien faire ! Ils veulent toujours tout savoir. En plus, ils ne sont jamais contents. Ils me critiquent sans arrêt pour un oui ou pour un non. Parfois j'ai vraiment envie d'atteindre la majorité pour pouvoir me casser de chez mes parents !!

Julien, Toulouse - 16 ans

Pour moi, la famille c'est sacré. Je fais partie d'une famille nombreuse (nous somme 5 frères et sœurs) et nous partageons tout. Ma famille est toujours là dans les moments difficiles et je peux compter sur mes parents. C'est important. Je ne sais pas ce que je ferais sans ma famille ! Certains de mes amis ne s'entendent pas avec leurs parents. Je trouve que c'est dommage. Ils devraient faire un effort pour essayer de les comprendre.

Arthur, Lille- 17 ans

J'ai la chance d'avoir des parents très compréhensifs et ouverts. Ils me font confiance et me soutiennent dans mes choix. Ils me guident et me conseillent mais me laissent prendre mes décisions toute seule. Si je me trompe, ils ne me jugent pas mais m'aident à résoudre mes problèmes. Je suis fille unique et c'est peut-être pour ça que ma relation avec mes parents est aussi ouverte. En tout cas, je ne leur ai jamais menti et je pense qu'il est très important que vous respectiez vos parents si vous voulez qu'ils vous respectent et vous traitent en adultes responsables.

Marie, Lyon- 15 ans

La vie de famille...c'est loin d'être facile ! Mes parents sont divorcés et ma mère s'est remariée il y a deux ans. Je m'entends bien avec mon beau-père mais je ne vois pas mon père très souvent et il me manque. En plus, ma mère me couve un peu trop. Elle m'interdit de sortir en boîte avec mes copains le samedi soir sous prétexte que je suis trop jeune !! Je pense qu'elle a peur que je grandisse trop vite et que je fasse de mauvaises rencontres! Je crois qu'elle redoute que j'aie de mauvaises fréquentations. Je la comprends mais ça m'agace de ne pas pouvoir faire ce que mes copains font ! J'aimerais parfois qu'elle se souvienne qu'elle aussi elle a été jeune et qu'elle aimait sortir !

Elodie, Marseille- 16 ans

1. Quelle expression tirée du témoignage d'Olivia, signifie "*démodés* » / « *ringards* » :

....

2. Quel verbe tiré du paragraphe de Marie signifie « *je fais une erreur* » :

....

3. Que signifie l'expression « *ma famille me tape sur les nerfs* » (paragraphe de Julien) :

   a. ma famille me fait mal / me frappe
   b. ma famille me dispute sans arrêt ☐
   c. ma famille m'énerve / m'agace
   d. ma famille me surveille tout le temps

4. Dans le paragraphe de Marie, à qui se réfère « *leur* » dans « *Je ne leur ai jamais menti* » ?

....

5. Dans le paragraphe d'Élodie, à qui se réfère « *la* » dans « *je la comprends* » ?

....

6. Dans le paragraphe d'Arthur, à qui se réfère « les » dans « *Ils devraient faire un effort pour essayer de les comprendre* » ?

....

NB:

- *It is worth noting again that all the examples given above and below are not genuine IB texts or even "genuine texts". They have been made up for the sole purpose of this revision guide. In the exam paper, texts will be genuine articles / interviews, etc. or, at least, they will be adapted from a range of original sources and not made up from scratch.*

- *Even if the texts have been here created for the purpose of the guide and therefore some of the statistics or even some of the facts, for example, are not necessarily accurate, the topics and vocabulary used in each and every single one of these examples are relevant to the IB themes and types of texts.*

- *In the exam, all the lines in the texts will be numbered and, sometimes, a reference to a specific line will be made.*

- *In some of the examples, only one question is being asked for practice purposes. This would not happen in the exam; you will always have a few questions on each text (sometimes even more than 10 questions).*

- *On page 55 of this guide, you can find a practice example of an exercise where you need to fill in the missing titles. This type of exercise is quite common but bear in mind that you will be given the full title and not be required to conjugate the verbs.*

- *Most of the types of questions that can come up in the exam have been covered and this should give you a pretty good idea of the exam format and therefore hopefully what to expect in the exam. However, although it is a good start to your revision process, it will not prove sufficient on its own and I would strongly advise you to ask your teacher for "genuine" IB past papers to practise on. It is essential that you are fully familiar with the format of a full paper.*

The last type of questions I am going to deal with in this guide is the fill in the blanks exercise. As you know, you may be given a text in which words are missing. These missing words will always be grammatical words such as link words (*cependant / bien que,*). The context will undoubtedly help you find the right link words but knowing what they mean and which nuances they bring to the sentence (*cause / consequence / chronology... etc. see list on pages 76-77*) will certainly help you narrow the possibilities! Equally, some on these words are always followed by a subjunctive (bien que / avant que), others by a verb in the infinitive (*afin de*), some by a substantive (grâce à). This will also help you... provided you know!
Be aware that you will always be offered more possibilities than you actually need.

Below is an example of a text in which some link words have been taken out. Try and put the right ones back where they should be!

- L'écho du Midi - - Samedi 12 juillet 2008 –

Pour passer l'été en toute sécurité…

*On le sait tous, **[-X-]** l'été est souvent synonyme d'insouciance, en matière de sécurité, il rime également avec baisse de vigilance. Il n'est **[-1-]** pas rare de se voir dépouiller de ses effets personnels par un opportuniste ou pire encore.*
*Cet été, **[-2-]** une initiative du conseil régional de la Drôme, les touristes pourront passer des vacances en toute tranquillité.*

En été, les balades en pleine nature sont privilégiées et un plus grand nombre de personnes fréquente des lieux habituellement désertés et qui sont très souvent retirés, ***[-3-]*** isolés. Cet isolement attire parfois des individus mal intentionnés pour qui une occasion d'abuser les touristes ne se rate surtout pas. Le conseil régional de la région a décidé de s'attaquer au problème à partir de cette année. Tous les gendarmes ont en effet été équipés d'un vélo.

Les gendarmes peuvent ***[-4-]*** patrouiller tous les coins paisibles (*et situés en retrait des zones très fréquentées où les risques sont moindres*) ***[-5-]*** veiller à la sécurité de tous. Le vélo permet une approche discrète des lieux. Un moyen simple, pratique et efficace d'assurer la sécurité des touristes et la baisse de la délinquance.
[-6-], ce mode de transport écologique est très utilisé pour les recherches de personnes disparues, ***[-7-]*** en forêt. La taille du vélo permet aux gendarmes d'accéder à des endroits difficiles où les véhicules traditionnels ne peuvent pas passer.
[-8-] les risques de vol, attaque et disparition n'aient pas complètement disparu, l'introduction de cette patrouille à deux roues devrait contribuer à renforcer la sécurité de tous cet été.

Touristes et amateurs de coins tranquilles, vous pouvez partir sereins et profiter de la nature en toute quiétude !

par Marie Deschamps

PARCE QUE ***NOTAMMENT*** ***SI*** ***VOIRE*** ***CAR***

AINSI ***BIEN QUE*** ***À CAUSE DE*** ***GRÂCE À*** ***POUR***

EN EFFET ***POURTANT*** ***PAR AILLEURS*** ***AFIN DE***

EXEMPLE : [-X-] …SI…

1. ………………………
2. ………………………
3. ………………………
4. ………………………
5. ………………………
6. ………………………
7. ………………………
8. ………………………

Let's practise further !

Below are a few more examples to help you get to grip with this type of exercise. Just read the short paragraphs and complete them appropriately. And don't forget; getting your hands on some past papers will be a useful idea too!

A)

CRI DU COEUR...

Je suis en colère...je suis très en colère...
...contre toutes celles et ceux qui osent clamer haut et fort qu'ils ne sont pas racistes **[-1-]** qui accusent les étrangers de tous les maux.
...contre celles et ceux qui préfèrent détourner ou baisser la tête quand ils croisent un étranger **[-2-]** de lui sourire.
...celles et ceux qui éprouvent du dégoût **[-3-]** par accident ils effleurent la main d'un maghrébin ou d'une maghrébine dans le métro.
....contre celles et ceux **[-4-]** qui employer une personne à la peau basanée est un sacrilège.
...contre tous les racistes ordinaires qui n'ont même pas la décence d'avouer que l'intolérance et la haine font partie de leur quotidien !

LORSQUE - PARCE QUE - POURTANT - MAIS -

POUR - SI - PLUTÔT QUE –

1. ....
2. ....
3. ....
4. ....

B)

COURRIER DES LECTEURS* - *Questions / réponses

"J'aimerais partir en vacances avec des potes l'été prochain mais mes parents refusent de me laisser partir sans eux **[-1-]** *je suis trop jeune. J'ai l'impression qu'ils ne me font pas confiance. »*

Sébastien, 16ans.

Cher Sébastien,

En lisant ton message, ça m'a rappelé de (mauvais !) souvenirs...Moi **[-2-]**, comme toi, je voulais partir en vacances avec des copains l'été dernier. Mes parents refusaient de me donner l'autorisation. Les convaincre n'a pas été facile !! J'ai tout fait pour leur montrer que j'étais capable de me débrouiller sans eux et que j'étais digne de leur confiance. **[-3-]** insister sans arrêt, ils ont fini par céder. Tout s'est bien passé et cet été, c'est eux qui m'ont demandé où je partais avec mes amis...comme quoi, tu vois, il ne faut jamais désespérer !!

Xavier, 17 ans.

Salut Sébastien,

J'ai le même problème que toi. **[-4-]**, j'ai demandé à mes parents l'autorisation de partir dans le sud de la France avec des copines **[-5-]** ils ont refusé. **[-6-]** ils connaissent mes amies et les apprécient. J'ai du mal à comprendre leur réaction. **[-7-]**, je suis une élève sérieuse et j'aide ma mère régulièrement avec les tâches ménagères. **[-8-]** je sois déçue, je ne désespère pas car tu connais le dicton « il n'y a que les imbéciles qui ne changent pas d'avis »... !

Magalie, 16 ans.

EN PLUS - POURTANT - AVANT QUE - EN EFFET -

MAIS - SOUS PRÉTEXTE QUE - AUSSI - BIEN QUE –

À CONDITION QUE - À FORCE DE / D' -

1. ....
2. ....
3. ....
4. ....
5. ....
6. ....
7. ....
8. ....

The following texts are authentic texts. They have been put together to try and give you an opportunity to practice a full . aper 1 type exam. Well...one more on top of the past paper practices you have already done or are about to do!

Note that there are only four texts and the total number of marks is 45. It therefore means that, in design, it is more a SL type paper than a HL type practice paper as at HL you have one more text (total of 60 marks); a literary text. Unfortunately, for copyrights reasons, it has not been possible to use a literary extract in this first version of the revised guide. However, it is still good practice for you if you are studying French at HL because the 4 other texts that will constitute your Paper 1 will be similar to the ones that follow. Same advice as before, ask your teacher for past papers and get going on practicing with literary texts.

.More specific to HL students...

A few tips to approach the literary type texts...

Remember that those extracts are taken from a wide range of francophone literature and that therefore they will vary in style. I recommend that you read as much as possible all the way through your IB studies. I hope it is not too late! If it is, no need to panic! Read the following tips and use your common sense on the day of the exam.

- ☑ Some of these texts may contain verbs conjugated in the *passé simple.* Be sure to be familiar with this tense to avoid getting stuck on the verbs. (*see grammar section for help*)

- ☑ Often (*although the register can be informal too*), literary texts will use a slightly more formal register of language. Be sure to revise synonyms of the words you may know in different registers of languages. If you are at an early stage of your French studies, get into the habit of looking up synonyms of new words in different registers if they exist. (*see chapter on register of language*)

- ☑ Like for any other type of texts, always check the meaning of words in context.

- ☑ Bear in mind that translations very rarely work words for words. Literary texts may be richer in images. Don't get caught out and use your common sense.

- ☑ Like for any other type of texts, take the time to read the text and get a feel for it before rushing onto the questions.

"What is the best thing I can do to prepare?" is the question I am sure you are burning to ask. Well...just go and practice with past papers and carry on reading and building your vocabulary. It will also almost certainly help you become more familiar with a range of idiomatic expressions and help you develop your intercultural understanding of Francophone cultures.

See the list of suggested reading provided at the back of this guide for inspiration.

TEXTE A

Les Restos du cœur en difficultés !

100 millions de repas distribués l'hiver dernier…

Depuis 25 ans, les Restos du cœur essaient de pallier à la misère quotidienne, mais ils finissent par s'épuiser eux-mêmes. Devant l'ampleur grandissante de la pauvreté et de la précarité, les Restos du cœur ont du mal à assurer financièrement leurs missions.

Les Restos du cœur viennent de lancer leur 25e campagne d'hiver. « *[-X-]* printemps et de l'été derniers, la fréquentation de nos centres de distribution a augmenté de 20 % sur un an, on s'attend à une forte hausse de la demande, qui avait déjà progressé de 14 % l'année dernière », a expliqué le président des Restos, Olivier Berthe. Face à cela, l'aide de l'Europe pour les Restos va baisser d'un million d'euros, a ajouté M. Berthe, rappelant que le gouvernement avait accordé l'an dernier aux Restos une enveloppe exceptionnelle de 10 millions d'euros, *[-6-]* faire face à l'augmentation des prix pour l'aide alimentaire. Cette année nous avons demandé une augmentation de cette enveloppe. Non seulement nous n'avons pas reçu un euro, *[-7-]* le gouvernement ne nous a même pas répondu, a-t-il déploré.

Compétent pour les Restos du cœur, le secrétariat d'Etat au logement a indiqué le samedi 28 novembre que le secrétaire d'Etat avait reçu un courrier le 24 novembre et répondu à M. Berthe vendredi, et que la question des 10 millions d'euros ferait l'objet d'une réunion le 7 décembre.

Les Restos du cœur ont distribué l'hiver dernier 100 millions de repas, 800 000 personnes ont été accueillies par 55 000 bénévoles dans 2 028 centres et antennes. Le budget a été de 142,8 millions d'euros en 2008-2009. La courbe de la demande suit, avec quelques mois de décalage, la courbe de l'augmentation du chômage, lorsque les gens arrivent en fin de droits, souligne M. Berthe, qui précise que les chiffres nationaux détaillant l'augmentation de la demande seront connus à la mi-décembre.

[-8-] ces difficultés, *[-9-]* s'ajoutent celles grandissantes pour trouver de nouveaux lieux de distribution et de stockage, l'association s'est engagée à ne pas rogner sur la qualité des produits distribués.

Les Restos rappellent aussi que le gouvernement s'était engagé à une sanctuarisation des lieux d'aide humanitaire, notamment au sujet des bénévoles étrangers, mais disent avoir constaté que les forces de police continuent d'intervenir sur des sites d'activité des Restos ou à proximité.

Les Restos comptent encore sur un sursaut de générosité des Français, tout en se demandant combien de temps encore pourront-ils faire face ?

Reproduit avec l'aimable autorisation de: http://www.zurbains.com

Indiquez dans la case de droite la lettre qui correspond à la réponse correcte.

1. Le but de ce texte est…

   A. de dénoncer l'inefficacité des Restos du cœur ☐
   B. de mettre en évidence la mauvaise gestion des Restos du cœur
   C. de dresser le bilan de l'association
   D. d'exposer les difficultés rencontrer par l'association et appeler aux contributions

Répondez aux questions suivantes.

2. Selon le 1er paragraphe, quel est le but des Restos du cœur.

   ....

3. Selon le 1er paragraphe, qu'est-ce qui empêche les Restos du cœur d'assumer au point de vue financier.

   ....

4. Selon le 2e paragraphe, pour quelle raison l'association a-t-elle sollicité l'aide du gouvernement.

   ....

5. Parmi les phrases suivantes, **deux** sont conformes aux idées exprimées dans le texte. Indiquez les lettres correspondantes dans les cases de droite.

   A. Il y a de plus en plus de personnes qui ont besoin de l'aide des Restos.
   B. L'Europe va accorder plus d'aide financière aux Restos.
   C. Le coût de l'aide alimentaire reste inchangé. ☐
   D. Le gouvernement n'a pas répondu à l'appel à l'aide.
   E. La demande d'aide est associée à l'augmentation du chômage. ☐

Ajoutez les mots qui manquent dans le texte en les choisissant dans la liste proposée ci-dessous. ATTENTION : il y a plus de mots que d'espaces et chaque mot ne peut être utilisé qu'une seule fois.

POUR QUE	ET	MÊME SI	AUXQUELLES	PENDANT
EN DÉPIT DE	MAIS	AU COURS DU	À QUI	AFIN DE

Exemple : [-X-] .... Au cours du

6. ....

7. ....

8. ....

9. ....

TEXTE B

Animaux de compagnie au Canada

Les chiens jouent depuis toujours un rôle important dans la vie des gens des Premières Nations. Pendant des siècles, on comptait sur les chiens pour chasser, travailler, manger, avoir de la laine et de la compagnie. Ils étaient le sujet de mythes et légendes que l'on se transmettait de génération en génération.

Aujourd'hui, même si les chiens jouent toujours un rôle important dans la vie des Premières Nations, les communautés ont de la difficulté à régler les problèmes de surpopulation des chiens et de chiens errants. Plusieurs communautés sont éloignées avec peu ou pas d'accès aux vétérinaires, et par conséquent, les chiens sont généralement en mauvaise santé.

Le coût des services vétérinaires et l'emplacement des cliniques animales (certaines à des centaines de kilomètres) font que la vaccination, la stérilisation et les soins d'urgence pour les animaux blessés sont presque impossibles. Sans ces services, prévenir les naissances non voulues et garder les chiens en santé est pratiquement impossible.

L'abandon est un autre problème grave. Les propriétaires qui ne sont pas capables de donner de la nourriture et un abri à leurs chiens les laissent se débrouiller eux-mêmes – parfois dans des températures extrêmes. Même si la plupart de ces chiens sont amicaux et socialisent bien, ils risquent de créer des bandes pouvant présenter un danger sur le plan de la santé et de la sécurité pour la communauté.

La triste réalité est que bien des communautés sont forcées de contrôler les chiens de façon cruelle. Sans accès aux vétérinaires ou à l'éducation faisant la promotion de la propriété responsable des animaux, des milliers d'animaux sont tués cruellement chaque année. La plupart des gens dans ces communautés ne sont pas heureux de cette situation, mais ils trouvent souvent qu'ils n'ont pas d'autres choix.

Histoire du travail de la WSPA avec les chiens des Premières Nations

Depuis 1999, la WSPA travaille avec les communautés des Premières Nations au Canada dans le but de créer des cliniques de stérilisation, d'offrir des vaccins, de renseigner les enfants sur les méthodes non cruelles de contrôle et de former les agents de contrôle des animaux. Des centaines de chiens ont été stérilisés, ce qui évite les naissances non voulues de milliers d'animaux.

En 2007, la WSPA a réuni des gens des Premières Nations, des organismes de protection des animaux, des vétérinaires, l'Assemblée des Premières Nations et les Chefs de l'Ontario pour discuter des chiens vivant sur les territoires des Premières Nations. Pour la première fois, ces intervenants ont pu se réunir pour discuter d'un problème qui existe à l'échelle nationale.

En 2008 et 2009, Josey Kitson de la WSPA Canada a visité une clinique de stérilisation gérée par notre société membre, l'Alberta Spay Neuter Task Force.

En 2009, Michelle Cliffe et Josey Kitson ont participé à des cliniques pour les animaux dans la communauté des Premières Nations Bella Bella en Colombie-Britannique gérées par notre société membre Big Heart Rescue.

En septembre 2009, la WSPA et la société membre Big Heart Rescue ont visité la communauté Bella Coola des Premières Nations pour organiser une clinique axée sur la santé des chiens et des chats. Plus de 241 animaux ont été vérifiés en l'espace de deux jours.

L'avenir

Au cours des prochaines années, la WSPA va travailler avec les intervenants pour élaborer une stratégie nationale pour les chiens des communautés des Premières Nations. Une partie de la stratégie consiste à aider nos sociétés membres à travailler sur le terrain.

Une fille à la clinique ASNTF © WSPA

Article adapté du site : http://fr.wspa.ca – avec l'aimable autorisation de la WSPA.

Répondez aux questions suivantes.

10. D'après le 3e paragraphe, citez **une** des raisons pour lesquelles il est difficile de soigner les chiens.

....

11. À qui se réfère « les » *(ligne 14)* dans « **les** laissent se débrouiller eux-mêmes ».

....

En vous référant au 5e paragraphe, complétez la phrase suivante. Citez **une** raison.

12. Les contrôles de chiens se font malheureusement de façon cruelle parce que ....

....

Reliez chacun des mots du texte se trouvant dans la colonne de gauche à son équivalent qui se trouve dans la colonne de droite. ***ATTENTION*** *: il y a plus de mots proposés que de réponses possibles.*

13. errants *(ligne 7)*	☐	A. niche
14. éloignées *(ligne 7)*	☐	B. s'évertuer à
15. abri *(ligne 14)*	☐	C. rapprochées
16. se débrouiller *(ligne 14)*	☐	D. adoptifs
		E. lointaines
		F. s'en sortir seul
		G. vagabonds

Répondez aux questions suivantes.

17. D'après le 6e paragraphe, pourquoi des chiens sont-ils stérilisés ?

....

18. Selon le dernier paragraphe, quel est le but futur de l'association ?

....

TEXTE C

Étapes d'organisation d'une Fête

L'idée d'organiser une Fête des voisins vous sourit? Excellent!

① **Parlez-en à vos voisins**

Préparez la fête en collaboration avec vos voisins. Répartissez-vous les tâches, partagez vos idées, discutez-en. Cette préparation en commun, c'est déjà un peu la fête! Vous n'osez pas les approcher? Pour une première année, initiez seul la Fête en déterminant un endroit, en faisant les invitations. Mais rappelez-vous que pour susciter la participation, rien de mieux que d'impliquer les gens!

② **Déterminez quelle forme aura la fête**

Un 5 à 7, un BBQ, un pique-nique avec des jeux pour les enfants ? Chacun apporte un plat ? On fait des hot-dogs pour tous ? Déterminez le lieu de la fête : un parc ? Une cour arrière ? Dans la rue (assurez-vous d'obtenir les autorisations nécessaires auprès de votre municipalité au moins un mois en avance). Rappelez-vous que plus c'est simple, plus c'est facile à organiser!

③ **Faites les invitations**

Distribuez les cartons dans les boîtes aux lettres de vos voisins quelques semaines avant le jour J. Installez une affiche annonçant la fête autour de votre propriété.

④ **Le jour de la fête : accueillez les gens et faites connaissance!**

Tout dépendant de la formule de fête choisie, il y aura peut-être des préparatifs à effectuer la veille ou le matin-même. Partagez les tâches entre voisins.

Autres conseils pratiques

[-X-]

Les enfants adorent les fêtes. Associez-les à l'organisation, vous verrez, ils auront plein d'idées. Confiez-leur des responsabilités : décoration, accueil, distribution des cartons d'invitations, etc. Prévoyez des choses avec et pour eux : jeux, animation, musique, etc.

[-22-]

Que ce soit dans la cour de votre maison, dans le hall, la salle commune ou la cour de votre immeuble, choisissez l'endroit qui vous paraît le plus approprié. Prévoyez une stratégie de repli en cas de mauvais temps. Vous vivez dans un quartier urbain où il y a peu d'espace disponible? Voyez auprès de votre municipalité si vous pouvez organiser la fête sur le trottoir ou dans la rue (autorisation préalable nécessaire).

[-23-]

La Fête des voisins c'est simple et chacun fait sa part. Que vous organisiez votre fête sous la forme d'un 5 à 7 ou d'un buffet, une bonne formule est d'inviter les gens à apporter quelque chose à manger et à boire. Mais que ce ne soit pas une condition de participation.

[-24-]

Pensez aussi à la décoration (guirlandes, ballons, fleurs,...) et à la musique (il y a peut-être des musiciens parmi vos voisins). Mais attention à ne pas importuner les voisins qui ne participeraient pas à la fête; ce n'est pas le jour pour créer des problèmes de voisinage...

[-25-]

Le jour de la fête, faite ressortir l'altruiste en vous, ne soyez pas réservé. Le but est de mieux connaître vos voisins, alors faites les premiers pas et présentez-vous. Les timides vous en seront certainement reconnaissants.

Inscrivez votre fête
La fête des voisins, c'est des centaines de personnes qui, en simultané, soulignent l'importance du bon voisinage. Pour qu'on sache que vous faites partie du mouvement, inscrivez votre fête (de façon anonyme ou non). Si votre municipalité est participante, informez-là aussi.

Texte reproduit avec autorisation - http://www.fetedesvoisins.qc.ca

Répondez à la question suivante.

19. Le but de ce texte est de donner des conseils pour:

   A. organiser une fête qui ne gênera pas vos voisins.
   B. organiser une fête entre voisins.
   C. éviter les fêtes de voisinage.
   D. inviter vos voisins à une fête.

☐

Les phrases suivantes basées sur les 4 premiers paragraphes du texte, sont soit vraies, soit fausses. Cochez la réponse correcte. Justifiez votre réponse par des mots du texte.

	vrai	*faux*
20. Mieux vaut préparer une fête seul pour éviter les problèmes.	☐	☐

Justification : ....

21. Il faut demander l'autorisation à la mairie 3 semaines avant la fête.	☐	☐

Justification : ....

En vous basant sur la deuxième partie du texte, reliez chaque titre au paragraphe qui lui correspond. ATTENTION : il y a plus de titres que de paragraphes.

Exemple : [-X-]- ......D ....

22. ....

23. ....

24. ....

25. ....

A. Un repas ?

B. Évitez vos voisins le plus possible

C. Utilisez n'importe quel local

D. Associez les enfants aux préparatifs

E. Créez une ambiance de fête

F. N'hésitez pas à faire connaissance

G. Identifiez un endroit approprié

H. Faites des économies

TEXTE D

Au Sénégal, la solitude des femmes d'émigrés

Mariées à des hommes partis émigrer en Occident, des milliers de Sénégalaises passent des années sans voir leur mari. Elles doivent gérer la pression familiale, le manque d'argent et l'absence d'amour.

Assise sur un canapé en cuir beige, ses longues jambes se balancent sur l'accoudoir. C'est dans son salon qu'Awa (les prénoms ont été changés) déroule sa vie de femme mariée à un « modou-modou », comme on appelle les émigrés au Sénégal. Le couple a un garçon de 3 ans. Son père ne l'a jamais vu. Jusqu'à présent, faute de papiers, il n'a pas pu revenir au Sénégal. Ce serait prendre le risque de ne plus pouvoir repartir. En attendant, coup de téléphone quotidien et envois de vidéos de la vie d'ici maintiennent le lien. Awa s'interroge : « En dix ans de mariage, nous n'avons vécu que quatre mois ensemble. Sans cette séparation, combien d'enfants aurions-nous pu avoir ? Combien de choses aurions-nous pu faire ? »L'indignation l'emporte quand elle raconte combien il est dur et humiliant d'obtenir un visa de tourisme pour rendre visite à son époux. Awa a attendu trois ans avant de pouvoir partir pendant ses vacances.

Elles n'ont pas vu leur mari depuis deux, quatre... voire dix ans

Son histoire est celle de la plupart des femmes de Louga, à 200 km au nord de Dakar, la capitale. C'est dans cette ville de 200 000 habitants que les émigrés sont les plus nombreux. Poussées par la famille, par les amies, beaucoup de jeunes filles croient qu'en épousant un modou-modou elles n'auront pas de souci matériel. Et si la crise économique mondiale a compliqué ce schéma, les idéaux restent tenaces. Awa relate :

« Entres elles, les filles se disent : "Si ce n'est pas un émigré, ne te marie pas avec lui". Certaines quittent même leurs petits copains pour un modou-modou qu'elles connaissent à peine. » Le modèle est si fortement ancré dans la société que dans la région du Fouta (nord du Sénégal), « les hommes se plaignent de ne pas trouver de femmes car ils ne sont pas émigrés », explique Fatou Sarr Sow, sociologue. Au bord des routes, de grandes villas poussent, les derniers modèles de 4x4 se pavanent dans les rues de cette ville aux allures de gros village. Les émigrés ayant fait fortune sont loin d'être majoritaires, mais ils entretiennent le fantasme.

Comme en Occident au temps des guerres, une grande majorité de la population de la ville est composée de femmes qui n'ont pas vu leur mari depuis deux, quatre, six voire dix ans.

« Je lui ai demandé : "Qui s'est marié ?" Elle m'a répondu : "toi" »

Awa est une exception, car son union est un mariage d'amour. A 13 ans, Fatimata a été mariée de force par sa tante, persuadée qu'une alliance à un modou-modou permettrait des revenus financiers assurés. Les trois quarts des mariages scellés avec des émigrés sont des mariages forcés. Aujourd'hui, Fatimata a 20 ans. Elle n'a cessé de réclamer le divorce à un mari qui l'ignore. Droite et fière, installée en tailleur sur le lit de sa patronne, elle raconte son mariage : « Un jour, je discutais avec mes copines sur la terrasse. Ma tante arrive avec des noix de kola, qu'on distribue traditionnellement pour célébrer un mariage. Je lui ai demandé : "Qui s'est marié ?" Elle m'a répondu : "toi". »

Dans la religion musulmane, pas besoin de la présence des deux époux pour célébrer le mariage. L'adolescente voit son mari une fois, puis celui-ci repart en Europe. Envoyée manu militari dans la maison de sa belle-famille, personne ne la soutient. Pendant six mois, son mari ne lui enverra pas d'argent et ne lui téléphonera pas. Trois ans plus tard, elle lui arrache enfin un divorce, plus facile à obtenir car ils n'ont pas eu d'enfants.

Un taux d'infanticide élevé

Conséquences de ces mariages précoces et forcés : un taux d'infanticide élevé lié à des grossesses extra-conjugales.

Depuis 2008, six cas connus d'infanticides ont été répertoriés dans la région, et les journaux sénégalais font régulièrement écho de ces faits divers. Au Sénégal, concevoir un enfant hors-mariage est considéré comme une honte. Les infanticides ont souvent lieu dans le milieu rural. Ces femmes sont dans des états de dépression tels qu'on ne peut pas parler d'acte choc. « De temps en temps, l'infanticide est camouflé par la famille. Le plus souvent, ces femmes enterrent leurs nouveaux-nés, les jettent dans un puits ou les abandonnent dans la rue », rapporte le capitaine.

A Louga, il n'existe pas d'associations ou de services d'assistance sociale pour leur venir en aide.

Adapté (avec l'aimable permission de l'auteure) de l'article d'Aurélie Fontaine sur le site : http://www.rue89.com

Répondez aux questions suivantes.

26. Pourquoi certaines femmes sénégalaises ne voient pas leur mari pendant plusieurs années ?

....

27. Le mari D'Awa ne peut pas revenir au Sénégal parce que…

   A. son fils n'a pas de papiers. ☐
   B. sa femme ne veut pas le voir.
   C. c'est risqué car il a des faux papiers.
   D. c'est risqué parce que sa situation n'est pas légale, il lui manque des papiers.

28. Pourquoi Awa ne va-t-elle pas rendre visite à son mari ?

....

Les phrases suivantes basées sur les lignes 15 à 25, sont soit vraies, soit fausses. Cochez la réponse correcte. Justifiez votre réponse par des mots du texte.

	vrai	*faux*
29. Aucune pression n'est exercée sur les jeunes filles ; elles font le choix d'épouser un émigré seule.	☐	☐

Justification : ....

30. Certaines filles rompent avec leur petit ami parce qu'elles sont tombées amoureuses d'un émigré. ☐ ☐

Justification : ....

31. La région du Fouta est dominée par les émigrés qui sont devenus riches. Ils sont les plus nombreux dans la région. ☐ ☐

Justification : ....

Répondez à la question suivante.

32. Selon le 3e paragraphe, pourquoi Awa est-elle différente des autres femmes ?

....

En vous basant sur le 3e paragraphe (lignes 29 à 41), reliez chaque début de phrase à la fin qui lui correspond. ATTENTION ; il y a plus de fins que de débuts.

33. Un mariage avec un émigré permettrait ... ☐

34. Les trois quarts des unions consacrées .... ☐

35. Fatimata ... ☐

36. Selon la religion musulmane, il est possible... ☐

37. Sans enfant, il est plus facile ... ☐

a. veut quitter son mari.

b. sont consensuelles.

c. de retrouver un nouvel époux.

d. d'assurer la santé économique du foyer.

e. veut que son mari arrête de l'ignorer.

f. sont des mariages forcés.

g. de divorcer.

h. se marier sans être présent/e à la cérémonie.

Répondez aux questions suivantes.

38. Selon le 4e paragraphe, pourquoi beaucoup d'enfants sont-ils tués au Sénégal ?

....

39. Selon le 4e paragraphe, où les infanticides se produisent-ils le plus souvent ?

A. dans les grandes villes
B. dans les banlieues
C. dans les villages
D. dans les petites villes

☐

40. Qui sont les auteurs de ces infanticides ?

....

Complétez le tableau suivant en indiquant à qui ou à quoi se rapportent les mots soulignés.

Dans la phrase...	***Le mot...***	***se rapporte à ....***
Exemple : « à un mari qui l'ignore » (ligne 33)	« l' »	............***Fatimata***..........
41. « Je lui ai demandé » *(ligne 36)*	« lui »	....
42. « personne ne la soutient » *(ligne 40)*	« la »	....
43. « elle lui arrache enfin un divorce » *(ligne 41)*	« lui »	....
44. « les abandonnent dans la rue » *(Ligne 51)*	« les »	....

Total : 45 points

As you know, if you are studying French at HL, you will have one more text to deal with; a literary text and your Paper 1 exam will be out of 60.

As it is not possible to use a literary extract in this version of the guide, I am adding one more text for you to practice. This text is slightly longer than the texts you will find in your Paper 1. If you are studying French at SL, please don't feel restricted / limited to the previous 4 texts and have a go at the next one too! After all, "*C'est en forgeant qu'on devient forgeron*" ("practice makes perfect")!

TEXTE E

" AU-DELÀ DES MOTS, IL Y A LES GESTES "

Campagne sur la désertification et pour la construction de puits au Mali

Bonjour,

C'est avec grand plaisir que nous vous invitons à vous joindre à la campagne « Au-delà des mots, il y a les gestes » avec les élèves de votre école. Ce projet offrirait à vos étudiants l'opportunité de vivre une expérience concrète de solidarité internationale, tout en faisant l'acquisition d'un bagage de connaissances sur la réalité des pays en développement et les impacts des changements climatiques. Ils seront également invités à poser des gestes d'écosolidaires au niveau de leur consommation d'eau et d'énergie.

Problématique de la désertification

La désertification, phénomène qui affecte directement près de 110 pays du monde, constitue une des problématiques les plus préoccupantes en lien avec le réchauffement de la planète. Elle consiste en la dégradation, l'appauvrissement des sols fertiles lorsqu'ils sont surexploités, déboisés, mal entretenus et/ou exposés à une sécheresse ou une intense pollution. Ceux-ci finissent alors par s'assécher et devenir du sable, comme un désert. Ce phénomène peut avoir des conséquences désastreuses sur les écosystèmes naturels et les populations des zones touchées, victimes de l'impossibilité de cultiver leurs terres et de bénéficier des récoltes qui assurent généralement leur survie.

Au Mali, les impacts de la désertification sont ressentis d'une façon particulièrement importante. Les 2/3 du territoire sont constitués de zones arides ou semi-arides et près de 85 % de la population y est localisée. Les gens sont contraints à abandonner leurs terres puisqu'ils ne peuvent plus les cultiver et que presque aucune forme de vie n'arrive à survivre dans un environnement aussi hostile. On assiste donc à un exode rural et à une inquiétante paupérisation de la population, tout cela dans un contexte de crise alimentaire au niveau mondial.

Projet de construction de puits

Pour mener à terme le présent projet, le Comité de Solidarité/Trois-Rivières a établi un partenariat avec Kilabo, une organisation malienne dévouée au développement du monde rural et de la paysannerie au Mali. Les fonds amassés dans le cadre de la campagne permettront de construire des puits qui viseront à lutter contre les impacts de la désertification dans la communauté malienne d'Ouelessebougou.

Ouelessebougou, située au sud de la région de Koulikoro, est actuellement fortement touchée par le phénomène de la désertification. Étant donné la pauvreté du sol et l'accès difficile à de l'eau potable et/ou d'arrosage, la production agricole locale est souvent insuffisante pour combler les besoins alimentaires de la totalité de la population. La sécheresse, la surexploitation des sols et le déboisement sont en grande partie responsables de cette situation préoccupante. Le projet « Au-delà des mots, il y a les gestes » vise donc à assurer la sécurité alimentaire et la bonification de la production agricole locale afin de garantir une meilleure valeur nutritionnelle au régime alimentaire des habitants d'Ouelessebougou.

Les retombées du projet

Le projet de coopération expliqué ci-haut permettra de soutenir les activités maraîchères et individuelles quotidiennes des habitants de la commune d'Ouelessebougou.

(…)

Les élèves auront l'opportunité de tirer un grand profit d'une telle expérience de solidarité internationale. Au terme de la campagne :

- ✓ Ils seront informés sur les problématiques de la déforestation et des changements climatiques.
- ✓ Ils auront acquis une ouverture d'esprit et une familiarité avec une réalité culturelle différente.
- ✓ Ils auront développé une confiance en leur capacité d'influencer le sort de la planète.
- ✓ Ils auront réussi à mener à terme un projet de solidarité rassembleur dans leur milieu.

Les élèves seront également introduits à la problématique de la surconsommation des ressources naturelles québécoises. Par le biais d'outils pédagogiques adaptés, ils seront en mesure d'acquérir des connaissances sur les réalités énergétique et hydrique au Québec. Des gestes écoénergétiques et écoresponsables concrets pourront par ailleurs être mis en œuvre par les jeunes et leur entourage afin de lutter contre les impacts négatifs de la surconsommation locale de l'énergie et de l'eau.

Pour participer, il suffit de remplir le formulaire d'inscription disponible par notre site Internet au www.in-terre-actif.com. Vous pouvez également communiquer avec nous par téléphone afin de permettre à votre école de prendre part à la campagne.

En souhaitant avoir l'occasion de collaborer avec vous et les élèves de votre école, veuillez agréer, Madame, Monsieur, nos salutations les plus chaleureuses.

Richard Grenier
Coordonnateur
Réseau In-Terre-Actif

Texte reproduit et adapté avec l'aimable autorisation du réseau in-Terre- Actif – www.in-terre-actif.com

Répondez aux questions suivantes.

45. Cette lettre s'adresse :

A. aux parents d'élèves
B. aux élèves
C. aux responsables des autorités locales
D. aux professeurs

☐

46. Le but de cette lettre est :

A. d'informer les parents au sujet du problème de la désertification au Mali.
B. de présenter la campagne sur la désertification et inciter les écoles à participer au projet.
C. de solliciter des dons de parents d'élèves pour aider l'association Kilabo.
D. d'inciter les professeurs à récolter de l'argent pour l'association Kilabo.

☐

47. Selon le 1er paragraphe, citez deux actions que les élèves pourront faire.

A. ……………………………………………………………………………………

B. ……………………………………………………………………………………

48. Quel mot du 3e paragraphe indique qu'au Mali les sols sont desséchés ?

……………………………………………………………………………………………

49. Quel mot du 3e paragraphe signifie « adverse » ?

……………………………………………………………………………………………

50. À la ligne 17, à quoi se rapporte « ***y*** » dans « ***y*** est localisée » ?

……………………………………………………………………………………………

51. À la ligne 18, à quoi se rapporte « ***les*** », dans « puisqu'ils ne peuvent plus ***les*** cultiver » ?

……………………………………………………………………………………………

52. Selon le 5e paragraphe, citez l'**une** des conséquences de la désertification sur la population malienne.

……………………………………………………………………………………………

Reliez chacun des mots du texte se trouvant dans la colonne de gauche à son équivalent qui se trouve dans la colonne de droite. ***ATTENTION*** *: il y a plus de mots proposés que de réponses possibles.*

53. amassés *(ligne 24)*	☐	A. abandonner
54. lutter *(ligne 25)*	☐	B. satisfaire à
55. combler *(ligne 28)*	☐	C. accumulés
56. garantir *(ligne 31)*	☐	D. combattre
		E. détruits
		F. assurer

En vous référant aux lignes 48 à 58, répondez aux questions suivantes.

57. Qu'est ce qui va permettre aux élèves de comprendre les réalités énergétiques du Québec ?

....

58. Qui, en plus des jeunes, pourra participer concrètement au combat contre la consommation excessive des ressources énergétiques et hydrauliques locales ?

....

Total : 60 points

General comments on Paper 1

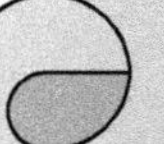

- Always bear in mind that it is a reading comprehension paper- **ALL of** the answers are in the texts and you must refer to the texts all the time.
- Do **not panic** if you don't understand every single word. Try and guess the meaning from the context.
- Remember that it is **not essential to understand all the words** anyway to get the gist of a given text.
- **Read all** the questions carefully before throwing yourself into the paper.
- Questions follow the order of the texts and line references will be provided. Make sure that you take notice of those line references in order to avoid looking for an equivalent of a word in the wrong paragraph for example… **and read the instructions**!
- Don't write full sentences when only one word or expression is required! You could end up losing / not getting your marks! Don't try and rephrase either. Use the words from the text.
- If you make a mistake and / or change your mind about an answer to a question, make sure you make it very clear which answer is your definitive one, for your examiner will not make this choice for you!
- Remember that at **Higher Level**, there will always be a text of a literary nature. No such examples have been provided in this guide for copyright reasons but do look at past papers as this will give you a fair idea of the types of texts, and do keep reading as much as possible on a regular basis too!
- Use a black or blue pen to answer the questions (***no pencil***)
- Manage your time
- Answer **ALL** questions

Chapter 2 **Paper 2 or written production** ***(productive skills)***

A) **The questions**

Depending on the level at which you are studying the language, the requirements for Paper 2 will vary.

You will have 1h30 to complete this paper *(+ 5 minutes reading time)* whether you are a SL or HL candidate.

This Paper is worth 25% of your final mark.

At SL, you will only have one section with a choice of 5 questions (*one per option*) to complete. You only choose **one** question.

At HL level, your paper will comprise of 2 sections:

- Section A: similar to the SL paper so a choice between 5 questions (*one per option*)
- Section B : *argumentation raisonnée* (reasoned argument). You will not have any choice. Section B is linked to the Core (*Tronc Commun*) part of the programme. (see section on Section B).

Paper 2 (for SL and HL Section A) is linked to the study of the **Options**: *Diversité culturelle, Loisirs, Coutumes et traditions, sciences et technologie, santé*. You will have formally studied only 2 of these options; although you will undoubtedly have worked on some aspects of the others and have enough vocabulary knowledge to choose any topic you want so **no need to panic** and get into the whole negative thinking scenario of what if none of the topics or sub-topics I have formally studied come up! In any case, one of the more specific themes you have covered in class may come up but you may not like the style of writing associated with it. You can choose any question you want - so take the time to **read all the questions** carefully in order to choose the best one for you and avoid potentially wasting time further down the line.

Each question should target a different type of text (*letter, guide, speech, etc.*).

Paper 2 SL and HL Section A is marked out of 25. A maximum of 10 marks is awarded for Language, 10 for Message and 5 marks for Presentation (type of text).

It is essential to familiarise yourself with the markscheme which you should be able to get from your teacher or IB coordinator. The markscheme will be invaluable as it will give you an indication of what you need to address in order to improve a given grade for a piece of work. It will also tell you what is required of you in order to achieve the best possible grades in each one of the criteria.

At SL and for HL Section A, you are required to write between 250 and 400 words.
The **minimum of 250 words** is a requirement as stated above and it may be helpful to know that, if you fail to reach this minimum, you will automatically loose one mark. ***So make sure you reach the minimum required if you want to avoid losing marks unnecessarily!!*** There should be no penalty if you exceed the upper limit but if there is an upper limit, it is not for it to be ignored! Writing too much is often counterproductive as the quality of your written language tends to suffer. So stick to the requirements and only write between 250 and 400 (quality) words.

Examples SL and HL Section A questions[1]:

Santé

Une de vos camarades de classe souffre d'un problème d'obésité et est constamment la victime de moqueries de la part du reste de la classe. Vous la savez déprimée et cela vous inquiète mais vous ne savez pas quoi faire pour l'aider. Vous vous confiez à votre journal intime.

→ *One of your school friends is suffering from a problem of obesity. She is constantly being teased by the rest of the class. You are aware that she is depressed and you worry about it but you are not sure of what to do. You confide in your personal diary.*

Loisirs

Vous venez de rentrer d'un voyage humanitaire organisé par votre lycée. Vous écrivez à un ami pour lui raconter votre séjour et pour l'inciter à participer au même genre de projet.

→ *You have just come back from a humanitarian trip with your school. You write to a friend to tell him / her about your experience and to convince him / her to join such a project.*

Sciences et technologie

Vous avez lu dans un journal un article condamnant vigoureusement l'euthanasie. Bien que vous soyez d'accord avec certains arguments avancés dans le magazine, vous avez un avis un peu plus mitigé sur la question. Ecrivez une lettre au rédacteur pour exprimer votre point de vue.

→ *You have read an article in a magazine in which the journalist was expressing a very strong opinion against euthanasia. Even though you share some of the points of views expressed, you have more mixed views on others. Write a letter to the editor of the magazine to explain your point of view.*

Diversité culturelle

En tant qu'étudiant/e de français et linguiste talentueux/euse, on vous a demandé de faire une présentation aux élèves des classes du collège pour leur parler de l'importance de l'apprentissage des langues et de la diversité linguistique. Vous voulez les convaincre de continuer l'apprentissage d'une langue.

→ *As a French student and talented linguist, you have been asked to give a presentation to younger students to talk to them about the importance of language learning and linguistic diversity. Your aim is to convince them to continue learning a language.*

Coutumes et traditions

Vous venez d'apprendre que la mairie de votre ville a décidé d'annuler la célébration du festival traditionnel qui, chaque année depuis plus de 50 ans, célèbre les traditions de votre région. Révolté/e par cette décision, vous décidez de rédiger un tract pour informer les habitants de votre ville et les inciter à réagir.

→ *You have just learnt that the local authority of your town have decided to cancel the annual traditional festival which, each year for over 50 years, has been celebrating the traditions in your region. You are outraged by this decision and take the initiative to write a tract in order to inform your fellow citizens and urge them to react.*

---

[1] All the examples are IB type questions but they are not actual exam questions.

How to choose the best question for me?

As you only have 1h30 to complete this paper, it is essential to devote some quality time at the beginning in order to read and "analyse" the questions (*you will be given 5 minutes reading time on top of the 1h30*). This will hopefully help you choose the right question for you and should avoid you embarking on a question on which you are going to be stuck an hour later! You should probably spend between 5 and 10 minutes choosing the right question. This might seem a lot but it is time well spent.

Read each question one after the other *(regardless of which option they relate to)* and for each one of them, ask yourself the following questions:

- What type of text is it?
- Who is the intended audience? (*this will help you decide on the correct register to use*)
- Who are you meant to be? (*yourself? A character from a book? A journalist? Etc.)*
- What is the aim of the task?
- What is the topic of the task?

NB: Don't be afraid of underlining key words and writing notes in the margins if it helps you.

topic: linguistic / cultural and personal enrichment — *Indication about who you are*

*Vous venez de rentrer d'un séjour linguistique au Québec où **vous** avez **découvert beaucoup de choses sur la langue et la culture** de ce pays. Ce voyage vous a aussi ouvert les yeux sur vous-même et **appris à mieux vous connaître**. Vous rédigez un **article pour le journal de l'école** dans lequel vous **racontez** votre expérience et **donnez des conseils** aux jeunes qui envisagent de partir en séjour linguistique.*

task — *type of text* — *audience and register*

- ***type of text*** *: article*
- ***targeted audience*** *: journal de l'école- so younger audience: the register can be familiar*
- ***Who you are****: a student in the school (enriched by a new experience)*
- ***Task****: report / describe your experience (résumé / rapport) AND give advice.*
- ***Topic****: cultural and personal discoveries / enrichment after a linguistic stay*

So once you have done that for each question you should be in a position to decide if you know enough about a particular topic and style of writing to choose the question.

⇨ *Now you can practise. Try and do the same with the questions given earlier but before you do so, it might be worth having a quick look at the following part of this writing section as you will find pointers about the format of each individual type of text as well as notes on registers of language.*

NB: *regardless of the topic of your chosen question, remember to* ***spare a few minutes at the end*** *before you have to hand your work in so that you can reread your work and* ***check*** *for any mistakes that might have crept in.*

And...

- Remember to bring a black or blue pen as well on the day of the exam to write with.
- Don't forget that this is an exam and drawings and / or irrelevant comments in the margins must be avoided if you want to create the right impression.
- try and take care of both your handwriting and the presentation of your work.
NEVER write in pencil.

More specific to HL students…

SECTION B

At HL, Paper 2 is divided into 2 sections:

- Section A: choice of one question amongst 5 / linked to options / 250 to 400 words
- Section B: a personal response ("***argumentation raisonnée***") to a given statement

What do I need to know about Section B?

- ☑ based on one (aspect) of the Core topics (***Relations Sociales / Communication et Medias, Questions Mondiales***)
- ☑ personal response to a given statement (*it could be a news headline, a famous person's statement etc.*)
- ☑ The statement could be one line or a couple of lines so be sure to read it carefully to ensure that you understand fully its implications.
- ☑ No choice
- ☑ your response must be a personal reaction to the statement. It therefore has to be structured and linked to the statement. By "linked to the statement", I mean that it needs to be focused on the main aspects / elements of the statement. If for example, you have the following statement given to you:

> *"Bien au chaud dans la poche de notre veste ou au fond de notre sac à main, allumé en permanence, le téléphone portable semble être devenu un accessoire indispensable dans la vie de tout citoyen. »*

Like for Section A, you need to take a few minutes to « analyse» the statement. What is it about? Mobile phones, of course, but what precisely about mobile phones do I have to react about? The key part of the statement here is "*indispensable dans la vie de tout citoyen*"- are mobile phones indispensable? Could we live without them today? So it isn't just a paragraph about mobile phones, the potential health risks link to them etc. or you would be missing the point of the statement.

- ☑ It is a personal response to the statement, **your** personal response, so there is no right or wrong answer as long as your response is structured, linked closely to the original statement, expresses opinions and illustrates and justifies them. You can choose to be in agreement or disagreement with the given statement or to express a mixed opinion.
- ☑ You are free to choose to write your personal response in any text type officially listed in the guide. However, remember that you are reacting to a statement and that your response must be justified and structured. This is why I would strongly recommend that you write your answer in a "mini" argumentative essay style or at least in one of the types of texts that is going to allow you to successfully and meaningfully express opinions and justify them in 250 words maximum (*speech, article, letter maybe to a push*).

- ☑ You must write between 150 and 250 words. If you fail to reach the minimum required, you will lose one mark. Again, there is no official penalty if you go beyond the upper word limit but stick to the requirements and word limit would be my advice.

- ☑ As / even if you are writing a fairly short answer (250 words maximum) in response to a written stimulus, it still needs to be meaningful. Your answer should not come across as simply a catalogue of ideas. You will need to be concise and precise and therefore be selective in your choice of ideas / opinions and supporting examples. Sometimes less is more and carries more meaning.

- ☑ Your essay / writing must be organised and coherent. You do not want to confuse yourself or your examiner. You can, as mentioned before, choose to look at the pros and cons of the statement or you can choose to stick to one side of the "argument". Whatever you decide, ensure that you are clear and coherent within the word limit. Plan to avoid losing your thread of thought and confuse everyone including yourself!

- ☑ Section B carries 20 marks (10 for the quality of language and 10 for your ability to develop and justify ideas in a structured way). It is important, like for Section A, to get hold of the marking criteria and familiarise yourself with them.

Examples of Section B statements:

Relations sociales	✓ *Dans nos sociétés modernes, les gens ne pensent qu'à eux et sont de plus en plus égoïstes. C'est la dictature du « moi d'abord », et les autres après. La solidarité n'a plus sa place.* ✓ *La religion est de moins en moins importante dans la vie des gens aujourd'hui. Le mariage religieux est donc une institution démodée qui n'a plus sa place dans notre société actuelle.*

Communication et médias	✓ *La violence est omniprésente dans les médias. Les jeunes y sont beaucoup trop exposés. On devrait interdire toute représentation de la violence à la télévision.* ✓ *La publicité est un fléau qui ne fait que tromper le public. Elle devrait être interdite.*

Questions mondiales	✓ *Chaque année, les Français donnent 3 milliards d'euros aux causes humanitaires. La majorité de ces dons est dépensée en publicité et autres frais superflus. Les personnes et les pays qui en ont besoin ne profitent pas de ces dons. Il faut arrêter de donner de l'argent aux associations caritatives.* ✓ « Désespéré, un couple a recours à la filière illégale du trafic d'organes pour tenter de sauver leur enfant ». Coupable ou innocent ?

Example of an answer to Section B

Rédigez une réponse personnelle en réponse à l'affirmation ci-dessous. Exprimez votre opinion personnelle et justifiez-la. Choisissez un des types de textes étudiés en classe. Écrivez entre 150 et 250 mots.

La publicité est un fléau qui ne fait que tromper le public. Elle devrait être interdite.

intro

Dans la société de consommation actuelle, la publicité est partout : à la télévision, dans les magazines, sur les murs de la ville, à la radio, dans les stades etc. Certaines personnes pensent qu'elle se répand comme une maladie infectieuse qui influence les gens. Elle sert à vanter des produits mais au lieu d'informer objectivement le public, elle trompe souvent le consommateur et créé un besoin superflu. On peut **donc** se demander s'il ne vaudrait pas mieux l'interdire.

mots de liaisons

S'il est vrai que la publicité peut être mensongère et cacher une partie de la vérité comme **par exemple** dans les publicités pour les voitures où tous les détails ne sont pas révélés, je pense qu'elle est utile **car** elle permet de faire connaître une diversité de produits et **donc** permet la compétition entre les fabricants d'un même type de produit. **Par conséquent**, cela incite les fabricants à toujours améliorer leurs produits pour rester compétitifs et ça permet **aussi** de contrôler les prix.

Par ailleurs, la publicité est un mode de communication entre les acheteurs potentiels et ceux qui fournissent les biens de consommation. **Même si** elle est omniprésente, elle ne nous est pas imposée et en tant qu'individu on peut choisir de la regarder ou pas.

conclusion

En conclusion, **même si** la publicité peut nous tromper, il me semble inutile et injuste de l'interdire. C'est à nous de choisir d'y croire ou non. C'est à nous d'exercer notre esprit critique et de savoir faire la part des choses.

246 mots

You should now feel able to tackle section B confidently.

Bear in mind that although you have two Sections to your written paper and therefore 2 tasks to deal with, you still only have 1h30 minutes to complete the whole paper (+ 5 minutes reading time). It is therefore essential that you manage your time efficiently.
You can start with Section B if you want. It is entirely up to you but you need to be organised as you will be switching between tasks and topics.

<u>Types of texts to master for Paper 2</u>

Here is a checklist that will help you with your revision. Just tick the box as you revise each of these types of texts.

	Revised
A) le journal intime et le blog *(p.42 to 44)*	☐
B) un article (p. 45)	☐
C1) une lettre officielle *(p. 46 to 49)* (*lettre de réclamation, lettre de candidature, lettre à un auteur...)*	☐
C2) lettre à un ami *(p. 50)*	☐
C3) le courriel *(p. 51)*	☐
D) le discours *(p.52 -53)*	☐
E) le guide de recommandations, le dépliant, la brochure… *(p.54-55)*	☐
F) le compte rendu / le rapport officiel *(p. 56)*	☐
G) la critique d'un film / livre etc. *(p.57)*	☐
H) une interview *(p. 58)*	☐
I) le tract / l'appel *(p. 59)*	☐
J) la dissertation *(p.61-62)*	☐

This list is the official list that can be found in the official Language B guide. This means that those text types listed above are the only ones that can come up in Paper 2, be it at SL or HL.

However, when it comes to the ***Travail Écrit*** or Written Task (*dealt with in the next Chapter of this book*), you can choose other types of texts to if you wish to so the following ones are some extras so that you have more options.

Additional types of texts useful for the Written Task

Le journal intime

Le journal intime or diary is a piece of "personal writing" in which people often express their feelings about someone or a situation. It can be happiness or sadness or even anger, etc.
As the intended audience is primarily yourself, the writer, you can use some familiar expressions. What you write in your *journa*l *intime* will obviously depend on the question asked, BUT whatever the question is, a *journal intime* should always have **a date**, **"Cher journal"** and your style should be direct and expressive: you should pretend that you are conversing with a friend and address this friend directly. At the end, you should "conclude" by saying good night to your *journal* and you can sign as well if you wish, BUT if you do so, no need to use your last name as your diary "*knows*" who you are!

La date →

NB:
Here, Louis is writing directly to his diary. "**Tu** te rends compte, **journal**, " He expresses his anger very successfully by using a *variety* of grammatical and linguistic tools: "*Tu te rends compte*" (*vocab*), punctuation (!!), question. His style of writing is Informal : "*bon*", "*nuls*" but this does not mean that his grammar is incorrect or too simple. Indeed he has even used 2 subjunctives here: *aille* and *comprenne*.

Lundi 12 juillet 2007

Cher journal,

J'en ai marre de mes parents!! Ils sont trop strictes!! Ils sont toujours en train de me faire des remarques sur mes copains. Ce soir maman m'a interdit de sortir avec Maxime et Xavier sous prétexte qu'ils ne sont pas assez sérieux!! Tu te rends compte, journal, j'ai 16 ans et mes parents m'interdisent de sortir le soir!!! Tu crois que les autres parents sont aussi nuls?? C'est pas juste!!!...
(...)

Bon, il est tard , il faut que j'aille me coucher.
Merci de m'avoir écouté, journal, tu es vraiment le seul qui me comprenne!
Bonne nuit

a.1.) ***Journal intime et expression des émotions***

As mentioned previously. A lot of emotions are expressed in one's personal diary. Those emotions can be positive or negative. (***anger / frustration / surprise / happiness / disappointment / sadness / misunderstanding / feeling of injustice / regret / feeling of being fed-up***)

Let's practise! *(answers page 184)*

Below is a list of those emotions and a list of phrases that can be found in a diary page. Link each one of these phrases to one of the emotions (*some phrases can be linked to more than one emotion*).

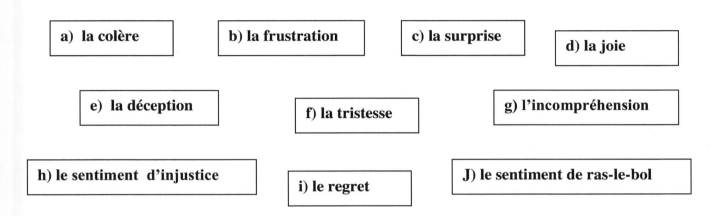

a) la colère

b) la frustration

c) la surprise

d) la joie

e) la déception

f) la tristesse

g) l'incompréhension

h) le sentiment d'injustice

i) le regret

J) le sentiment de ras-le-bol

1) Ça m'énerve !! Ils ne peuvent pas se mêler de leurs affaires / oignons !
2) On ne peut jamais discuter avec eux !
3) C'est vraiment génial !
4) Comment a-t-elle pu me faire ça à moi, sa meilleure amie !
5) J'en ai marre !
6) C'est pas juste ! C'est toujours la même chose avec eux !
7) J'aurais dû lui dire la vérité...
8) Ils sont toujours sur mon dos !
9) Je suis déçu.
10) Mais pourquoi a-t-il fait ça ?
11) Si seulement ils pouvaient me lâcher les baskets !
12) C'est énervant à la fin !
13) J'y crois pas !
14) Mon frère me prend la tête !
15) C'est plus fort que moi, je n'ai pas arrêté de pleurer depuis que j'ai appris la nouvelle.
16) Je n'en reviens toujours pas !
17) Je n'en peux plus ! Il est temps que ça s'arrête !
18) Elle m'agace à la fin ! Elle est toujours en train de pleurer pour un oui ou pour un non.
19) Je suis trop contente... Il m'a enfin téléphoné ! Je suis impatiente de le voir demain.
20) Ça arrive à tout le monde de se tromper/ faire des erreurs ? Qu'est-ce que tu en penses, journal ?

NB: *If you are stuck on the meaning of these phrases, turn to page 164 and you will find a translation for some of them.*

a.2) ***Le blog / blogue ou bloc-notes***

Instead of being asked to write a page of your / a diary, you might be asked to write a blog. So you might be asking yourselves the following questions: *What is a blog? How am going to approach it?* Well, if you think about it, a blog, is not very different from a "*journal intime*" and most of the task requirements will therefore be similar. Like the *journal intime*, It is a **personal** page in which emotions / opinions about a specific issue perhaps are likely to be expressed. The main difference is that your diary page is not meant to be read by anyone. However, your blog page is a personal page - true, but it is one which is meant to be on a **website** so, therefore, its purpose is to **share** your thoughts and emotions with others. So, you might not want to be as open with your thoughts and emotions as you are in a personal diary.

The blog is a personal page so familiar language can be used (*see example below*) but then again, it very much depends on the nature and audience of the website on which your blog is going to be posted. In some contexts (for example on a newspaper website like *Le Monde*), the use of formal register might be more appropriate.

As for the diary, your blog entries must be **dated**. However, it is important to note that unlike the diary entries, the most recent entry will be at the top of your page as it appears on your computer screen in **reverse chronological order**.

Photos can be posted on a blog but remember that you are not judged on your artistic talent in a French exam, so don't waste your time drawing!

Note that an entry on a blog page is called "**un billet**". A person who writes a blog is called "**un blogeur**". An entry can be modified or updated and this change is then called "**une mise à jour**". There might also be a list with links to other blogs on the site, such a list is called "**une blogliste**" and generally appears in a menu on the side.

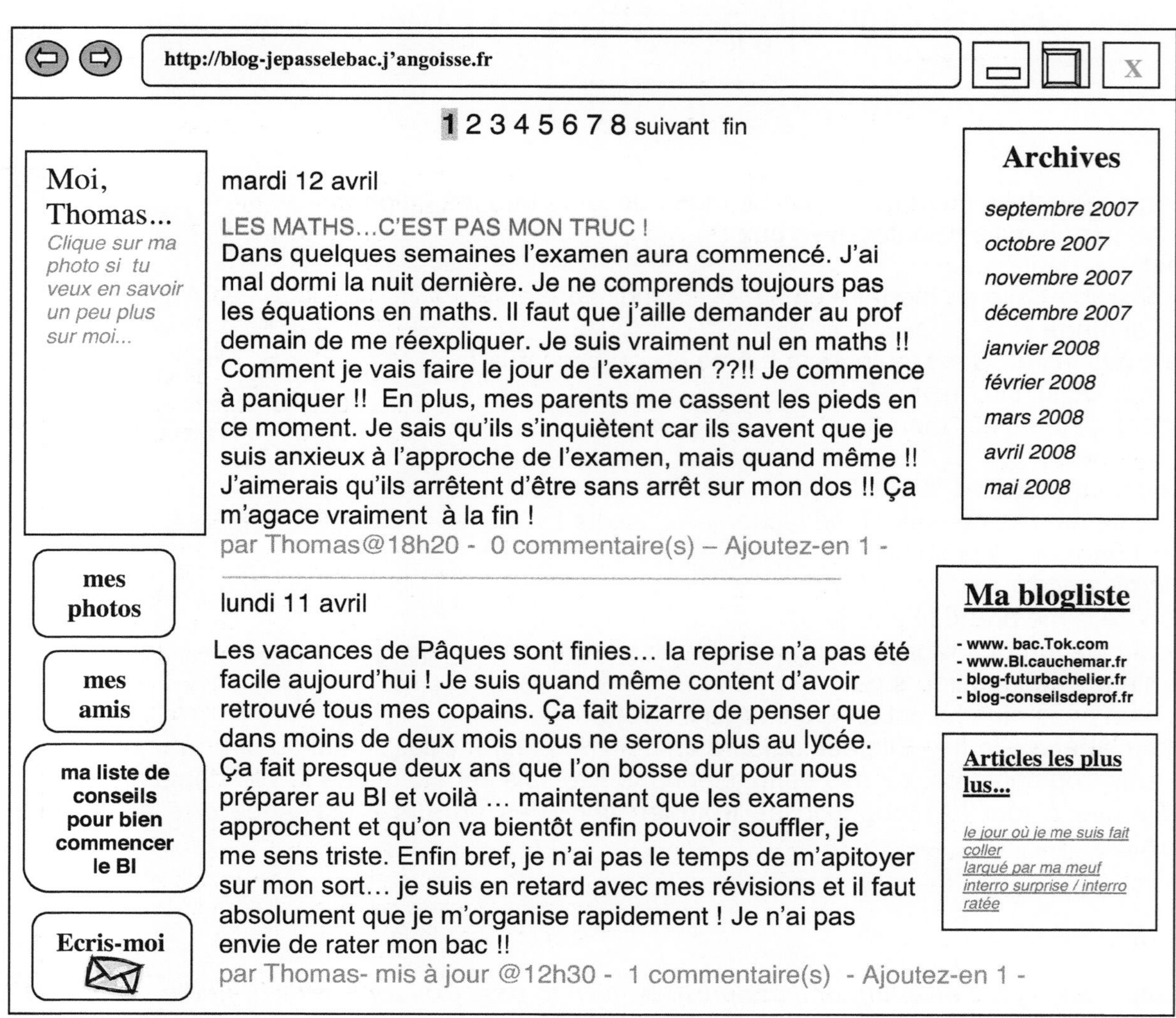

B) **L'article**

An article is a piece of written work in which the journalist is going to give information about someone / an event (etc.). The tone of an article can be neutral but it can also be subjective and therefore express a strong opinion about something. The register of language used can be very formal (*if you are writing an article for Le Monde for example*) or can be more familiar (*School newspaper*).
All of this will depend entirely of the targeted audience and the type of newspaper you are meant to be writing for.

An article may also take different forms: it can be one relatively short paragraph; it may be divided in columns. Just pick up a newspaper and see for yourself: whatever the language, the apparent structure of an article is very specific and recognisable and so should yours be.
So even if the content and style of language may vary from one article to another, an article should always have:

- a main title (*gros titre*)
- a date
- the name of the journalist
- as your articles will be a least 250 words long, you really ought to think of divided it into paragraphs with sub headings (*sous-titres*)
- examples or percentages to reinforce your message

An article may also contain:

- a brief introduction
- pictures BUT don't waste your time drawing pretty pictures(!)- just draw a box and write a caption.
- depending on the type of article, humour can be used as well
- invented quotations from interviewed people.
- use of the conditional tenses to expose unverified facts (*Un vol* ***aurait été commis*** *chez le grand bijoutier Cartier ce matin, mais les faits n'ont pas encore été confirmés*).

gros titre → **L'eau, une ressource inépuisable ?** -La gazette des écolos -26 mai 2008 - ← date

"chapeau" → ***Nous le savons tous… sans eau… pas de vie sur terre! L'eau est une ressource très précieuse. Mais à une époque et dans une société matérialistes où tout est produit en abondance, l'eau est-elle vraiment une ressource inépuisable ?***

"introduction" → *Quoi de plus naturel que de prendre une douche ou de se faire couler un bain ? Tout aussi normal de voir une eau claire et limpide s'écouler du robinet… Pourtant, plus d'un milliards d'êtres humains n'ont pas ce privilège ! Pourquoi ? Comment cela est-il toujours possible à notre époque ?*

chiffre / exemple

sous-titres

Manque de ressources
Dans beaucoup de pays du tiers monde (*notamment en Afrique*), les habitants n'ont pas accès régulièrement à une eau potable. En raisons de conditions climatiques et / ou géographiques, l'eau y est une denrée plus rare. Par ailleurs, un manque de moyens financiers vient encore s'ajouter à ce problème naturel. Sans argent, impossible de mettre en place des systèmes d'assainissement tels les stations d'épuration ou encore les égouts.

Conditions de vie difficile

Qui dit manque d'eau, dit difficultés quotidiennes. Des actes aussi banals que se laver les mains, faire la vaisselle, laver le linge deviennent synonymes de manque d'hygiène. Ce problème est également à l'origine de maladies et parfois d'épidémies. Ceci constitue aussi un frein au développement économique de ces pays.

Mais nous n'avons rien à craindre !
Si ces problèmes n'affectent pour l'instant que les pays en voie de développement, le problème risque de se généraliser dans les années à venir. En effet, non seulement la population mondiale continue à augmenter, mais la pollution et les effets néfastes du réchauffement climatique commencent à se faire sentir. L'eau se raréfie notamment à cause de notre surconsommation ! Cessons enfin d'être égoïstes et de ne penser qu'à nous ! Montrons-nous responsables car il est urgent que nous arrêtions de gaspiller et commencions à partager cette ressource si précieuse: l'eau.

par Laure Lasource ← nom du journaliste

C) La lettre

A letter can be formal or informal.

1) Presentation of a **formal letter**:

Whether you are meant to be writing a formal letter to *apply for a job, ask for information, complain about something, congratulate someone or thank someone*, the "traditional" presentation of the formal letter will have to be respected.

Nom et adresse de l'expéditeur

Nom et adresse du destinataire

OBJET: *

PIÈCES JOINTES: *

Lieu, et date

Formule d'appel,

-

Formule de politesse

signature

*Both boxes marked by an asterisk will only appear in some types of letters (*lettre de motivation* ou de *plainte* for example). When they are appropriate and you need to use them, you must write "**Objet:**" and "**Pièces jointes**:".

You will also have gathered that the boxes are there to show you where to put which information but they are not to be drawn on your letter on the day of the exam, nor do you need the word for what each section is called!

But do you know what they are and how to formulate them...?

Let's practise!

Match each example with the right category.

1) nom et adresse de l'expéditeur	☐	**a) C.V.**
2) nom et adresse du destinataire	☐	**b) Lyon, le 12 juillet 2008**
3) lieu et date	☐	**c) Je vous prie d'agréer, Monsieur, l'expression de mes sentiments distingués.**
4) objet :	☐	**d) Ton / votre nom Ton / votre adresse**
5) pièces jointes :	☐	**e) Madame,**
6) formule d'appel	☐	f) Jules Laforgue
7) formule de politesse	☐	**g) demande de renseignements**
8) signature	☐	**h) Hôtel Arc-en- ciel 16 avenue du Général de Gaulle 69 000 Lyon**

A few more details about the format of the formal letter:

1) The "***formule d'appel***" is linked to the "***adresse du destinataire***". There are 3 possibilities:

a) If you know the name of your "*destinataire*" (*Madame Dupont*) and have mentioned it in the address, you will start your letter with: "***Madame,*** "

b) You know the position / job title of your "***destinataire***" in the firm and have mentioned it in the address (*Monsieur le Directeur Général*), you will then start your letter with: "***Monsieur le Directeur,***".

C) You do not the name the function of your "*destinataire*" and you do not know if your are addressing your letter to a man or a woman, so to avoid offending anyone, just start your letter as follows: "***Madame / Monsieur,***"

NB: *Please avoid using "Cher Monsieur," / "Chère Madame,"*

2) "***Formule de politesse***" :
There is obviously more than one formula and /or some possible variations of the one given above. However, do remember that it has to be used and used correctly. It does translate as "*Yours Sincerely*" and needs to be written in full in a formal letter.
Even if you are writing a letter to complain about something and your complaint is rather strong, you still need to finish your letter with the ***"formule de politesse"***.
Here is a variation of the structure. Learn one but learn it well (spelling included!).

Je vous prie de croire, Madame, en l'assurance de mes sentiments dévoués.

You can be asked to write different types of formal letters:

- lettre de remerciements / félicitations ***(Thank you / congratulation letter)***
- lettre de demande de renseignements ou informations → ***(asking for info)***
- lettre de motivation → ***(job application)***
- lettre de réclamation / pour vous plaindre → ***(letter of complaint)***
- lettre à un journal / au courrier des lecteurs → (***pour féliciter ou vous plaindre***)

Whichever type of formal letter you have to write, and regardless of the topic, you must bear in mind the following:

- Use the appropriate register of language- you will need to use the "***vous***" form and to be coherent all the way through your letter.
- Beyond the use of the "***vous***" form, you also need to choose your vocabulary and structures from the formal register (*see paragraph on registers of language)*
- Your letter must be **STRUCTURED** so use link words.
- Even if you are writing a strong letter of complaint, do not use swear words. The punctuation, your choice of vocabulary and your style of writing should convey your anger or disappointment.

→ ***Comment osez-vous affirmer dans votre publicité que votre voiture ne tombe jamais en panne ?!***

→ ***Je tenais à vous exprimer mon mécontentement.***

- If part of the question requirement is to congratulate, complain or even convince, don't forget to use examples to support your arguments and ideas.
- If you are writing to an author about a book or a character, or indeed have to put yourself in the shoes of one of a characters writing to its author, make sure you know enough about the book or the character to be convincing.

Here is a situation and one example of a formal letter: *a letter of complaint.*

Question: (Option loisir – tourisme)

Le conseil général de votre région vient de donner son accord pour la construction d'un nouvel aéroport. Bien que vous compreniez les enjeux économiques d'un tel projet pour votre région, vous êtes contre ce projet car cet aéroport va être construit à moins de 10 km de votre paisible village.
Vous décidez d'écrire une lettre au Président du conseil général de votre région pour protester contre la construction de ce nouvel aéroport.

Jean Aimarre
5 avenue Colère
32110 Nogaro

Monsieur le Président du
Conseil Général
12 rue Victor Hugo
32110 Auch

OBJET: construction de l'aéroport

Nogaro, le 16 mai 2007

Monsieur le Président,

Je me permets de vous écrire pour vous signifier mon opposition face à la décision de construction d'un aéroport près de Nogaro. En tant que maire du village de Nogaro, je me fais aussi le porte-parole de mes concitoyens par le biais de cette lettre. J'habite à Nogaro depuis plus de 30 ans et, comme vous le savez, l'un des attraits principaux de ce village a toujours été sa tranquillité. Tous les habitants s'accordent pour dire que la construction d'un aéroport à moins de 10 km du village ne pourra que contribuer à la dégradation de leur cadre de vie et de celui des habitants des communes voisines. **Bien que** nous comprenions les raisons de votre décision, nous ne pouvons rester silencieux et inactifs face à la menace écologique qu'un tel projet représente. **Certes**, nous ne contestons pas l'idée que l'impact économique lié à la construction d'un aéroport puisse être attrayante. **Par ailleurs**, nous ne nions pas que la construction de l'aéroport puisse faciliter et améliorer les transports dans la région et contribuer à les rendre plus accessibles aux touristes potentiels. Nous sommes **également** conscients que la construction d'un aéroport pourrait contribuer au développement de nouvelles infrastructures ainsi qu'à la création de nouveaux emplois. **Toutefois**, nous sommes farouchement opposés à la construction de cet aéroport aussi près de notre belle commune ou de toute autre zone habitée ! **En effet**, le niveau de pollution sonore engendré par un accroissement du trafic aérien ne peut qu'être nuisible à notre environnement. Tolèreriez-vous le passage incessant d'avions au-dessus de votre jardin ? Trouveriez-vous un tel niveau de bruit acceptable ? Permettez-moi d'en douter !

De plus, le bruit n'est pas le seul problème écologique qu'un tel projet engendrera. Avez-vous songé aux émissions de gaz produites par les avions ? Avez-vous pensé à la pollution engendrée par l'accroissement du transport routier nécessaire au succès de tout aéroport ? Est-il utile de mentionner les conséquences sur notre belle campagne qui se verra, sans aucun doute, défigurée par ce monstre technologique ?? Avez-vous considéré les effets, sans aucun doute nocifs, que le niveau de pollution créé par la construction de cet aéroport aura sur les générations futures? Ne devrions-nous pas plutôt être vigilants et agir pour la sauvegarde de la planète et dans le meilleur intérêt de nos enfants ?

C'est **donc** pour toutes ces raisons que nous vous demandons, Monsieur, de revenir sur votre décision et de reconsidérer l'emplacement initialement prévu pour la construction de ce nouvel aéroport. Nogaro est fière de sa qualité de vie et compte sur vous pour l'aider à la préserver.

Dans l'attente de votre réponse, je vous prie de croire, Monsieur, en l'assurance de mes sentiments distingués.

Jean Aimarre

2) The **informal letter**

As you know, a letter can be informal. An informal letter is a letter that you write to a friend, your parents, someone you know very well.
The types of informal letter that you could be asked to write are likely to be along those lines:

- letter to a friend to give advice
- letter to your parents to convince them of something
- letter to thank someone for helping you or for hosting a family
- letter to ask someone advice
- letter to a friend to talk about a specific event and express your emotions

Whatever the purpose of your informal letter, there are a few key points to keep in mind:

- *Informal or not, your letter needs to l**ook** and be structured **like a letter**.*
  This means that it needs to contain the following:
  - Addresses (*they are not essential in an informal letter but it looks good if you show you know where they go- at least in Paper 2. You can "forget" about them in Paper1)*
  - Place and date
  - « *formule d'appel* » – *(Cher Luc, / Salut François !)*
  - «*formule de politesse*» - *(à bientôt / écris-moi vite / je t'embrasse...)*
  - Signature *(and remember that your signature must be that of whoever you are meant to be! Be careful, especially if the letter is for the Written Response in Paper 1)*
- *Your use of **register** must be **coherent** throughout your letter.*
  You will be using the informal register. You can use the "***tu***" form or the "***vous***" plural form depending on who you are writing to.
- *Your letter needs to be logical and **STRUCTURED**.*
  However, you will need to be judicious in your choice of linking devices for some might be more suited to a formal context than an informal one!

Vous participez à un échange. Vous écrivez à vos parents pour leur parler de votre expérience.

M et Mme Lemaire
Allée des Acacias
36220 Toulon

Montréal, le 15 décembre 2008

Mes chers parents,

J'espère que vous allez bien et que David et Hélène vont bien aussi. Ça fait maintenant 10 jours que je suis ici à Montréal et j'ai décidé de vous écrire pour vous donner quelques nouvelles. Ma famille d'accueil est charmante. Mon corres, François est super rigolo et ses parents sont très gentils. Sa mère nous mijote de bons petits plats tous les soirs. Elle m'a fait goûter à des plats traditionnels et je vais vous ramener quelques unes de ses recettes ! Ici il fait très froid et j'ai un peu de mal à m'y habituer. Nous sommes allés faire une promenade en chiens de traîneau hier et les paysages étaient magnifiques ! Nous avons aussi vu une meute de loups et je n'étais pas très rassuré. Evidemment, François s'est moqué de moi et il m'a dit qu'il fallait que je sois plus courageux!
(...)
Je vous laisse pur maintenant et vous embrasse bien fort. À bientôt.
Guillaume

3) Le **courriel** ou **courrier électronique**

Instead of being asked to write a letter, the task requirement might be to write an email. An email, like a letter, can be either formal or informal. In effect, an email is a form of communication which is very close to the letter... It is an electronic letter! So what are the common traits and differences between the two? Below is a check list of what should appear in an email as far as the format is concerned.

Formal and informal emails:

	YES	NO
- ***Do I need to write the addresses in full at the top?*** *The addresses will be electronic ones and will appear in boxes at the top.*	☐	☑
- ***Do I need to write the place and date?*** *The date (and even the time) appear automatically in the recipient's email once opened. So draw those boxes and fill them in appropriately.*	☐	☑
- ***Do I need to use a "formule d'appel"?*** *Email or not, you still need to address the person who are emailing in an appropriate way.*	☑	☐
- ***Do I need to end my email with a "formule de politesse"?*** *Whether it takes the form of an email or not, the "formule de politesse" is compulsory. choose the appropriate one according to the type of email (formal or informal) you need to write (see paragraphs about letters).*	☑	☐
- ***Do I need to sign my email?*** *Even if your name will automatically appear in your recipient's email box when he / she receives it, it is polite to write your first name (informal email) or full name (formal email) at the end of your email.*	☑	☐
- ***Do I need to write "objet" or "piece(s) jointe(s)" at the top of my email if appropriate?*** *Like with the addresses, these pieces of information, if appropriate, will appear in some boxes at the top of your email but not in the body of your email.*	☐	☑
- ***If I am writing a formal email, do I need to use the "vous" form and the formal register and vocabulary?***	☑	☐
- ***If I am writing an informal email, can I use the "tu" form and the informal register?***	☑	☐

nouveau message | **envoyer** | **sauvegarder** | **attacher pièce jointe**

De:	*clairemessage@yahoo.fr*
À:	*hélènelavigne@wanadoo.fr*
Cc:	
Objet:	*Bonjour des sports d'hiver!*
Pièces jointes :	*une photo de moi sur les pistes!*

Chère Hélène,

Comment vas-tu? Je t'envoie un petit message de Courchevel où je passe mes journées sur les pistes. Il a neigé toute la nuit et ce matin la neige était poudreuse... des conditions idéales pour faire du ski !
Ce week-end je suis allée en boîte avec des amis et j'ai rencontré un mec super…
(…)
Bon je te laisse et je t'envoie plein de gros bisous. À dans deux semaines.
Claire

D) **Le discours**

A speech is primarily written to be said, therefore, it will have to be extremely well structured and clear. A speech is also generally meant to present facts and convince an audience of something (*for example, you might want to convince your audience to react against the rise in climate changes or maybe to join a specific group etc.*).

Examples of questions:

- Write a speech to inform young children about the dangers of drugs.
- Write a speech to raise awareness amongst your peers of the rise of violence in schools and the necessity to address the issue.

Whatever the context and topic, and whoever your audience is, there are certain elements that need to be respected when writing a speech.

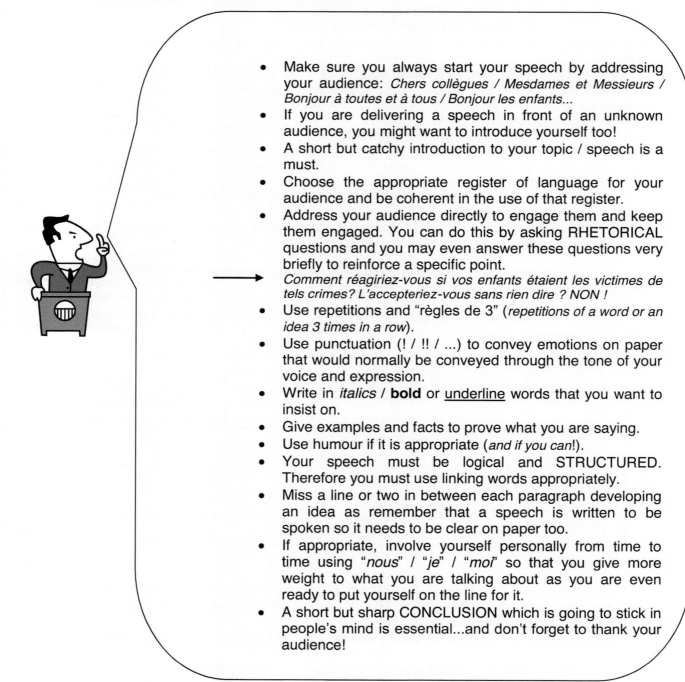

- Make sure you always start your speech by addressing your audience: *Chers collègues / Mesdames et Messieurs / Bonjour à toutes et à tous / Bonjour les enfants...*
- If you are delivering a speech in front of an unknown audience, you might want to introduce yourself too!
- A short but catchy introduction to your topic / speech is a must.
- Choose the appropriate register of language for your audience and be coherent in the use of that register.
- Address your audience directly to engage them and keep them engaged. You can do this by asking RHETORICAL questions and you may even answer these questions very briefly to reinforce a specific point.
  → *Comment réagiriez-vous si vos enfants étaient les victimes de tels crimes? L'accepteriez-vous sans rien dire ? NON !*
- Use repetitions and "règles de 3" (*repetitions of a word or an idea 3 times in a row*).
- Use punctuation (! / !! / ...) to convey emotions on paper that would normally be conveyed through the tone of your voice and expression.
- Write in *italics* / **bold** or <u>underline</u> words that you want to insist on.
- Give examples and facts to prove what you are saying.
- Use humour if it is appropriate (*and if you can*!).
- Your speech must be logical and STRUCTURED. Therefore you must use linking words appropriately.
- Miss a line or two in between each paragraph developing an idea as remember that a speech is written to be spoken so it needs to be clear on paper too.
- If appropriate, involve yourself personally from time to time using "*nous*" / "*je*" / "*moi*" so that you give more weight to what you are talking about as you are even ready to put yourself on the line for it.
- A short but sharp CONCLUSION which is going to stick in people's mind is essential...and don't forget to thank your audience!

Below is an example of a very famous speech made on the 18th June 1940 by the Général De Gaulle on the radio from London. The speech is what we call "*un appel*" to all French people to join the Resistance and fight back the Germans in occupied France. It is a very powerful and effective speech. Take a look at some of the devices use by the Général de Gaulle to convey his message and convince people.

Les chefs qui, depuis de nombreuses années, sont à la tête des armées françaises, ont formé un gouvernement. Ce gouvernement, alléguant la défaite de nos armées, s'est mis en rapport avec l'ennemi pour cesser le combat.

"***certes***" / "***mais***" → Mots de liaison

Certes, nous avons été, nous sommes, submergés par la force mécanique, terrestre et aérienne, de l'ennemi.

Infiniment plus que leur nombre, ce sont les chars, les avions, la tactique des Allemands qui nous font reculer. Ce sont les chars, les avions, la tactique des Allemands qui ont surpris nos chefs au point de les amener là où ils en sont aujourd'hui.

Questions Rhétoriques (+réponse brève)

Mais le dernier mot est-il dit ? L'espérance doit-elle disparaître ? La défaite est-elle définitive ? Non !

Croyez-moi, moi qui vous parle en connaissance de cause et vous dis que rien n'est perdu pour la France. Les mêmes moyens qui nous ont vaincus peuvent faire venir un jour la victoire.

Répétition (3 fois) →

Car la France n'est pas seule ! Elle n'est pas seule ! Elle n'est pas seule ! Elle a un vaste Empire derrière elle. Elle peut faire bloc avec l'Empire britannique qui tient la mer et continue la lutte. Elle peut, comme l'Angleterre, utiliser sans limites l'immense industrie des Etats-Unis.

Cette guerre n'est pas limitée au territoire malheureux de notre pays. Cette guerre n'est pas tranchée par la bataille de France. Cette guerre est une guerre mondiale. Toutes les fautes, tous les retards, toutes les souffrances, n'empêchent pas qu'il y a, dans l'univers, tous les moyens nécessaires pour écraser un jour nos ennemis. Foudroyés aujourd'hui par la force mécanique, nous pourrons vaincre dans l'avenir par une force mécanique supérieure. Le destin du monde est là.

« ***Moi*** » s'implique de façon personnelle →

Moi, Général de Gaulle, actuellement à Londres, j'invite les officiers et les soldats français qui se trouvent en territoire britannique ou qui viendraient à s'y trouver, avec leurs armes ou sans leurs armes, j'invite les ingénieurs et les ouvriers spécialistes des industries d'armement qui se trouvent en territoire britannique ou qui viendraient à s'y trouver, à se mettre en rapport avec moi.

Quoi qu'il arrive, la flamme de la résistance française ne doit pas s'éteindre et ne s'éteindra pas.

« conclusion » → brève et pertinente

Demain, comme aujourd'hui, je parlerai à la Radio de Londres.

E) Le guide de recommandations / le dépliant / la brochure

The main purpose of a guide or brochure is generally to give you (*the target audience*) advice about something or making you aware of a specific issue and asking you to help or act in a certain way. For example, you, as an expert, could be asked to write a guide to give advice on how to organise their time to students starting their IB. A guide can often be found under the form of a leaflet. However, you will not be able to fold your exam paper on the day of the exam, but you can still (although *this is not essential*) make it look like a folding leaflet simply by dividing your page into two or three columns. You know how guides look. They can be found everywhere and about everything these days. Just have a look and use your creative sense. However, whichever way you choose to present your guide, there are certain items of language and structures that you must be careful to use.

A guide always has a catchy / explicit or useful **TITLE**

- A guide must have a good **INTRODUCTION** which is going to make your targeted audience interested in reading your guide.
- **<u>SUBTITLES</u>**
  They may be used to divide your guide into distinctive parts / paragraph. The presentation must be clear and reader friendly.
- **HOWEVER**, your guide must also be **STRUCTURED**. Use link words.
- In your paragraphs, use **examples** and / or **facts** to prove that what your are saying. How can you convince someone if you don't have any proof!
- Use **punctuation** (? / ! / ...) to make your guide more convincing / interesting.
- Make sure that you are **consistent** in your use of **register** of language. You may use the collective "***vous***" or even "***nous***" to involve yourself but you can also use the "***tu***" for a younger audience to create a feeling of being addressed directly.
- **Engage your audience** by asking *question*s which are likely to make them think about specific ideas / issues.
- You can use **lists** of words or phrases in some paragraphs.
- You can **emphasise** some ideas or words by putting them in **bold** / *italics* or <u>underlining</u> them.

- If you need to give **advice**, vary your structures:

  - **Devoir / pouvoir** + infinitif
  - **Il faut** + infinitif (*il faut arrêter de fumer de toute urgence)*
  - **Il faut que** + subjonctif (*il faut que vous arrêtiez de fumer)*
  - **Il est important / essentiel** (etc.) que + subjonctif
  - **Impératif** (*mangez moins de chocolat !*)
  - Je te / vous **conseille** / **déconseille** / **suggère** / **recommande de** + infinitif
  - **Suggérer que** + subjonctif
  - **Pourquoi ne pas** + infinitif **?** → *Pourquoi ne pas en parler avec vos amis ?*
  - **Infinitifs** *(regarder la tété trop souvent n'est pas bon pour votre santé).*
  - **Structures en « si »**
    → *Et si vous arrêtiez de vous plaindre et commenciez plutôt à vous mobiliser ?*
    → *Si vous suivez ces conseils, vous réussirez votre guide de recommandations !*

- **Pictures**
  Just draw a box and add a caption!

- A short but to the point **CONCLUSION** is needed.

- **Contact details** :
  Pour plus de renseignements, contactez le numéro vert suivant: 08-50-00-64

Below is a mini Guide de recommandations *aimed at parents who are travelling with young children. The aim of the guide is to provide parents with advice to help them and their children have a good journey. Reconcile each title with the right paragraph and put the verbs in brackets in the imperative along the way! (you can look on page 91 for help!)*

Conseils pour voyager avec de jeunes enfants[2]

Voyager avec des enfants n'est pas toujours facile. Voyager avec des enfants, c'est aussi poser sur le monde le même regard émerveillé qu'eux…N'oubliez pas cependant que vous voyagerez à leur rythme et non au vôtre. Voici donc quelques conseils pour faciliter votre voyage.

1. ....

Si vous prenez l'avion, il est essentiel d'avoir des documents prouvant l'identité de votre enfant avec vous. (***vérifier***) la date de ces documents avant de partir.

2. ....

(***s'assurer***) qu'il a sur lui un document permettant de l'identifier au cas où vous seriez séparés. Pourquoi ne pas écrire son nom ainsi qu'un numéro de téléphone à l'intérieur de son sac à dos ?

3. ....

Si vous voyagez en voiture, (***s'arrêter***) souvent pour lui permettre de se dégourdir les jambes et de dépenser son trop plein d'énergie.

4. ....

Pour éviter que l'ennui ne s'empare de votre progéniture, (***ne pas oublier***) d'emporter des jeux et des livres pour le divertir pendant le voyage.

5. ....

Si vous voyagez avec de très jeunes enfants, n'oubliez pas les médicaments ainsi que tout le matériel nécessaire au bien-être de votre bébé.

6. ....

(***préparer***) des sandwichs avant le départ, (***emporter***) des barres de chocolat et autres friandises pour combler les petites faims.

7. ....

Si votre enfant voyage seul en avion, (***demander***) à ce qu'il soit accompagné par une hôtesse de l'air qui pourra le guider pendant le voyage.

8. ....

Si vous voyagez seul(e) avec votre enfant, (***se faciliter***) la vie en emportant le strict nécessaire.

Bon voyage !

a) (*Penser à*) **faire le plein de distractions**

b) (*ne jamais laisser*) **un jeune enfant sans surveillance**

c) (*prendre*) **des dispositions à l'avance avec la compagnie aérienne pour qu'il soit escorté**

d) (*emporter*) **une quantité suffisante de produits pour bébé**

e) (*s'assurer*) **que votre enfant a un passeport valide**

f) (*être*) **raisonnable;** (*se charger*) **le moins possible**

g) (*prévoir*) **les encas**

h) (*faire*) **des pauses régulièrement**

(answers page 184)

[2] D'après le guide : *Bon voyage, mais…*

F) Le compte rendu / Le rapport officiel

The « ***compte rendu*** » or « ***résumé*** » or **. ....** ***ort official"*** is an account / a summary of an event that you might have been involved with or taken part in or something that has happened. As it is an account, it is a **factual** report of an event. It should therefore be **objective** and as **precise** as possible. You could be asked, for example, to give an account of a sport or cultural event in which you have participated, or an account of a humanitarian trip or even an account of the preparation process before the trip. An account will therefore give **detailed information** about the event as well as **examples** and **proof** of what you are saying.
As it is a **structured** write-up about a past event, it should mainly be in the past, but obviously, other tenses and moods can be used too when and where appropriate. Having said that, one could envisage being asked to provide a "***compte rendu***" or a ***"rapport officiel"*** of a future event. In this case, they will take the form of a structured proposal and the future tense might then be more appropriate. When you write a ***"rapport officiel"***, you may have to draw a clear conclusion regarding the benefit or success of the event that has taken place for example.
The style and register that you need to use will vary according to the context, aim, purpose and your audience too (*for example, you could be asked to write a summary of a cultural activity in which you have taken part, like a play or a concert, for an article which will be published in a school newspaper. In this example, the use of a more informal register might then be appropriate.*)
The "***compte rendu***" might constitute only one part of another task (*guide / article / letter etc.*) or it might be a whole task. Whether it is a task in itself or not, it should be **structured** either **chronologically** or **thematically**. If it is the task itself, giving it a **title** might be a good idea too. It would also be useful to indicate who is the "**writer**" of this account / summary / report. A brief but sharp **introduction** to place the event in context as well as a short **conclusion** will also be useful.

The ***"rapport officiel"*** *should be a task on its own. It is usually more analytical than a* "***compte-rendu***" even if it is also factual.

Imagine that you have just been part of a team from your school who have just returned from a charity project in Africa. The aim of the project was to go and help a well-established charity whose aim is to improve housing in deprived areas. On your return, you have been asked to write a "rapport officiel" of the project to the Head Teacher of your school.

Below are two possible skeleton frameworks for how to present your "***rapport officiel***". (*These are only examples and a "compte rendu" or "rapport officiel" could take different forms according to the context.*)

Chronologically

Voyage humanitaire en Tanzanie 2008
par Luc Boncoeur

En janvier 2008, après 5 mois de préparation, un groupe de 15 élèves et 3 professeurs se sont rendus en Tanzanie dans le but de participer au projet « une maison décente pour tous ».

Avant le départ :
Pendant 5 mois, l'équipe a organisé des concerts et autres activités pour collecter les fonds nécessaires au bon fonctionnement d'un tel projet. (.....)

Le premier jour :
Nous sommes arrivés à......(...)

Le deuxième jour :
(....)

Le succès du projet est évident. En tout, l'équipe a construit 5 nouvelles maisons. Il est important qu'une expérience aussi enrichissante puisse être reconduite à l'avenir.

"Thematically"

Voyage humanitaire en Tanzanie 2008
Par Luc Boncoeur

En janvier 2008, après 5 mois de préparation, un groupe de 15 élèves et 3 professeurs se sont rendus en Tanzanie dans le but de participer au projet « une maison décente pour tous ».

La préparation au départ :
Avant le départ, l'équipe s'est rencontrée plusieurs fois. Il était important d'apprendre à se connaître pour le bon fonctionnement du projet. De plus, (...)

Le voyage :
(...)

Le chantier :
(...)

Le contact avec les villageois :
(...)

Le succès du projet est évident. En tout, l'équipe a construit 5 nouvelles maisons. Il est important qu'une expérience aussi enrichissante puisse être reconduite à l'avenir.

G) La **revue / la critique de film / livre**

The film or book review / critic can take different forms. As with all types of texts, you will first have to identify your audience and adapt to it. You might have to take a specific point of view. You might indeed be asked to write a neutral review but more often than not, you will be required to write a positive or negative one. If you are asked to write a positive review, this does not mean that you can't mention or allude to one or two negatives aspects (*and vice versa if you have to write a negative one*) but your review will have to be mainly positive.

Below is a list of points to bear in mind:

- Make sure you demonstrate your knowledge of specific vocabulary linked to films or books (*refer to the vocabulary section of this guide for some pointers*)
- Describe / talk about the characters / the plot / the special effects or the style of writing etc.
- Mention the writer or film director and actors
- Summarise the story / the plot (*make it exciting / full of suspense to give your audience the urge to go and see the film or read the book if appropriate*)
- Express your personal opinions about different aspects and justify them
- Indicate ratings if the review is to be published in a magazine
- If you are asked to write a book review, it is always better to choose a title from the French / Francophone literary world, especially if you have studied French at Higher Level.
- If you are required to write a film review, it does not necessarily have to be a Francophone film (*although it is always more impressive in a way*) and sometimes, you can even make up the plot of a film.
- If you are writing a review of the cinematographic adaptation of a book, compare it to the book.
- Make references to previous films / novels / plays / etc.
- **STRUCTURE** your review (*use appropriate linking devices*)

- **La revue des cinéphiles** -   - semaine du 16 mai 2007 –

ENSEMBLE, C'EST TOUT ☆ ☆ ☆ ☆

Réalisateur : Claude Berri
Film français en couleur –
- Sortie mars 2007 –
Durée : 1h37
Avec : Audrey Tautou et Guillaume Canet
D'après le roman **D'Anna Gavalda**

Photo des acteurs principaux

Adaptation du roman d'Anna Gavalda, ce film raconte l'histoire de Camille, une jeune fille douce et anorexique, Franck, un cuisinier au caractère difficile et Philibert le jeune aristocrate : trois êtres que la vie n'a pas épargnés. Lorsque Camille croise Philibert par un soir froid et pluvieux sur le palier de leur immeuble, le destin de ces 3 personnages bascule. (…)
Un film à la fois drôle, émouvant et attendrissant. L'intrigue est bien ficelée et la fin reste fidèle à l'œuvre originale d'Anna Gavalda. Le jeu des acteurs est excellent et Audrey Tautou campe une Camille attachante.
***De plus**, (…)*
***Toutefois**, (…)*

Un film à recommander à ceux qui croient encore en la générosité et l'entraide
Un film qui fait du bien !
À voir absolument !

par Paul Truffaut

H) L'interview

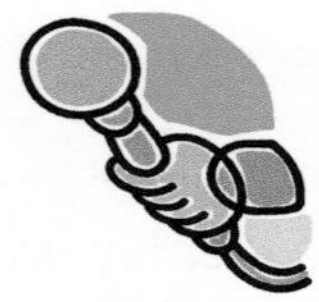

The interview is the written form of a question and answer session which has taken place between two people. When conducting an interview, you always have two sides:

- the interviewer : *the person who asks the questions*
- the interviewee: *the person / group who answers the questions.*

- The questions that will be asked will obviously depend on who is being interviewed, the purpose of the interview (*talking about someone's latest film or book / giving advice after an expedition or even an interview of the main character of a book etc.*) and where the script of the interview will be published (*target audience*). This will also determine the register of language used during the interview. However, it is important to bear in mind that the interview must be **interesting** and **meaningful**. A good interviewer has always researched its material beforehand and is able to gear the questions in a specific way and direction. Therefore, you might have general questions followed by shorter answers to start with, but it must then go further than a few personal questions.
- The interview must be conducted in a **STRUCTURED** and logical way.
- If the interview is being published in a magazine, a short introduction and conclusion will be welcomed, maybe even a title.
- Don't forget to thank the interviewee at the end.
- Try and use humour if appropriate.
- Include personal anecdotes from the interviewee if appropriate to lighten up the interview.
- Depending on the nature and purpose of the interview, personal views and opinions might need to be expressed, argued, illustrated, defended and even challenged by the interviewer.
- As it is the script of a conversation, use punctuation to reflect emotions and mood (*like in a diary*).
- And obviously... use of variety of grammar and linguistic tools as well as linking devices and a rich and specific range of vocabulary!

Imagine that you have to interview a fictional character for a teenage magazine. Opposite is the beginning of this interview and an example of layout. The brief conclusion and thanks are also missing.

***NB**: Remember that it would be better if you can (unless otherwise specified) to choose a Francophone character. Here, I have chosen Harry Potter as I am pretty confident that it is a point of reference for everyone.*

\- ado mag - - mai 2008 –

Interview avec Harry Potter!

Personnage sorti tout droit de l'imagination de JK Rowling, Harry Potter n'existe pas...et pourtant, l'équipe d'Ado Mag l'a rencontré…

***AM** : Harry, **tout d'abord** merci d'avoir accepté de nous rencontrer. Tu es très occupé en ce moment puisque tu es en plein tournage du prochain volet de la saga Harry Potter. Peux-tu révéler en avant première à nos lecteurs quels personnages nous quittent ?*

***HP** : Malheureusement, vous révéler quels personnages meurent serait vous gâcher la surprise. Je préfère donc vous laisser sur votre faim et vous inviter à aller voir le film dès sa sortie au ciné, Par ailleurs, un personnage ne meurt jamais... Il reste vivant au travers des livres, non ??*

***AM** : oui, ce n'est pas faux…C'est difficile d'être Harry Potter au quotidien ?*

***HP** : (…)*

I) Le tract / l'appel

"Le tract" (which is a type of brochure") and the "appel" are not very different from the guide in that they need to attract attention and convince. They don't necessarily appear as a leaflet and they might not have nice pictures designed to attract one's attention, but their aim is not too dissimilar. It is often to make people aware of an issue but most importantly, it is aimed at making people react either by joining a group, giving money (etc.). Tracts can be used as a tool for propaganda in certain contexts or to convince people to adhere to a political party for example. However, the aim of a guide is often to provide information and advice, whereas the aim of the tract or appeal is to give information, express strong opinions and convince / incite and sometimes even urge people to act about a specific issue. Their aim is sometimes to incite people to go on strike in France for example. This means that there is a need for these types of writing to:

- visually attract people's attention (***title / use of capital letters / words in bold / italics or underlined / bullet points / punctuation...***)
- be STRUCTURED- clearly and logically.
- be CONVINCING (*use of repetition / questions etc.*) – persuasive language.
- use appropriate and varied vocabulary and grammar items.

Note that the tract will make more use of bold letters (etc.) than the "appel" which will look more than one piece of coherent writing. An "appel" is often makes use of more sophisticated language. Note as well that a brochure can be strictly informative (brochure ou dépliant "touristique" for example) with no point of view expressed.

Look at this short example of a "tract". (*yours would be at least 400 words!*) Here the aim is clearly to make people aware of the problem of "**Filles esclaves**" as well as urging them to react and give their support by signing the petition.

Elles ont entre 8 et 12 ans.
Elles ne sont encore que des **enfants**
POURTANT...
Elles travaillent toute la journée,
subissent **brimades** et **sanctions**...

QUI SONT-ELLES ??

Les FILLES **ESCLAVES** du Maroc !

OUI, il s'agit bien d'une réalité. Elles sont plus de 80000 à être vendues par leurs parents pour de bien maigres soldes ! Leur salaire ne leur appartient pas et seul le mariage peut les délivrer de leur triste sort.
Leur quotidien ? Ménage, cuisine, repassage et autres corvées.
L'école ? Elles n'y sont jamais allées !
Jouer ? Un concept totalement inconnu pour ces petites filles.

Elles ont le même âge que nos filles...
Laisseriez-vous votre fille travailler toute la journée à cet âge et dans de pareilles conditions ?!

NON !
Réagissons contre cette atteinte aux droits des enfants. Aidons ces jeunes filles à sortir de la misère !

Aidez-nous à les aider en signant la pétition qui se trouve au dos de cette page.

Ensemble luttons pour que les droits de l'homme soient enfin respectés !!

- ***Association « Aidons les enfants du monde » - 5 avenue Charité- Paris -***

Let's keep the same topic but now have a look at one possible example of an "***appel***". This should hopefully give you a clearer idea of the difference between the "*appel*" and the "*tract*" as well as providing with some ideas about the general layout / format and language required in an "*appel*".

APPEL
pour la lutte contre
l'ESCLAVAGE moderne!

Cet appel vise à informer le plus grand nombre au sujet de la situation réservée aux « filles esclaves ».

Effectivement, dans certains pays comme au Maroc, des jeunes filles, à peine âgées de plus de six ans dans certains cas, sont vendues par leurs familles pour des sommes modiques.

Pourquoi ?

Tout d'abord, leur vente permet un apport immédiat d'argent aux familles. Cette vente représente également une bouche de moins à nourrir pour ces familles qui vivent souvent dans la misère la plus complète.

C'est donc plus de 80000 jeunes filles marocaines qui subissent chaque année le même sort. Leur quotidien est fait de corvées (*elles ont la charge de toutes les tâches ménagères, de la cuisine etc.*) et de brimades (*souvent exercées par les autres femmes du foyer*). Elles sont en effet souvent pincées, malmenées voire battues.

Par ailleurs, elles n'ont que peu de chance de s'en sortir car leur seule porte de sortie est le mariage... Elles n'ont que peu d'espoir...Alors sont-elles condamnées à souffrir en silence ??!

Non. **Nous**, membres du comité pour la défense des droits des enfants, **refusons** de laisser ces jeunes filles livrées à leur propre sort sans réagir.

C'est de l'ESCLAVAGE !! Au XXIème siècle !!

C'est pourquoi ...

PARENTS, CITOYENS DU MONDE, DÉFENSEURS DES DROITS DE L'HOMME ET DES ENFANTS,
MESSIEURS LES HOMMES POLITIQUES,
nous ne pouvons rester insensibles et inactifs face à cette situation !

Nous nous élevons contre ces pratiques ancestrales, archaïques et inhumaines !

Nous refusons d'accepter ces injustices... Les accepter, c'est s'en montrer complices !

Nous en appelons donc aux consciences des responsables pour agir en faveur du respect des droits de l'enfant.

Nous souhaitons que le gouvernement fasse pression sur le gouvernement marocain pour la mise en place d'une loi condamnant et interdisant la vente et l'achat de jeunes filles.

Ces jeunes filles sont des êtres humains, pas des marchandises !!

Si **vous** aussi **vous vous sentez concernés** et voulez nous aider à faire pression sur les autorités pour mettre fin à cette forme d'esclavage; signez la pétition qui se trouve au dos et renvoyez-là à l'adresse suivante :

Comité pour la défense des droits des enfants
16 Boulevard de la Paix
Paris

J) La dissertation (*particularly useful for HL section B*)

Whether you consider it a privilege or a poisoned chalice, the essay is nonetheless a type of texts at both HL and SL. Like any other types of text, it has its specificities and needs to be dealt with in a certain way.

The starting point of an essay question is of course...the question itself! It is often a general question about a specific aspect and you will be required to express points of view (*whether they are yours or more general ones*) and illustrate and defend them!
You will not necessarily have to be for or against an aspect of a topic. You may have to introduce different points of view and then conclude. The questions might be very specific or left open for you to interpret more generally. However, before you can decide on which point(s) of view you are mainly going to adopt and before you embark on your essay, you need to read the question carefully and consider it. The first step should therefore be to spend some time looking carefully at the question to analyse the key words. This way, you are less likely to miss out any aspect of the question. My advice would then be to jot down ideas on a rough piece of paper before you start thinking about structuring an answer. **DON'T** throw yourself into the writing before you have even understood all the subtleties of the question and pondered whether or not you have enough elements (*linguistic / grammatical / cultural or even ideas)* in hands to answer the question!

Examples of possible topics / questions:

- La télévision fera la perte de la littérature.
- L'influence de la télé sur les jeunes enfants est toujours néfaste. Discutez.
- Le clonage : pour ou contre ?

The starting point of the question might be a famous quotation and you might be asked to agree / disagree with it or comment it! Look back at a few past papers to get a better idea of this type of question.

However, whatever the question, the essay must be written in a certain way and must encompass the following points:

- An **INTRODUCTION** in which you must introduce the general theme, then the precise question and then your plan.
- A well-developed and **STRUCTURED** argumentation.
  Divide your arguments in paragraphs. The structure must be **CLEAR** and logical. Miss lines between different paragraphs. Don't forget that you must prove and defend your arguments if you want to be convincing, or at least credible. You therefore must ensure that you use examples / percentages etc. to develop and illustrate your arguments.
- A **CONCLUSION** in which you must summarise the main idea(s) / the main conclusion of your argumentation. Please note that you may hint to another aspect of the question in the conclusion but that it is too late to develop new ideas.
- Use **LINK WORDS** to link paragraphs together, introduce nuances and give coherence to your essay as a whole.
- Use some specific items of vocabulary according to the topic of your essay.
- Mind your language... an essay is a more formal piece of writing so no "*registre familier*" should be used.
- And again... as always you must be careful to vary your structures and linguistic tools (*verb tenses etc.*)

Let's look at the possible framework of an essay.
Let's imagine that we have to answer the following essay question:

Le clonage: progrès scientifique ou danger ?

Here, the topic is very clear: *cloning*. Two aspects are being mentioned; the aspect of scientific progress and / or danger. You will therefore need to mention **both** aspects of the question in your essay even if you agree more with one aspect than the other. Bear in mind that this is only one example and that variations are therefore possible. Don't forget either that, when writing your essay, the sub-headings will not appear. They are being used here to help you see the structure of the example. The conclusion will need to be developed too. Remember to use link words to structure your essay and examples to illustrate.
Please note, that in an essay, you need to express opinions and possibly your personal opinion too. However, the treatment of a question might not always require you to look at the "for and against" sides of that question.

INTRODUCTION:

a) Mise en contexte générale:

Aujourd'hui, force est de constater que des progrès considérables ont été faits dans le domaine de la science et de la médecine. Toutefois, tous les progrès réalisés ne font pas toujours l'unanimité.

b) Question spécifique soumise à notre étude:

C'est en effet le cas du clonage contre lequel beaucoup s'opposent notamment pour des raisons d'éthique et de morale.

C) plan :

Faut-il donc considérer le clonage comme un progrès scientifique et en défendre la cause ? Faut-il le voir comme un danger et le condamner ?

DÉVELOPEMENT DU DEVOIR / DE L'ARGUMENTATION :

b) Le clonage progrès scientifique :

1) reproduction de cellules et d'organes pour le traitement de maladies graves comme le cancer etc. (exemple : greffes etc.)

2) Domaine agricole et écologique : assurer la préservation de certaines espèces menacées d'extinction.

3) Permet également de pratiquer des expériences sur des sujets non vivants.

CEPENDANT

B) Clonage = danger :

1) Contre nature. Les questions morales et éthiques. Qui nous donne le droit de transformer / reproduire à l'identique ce que la nature a créé de façon unique ? (« science sans conscience n'est que ruine de l'âme »)

2) Les dérives du clonage… Jusqu'où peut-on / risque-t-on d'aller ? Quelles limites au progrès scientifique ? N'est-il donc pas préférable de refuser le clonage même si cette méthode peut mener à des avancées bénéfiques dans le domaine de la médecine ?

3) Donc : risque de problèmes et changements génétiques irréversibles pour les espèces humaines, animales et végétales.

CONCLUSION :

→ *Synthèse de l'argumentation. D'après ce que vous avez argumenté, le clonage est-il une découverte positive, à utiliser mais avec précaution ou faut-il le mettre au banc des accusés et le déclarer « hors-la-loi » ?*
+ Ouverture sur un autre aspect de la science par exemple.

Additional types of texts useful for the Written Task / Assignment

K) L'éditorial

An editorial is a type of newspaper / magazine article. It is usually published at the **beginning** of the magazine (*first or 2nd page*) and is written by the "rédacteur / rédactrice en chef" of the magazine, or a representative figure who will be the **voice of the magazine's views** about a particular issue. If you open any French magazine (*see suggested list in the "References" page*) you will probably find an editorial page. So be proactive. Go and find some French magazines in your school library and have a look at a few to get an idea of format and content! However, you can also find examples of "*éditoriaux*" on the web on magazines and newspapers websites...so you really have no excuse at all not to find one!

So what exactly is an editorial?

- An editorial is an article in which the journalist **discusses / gives his or her opinion, expresses his or her views** about a specific topic. It could be about an event that has happened the previous week or month. It could be about an important issue (*politics / environment / education / etc.*). As I mentioned above, the personal opinion of the "*rédacteur / rédactrice en chef*" can be very strongly expressed about the issue raised, but sometimes, the opposite views will also be mentioned / acknowledged in some ways in order to give a slightly more balanced outlook to the editorial or, at least, the issue will have been considered in a wider / more global perspective. It is also important to bear in mind that whatever opinion is being expressed, it is never an unfair or unreasonable one. So don't get carried away... after all, it is the magazine's reputation which is also at stake!
- It is also probably useful to mention that, often to conclude the editorial, you may find a summary of what is being published in this month's magazine / issue.
- As an editorial is about expressing clear opinions, your editorial will have to be well **STRUCTURED**. Use linking devices.
- You will need to give **arguments** to convey your views and of course, you will need to explain / detail / illustrate these arguments with examples / statistics /etc. Your editorial will need to be **CONVINCING**. Remember that the prime aim of an editorial is to raise awareness of a specific issue amongst its readers / convince them of the importance of an issue / challenge their way of thinking about a specific issue. Use some of the techniques used in a speech (***repetitions / rhetorical questions / address your audience directly if appropriate / involve yourself / punctuation /*** etc.)
- Don't forget to use a wide range of grammatical structures and vocabulary items.

- Réflexion Mag - - juillet 2008-

ÉDITORIAL

Le Mot du Rédacteur en chef... Stéphane Dupuis-

La Guerre ne prend pas de vacances !

Au moment où vous lisez ces lignes, la Guerre continue de faire rage aux quatre coins de la planète…en Irak, en Afghanistan… Qu'elle soit civile, idéologique ou religieuse, la Guerre continue de faire des victimes innocentes, de détruire et anéantir… un prix très cher payé !! Naît de la différence, du malentendu ou de l'ignorance ou encore de la haine, elle continue à engendrer… la Haine. Y pensez-vous ? Alors que les congés sont enfin là, qu'il est enfin possible de mettre en parenthèse la routine du train-train quotidien pour partir se reposer au soleil et en famille… Pensez-vous à ces familles déchirées par le conflit ? Car la Guerre, elle, ne part pas en vacances. Pas de répit pour les populations touchées par ce fléau ! Pas la peine de culpabiliser, vous n'êtes pas responsable, mais où que vous alliez cet été, ne les oubliez pas, ne l'oubliez pas ! Ainsi, lorsque fatigué du retour de la plage, vous sentez la dispute doucement s'immiscer pour une futilité, rappelez-vous que finalement, ça n'en vaut sûrement pas la peine !
Au sommaire de notre numéro ce mois-ci (…)

L) La déclaration à la police

You could be given 3 documents talking about "cyber-intimidation" or bullying for example, and choose to do for your ***Travail Écrit*** at SL a police report of the victim. Equally, at HL, you may have studied a piece of literature in which a specific event happens and you could decide to write the police statement made by one of the characters.

What sort of declaration can one imagine to write?
One can imagine any of the following:

- report of a theft / loss
- a witness account of an accident / burglary / murder / terrorist attack / incidents during a demonstration etc.
- a victim account of the above case scenarios

Those are only examples and do not constitute an exhaustive list at all.

Whatever the context, there are a few points to consider:

- a declaration to the police is an **official** document and as such, will need to be presented in a specific way.
- the **date(s)** (*and sometimes even **time** of incident and declaration*) / the **names** and the details of the victim(s) or the witness(es) and the name(s) of the person(s) taking the deposition / the **place** where the incident took place as well as where the declaration is being made.
- As an official document, it will need to be **signed** by the person making the deposition as well as the person taking it.

Apart from the details mentioned above which make the declaration to the police a very specific and official document, a declaration to the police will resemble in its format a **report**. Indeed, when you come to think of it, it is in fact an **account** / a report of something which has happened (*whether you have been the victim or the witness*). It is therefore advisable to organise it **clearly** - probably **chronologically** will be your best bet. You could have sub-headings to divide it into different sections. As it is an account of something which has happened, it will have to be **detailed and precise** and mainly in the past (*although a range of tenses needs to be included in some way*).

Below is one simple example of the general format that a report to the police could take. It could vary in its presentation as long as you don't forget to include the elements mentioned above.

- Commissariat de la ville de Nice –

Date de la déposition : ....

Nom de la victime / du témoin : ....
Adresse : ....
Nature de l'incident : ....
Date et heure de l'incident : ....
lieu: ....

Nom de la personne présente lors de la déposition :
....
Fonction : ....

Lundi 26 août 2007, aéroport de Nice, 3 hommes d'une vingtaine d'années, habillés en tenue militaire ont pénétré dans l'enceinte de l'aéroport. Les 3 hommes étaient armés. Le plus grand était chauve et avait une ancre tatouée sur le bras gauche. (...)
Au moment de l'irruption des trois hommes dans l'aéroport, j'étais assis tranquillement sur un banc à côté de la machine à café. J'attendais l'annonce de mon embarquement pour Athènes. (...)
*Les trois hommes ont **d'abord**...*
(...)

Signature du dépositaire : *Signature du témoin* présent :*

NB:
Note that instead of having the date and place of declaration at the top, you could have the following mentions at the bottom:

Fait à: ....
Le: ....

and then the signatures.

**"témoin" refers here to the person witnessing the declaration.*

M) L'anecdote

You could decide to write an ***anecdote*** but it is often a shorter piece of writing so I do not intend to spend too long on this type of text. But you could choose it if it was appropriate. *Pourquoi pas?*

What is an anecdote?
An anecdote is a short account / story of an often incongruous event. This event can be historical or personal. An anecdote is often retold because of its incongruity / originality, strangeness or humoristic nature.
The anecdote generally consists of the account itself. Generally, no opinion is clearly expressed.

So, how can it be approached?
Your best bet is to approach it the same way as any account / report. This means that it needs to be **STRUCTURED**, maybe chronologically. Give a lot of details and descriptions. Use the appropriate vocabulary and structure to make it interesting, full of suspense or even funny or sad, depending on the task.
The anecdote is a story and its strength is in the way it is rendered to the audience.
In its format, it is like an imaginative story in a way as in, there is no "real" specific "official" format".

N) La page internet

The internet page does not constitute a type of text on its own. It will always invariably come in conjunction with another format whether it is an article, a guide, a film review or even an imaginative story. You will therefore need to ensure that you respect the format and linguistic requirements of these types of texts while adapting them to the format of the internet page.

Here is a list of a few points to remember:

- an internet address box
- a menu
- some links to be clicked on as don't forget that the internet page is meant to be an interactive tool
- boxes for pictures if necessary
- it must be clearly and attractively presented

There is not just one way of presenting an internet page so do have a look for yourself at a few sites!

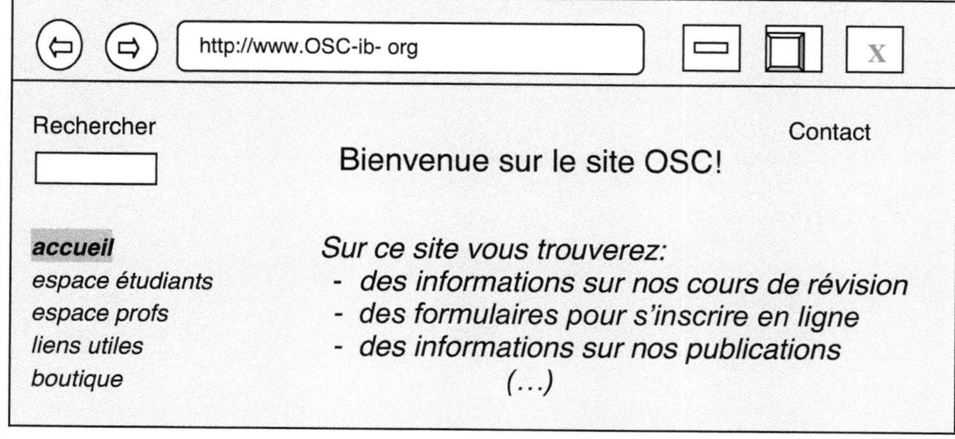

O) La proposition raisonnée

Let's imagine that you have been given 3 texts at SL about a specific environmental issue. You could then write a "*proposition raisonnée*" to propose / suggest solutions. A "*proposition raisonnée*" is in fact a kind of argued proposal whose aim is to achieve a precise goal. It is often aimed at making someone or a committee, for example, agree with a point of view or a concrete idea (*before a new law is adopted for example, a proposal is submitted to explain the law and its aims*). If the proposal is successfully presented to whoever its target audience is, it should bring concrete results (*the removal of something / the closing of a building / the opening of a building etc...*) Let's look at possible examples of questions to get a better idea.

- *Il y a deux ans, le maire de votre ville a interdit l'utilisation du skateboard sur la voie publique. Vous faites du skate et vous sentez frustré. Ecrivez une proposition pour la construction d'une piste de skateboard dans votre ville que vous présenterez au maire.*
- *Vous êtes maintenant en terminale et vous pensez que certains privilèges devraient vous être octroyés. Ecrivez le texte de la proposition que vous comptez soumettre à votre chef d'établissement.*

Whatever the topic or the exact context, below are a few points to bear in mind:

- A "*proposition raisonnée*" is a formal document so mind which register of language you use.
- Giving your proposal a **TITLE** might be a good idea as it will give your target audience an indication of the content / theme of your proposal.
- An **INTRODUCTION** to your proposal would also prove useful. *What is it about? Why? Give an indication of the context?*
- Indicate clearly who is submitting the proposal
- A "*formule d'appel*" (*such as one used in a letter*) might be appropriate to start with.
- Your proposal must be **CLEARLY** and **LOGICALLY** presented (*divide it in paragraphs; one per idea / miss lines...*)
- It must be **STRUCTURED** (link words!)
- You may want to use sub-headings as it helps the general presentation of your proposal.
- If you want to convince someone to accept your proposal and act on it, you need be **CONVINCING**. You must therefore argue and illustrate your points. You must also make sure that you use linguistic structures and devices which will help you achieve this aim. These could be repetitions, structures such as "*il est important / essentiel*" etc.)
- Provide your intended target with concrete / practical ideas of where / how (etc.) your project can be realised. That will help convince him / her or them.
- Be detailed in the description of your project / idea and as specific as possible.

NB:

If one looks at all the elements needed here, one could be tempted to think that in fact, this type of text comprises aspects of a letter, a speech or even or tract or appeal. Even though this might be true in some ways, don't forget that it is a type of text with its specificities in its own right, so don't start getting confused!

So, let's pretend that we are writing to the mayor of the town to convince him to allow the building of a skateboard park and take a look at the following example of a proposal.
Bear in mind that this is only one example of a possible layout and thread of argument. However, I hope that it gives you a clearer idea of what is meant by the concept of "*proposition raisonnée*".

Titre →

Proposition pour la construction
d'une piste et d'un parc de skateboard à Menton

présentée par Sébastien Roulette ← **Qui?**
Citoyen de Menton

Formule d'appel → *Monsieur Le Maire,*

"Intro"

Il y a deux ans, vous avez déclaré hors-la-loi les skateboards dans notre belle ville de Menton. De ce fait, leur utilisation est dorénavant interdite sur la voie publique et toute enfreinte à ce règlement est passible de lourdes amendes.

Toutefois, les adeptes du mode de transport qu'est le skateboard habitent toujours dans votre ville et en tant que citoyens de Menton, ces amateurs de skateboard se sentent exclus, voire victimisés par une décision injuste. Ne s'agit-il pas en effet d'une atteinte aux droits et libertés des citoyens ? Est-il normal que le droit d'exercer ce sport leur soit refusé sous prétexte que cette activité est dangereuse et pourrait être à l'origine d'accidents ?

Les skateurs acceptent certes que le trottoir appartient aux piétons qui ne devraient pas être gênés par l'apparition de mode de transport sur leur territoire.

C'est la raison pour laquelle ces adeptes réclament aujourd'hui le droit d'exercer leur activité, leur sport, leur passion. Ils aimeraient pouvoir l'exercer dans un environnement adapté et en toute sécurité.

C'est dans cette optique que je me fais aujourd'hui leur porte-parole pour vous soumettre ce projet de loi en faveur de la construction d'un parc de skate et que nous vous demandons de bien vouloir considérer et accepter ce projet.

PROPOSITION

Les raisons

La construction d'un espace réservé aux skateurs apparait comme une nécessité dans notre ville. En effet, plus de six cent jeunes sont inscrits au club des skateurs de la ville et il paraît aberrant qu'un espace spécifique pour la pratique de ce sport et loisir leur soit actuellement toujours refusé.

← **Exemple**

Sous-titres

Les objectifs

La construction d'un parc de skateboard a donc pour objectif principal de permettre aux jeunes adeptes du skateboard de pouvoir enfin exercer leur sport en toute tranquillité et en sécurité.

Les avantages

Les avantages à la construction d'un parc de skate sont multiples.

Mots de liaison

- **Tout d'abord**, le sentiment d'injustice ressenti par les jeunes se verra réparé.
- Ensuite, les jeunes ne traineront plus en ville puisqu'ils pourront enfin se consacrer à leur activité préférée. Ceci ne peut être qu'un avantage puisque bon nombre de personnes se plaignent actuellement des rassemblements de jeunes désœuvrés sur la voie publique.
- **Par ailleurs**, l'ouverture d'un parc de skate ne nuira en aucune façon aux citoyens de Menton puisque la création d'un espace réservé à la pratique de ce sport permettra d'assurer la disparition totale de l'utilisation du skate en ville. Les jeunes s'engagent en effet à ne faire usage de leur skate que dans l'enceinte du parc et à ne plus envahir le jardin public comme ils le font actuellement puisque c'est le seul endroit où ils ne sont pas encore inquiétés. Les habitants de Menton retrouveront donc leur jardin public et son calme.
- Les parents seront également rassurés puisqu'ils sauront désormais où et dans quelles conditions leurs enfants exercent leur activité préférée.
- De plus, l'ouverture du parc conférera sans aucun doute un statut de ville dynamique à Menton. Menton apparaitra comme une ville qui avance avec son temps et qui sait écouter ses jeunes.
- Finalement, la réalisation de ce projet rendra le sourire à six cent jeunes mentonnais, qui, ne l'oubliez pas, seront bientôt en âge d'exercer leur droit civique, celui de voter…

Où ?

La question du lieu est une question importante. Il est en effet essentiel que ce parc soit facile d'accès aux jeunes, donc assez proche du centre ville, sans pour autant interférer avec le bien-être des habitants. C'est la raison pour laquelle nous proposons le site de l'ancienne décharge municipale comme emplacement potentiel. C'est l'endroit idéal car il se trouve à 20 minutes à pied du centre ville. Il s'agit également d'un espace inutilisé et inutile pour le moment.

Financement

Il s'agit également d'un aspect important. Nous nous proposons de jouer une part active dans ce domaine et de contribuer au financement du projet par le biais de l'organisation d'actions destinées à collecter des fonds et sensibiliser le public.

Nous espérons donc qu'une suite favorable sera donnée à ce projet.

More specific to HL students…

P) **Le récit / continuer ou ajouter un chapitre d'un / à un livre**

This is a more creative type of text, perhaps one better suited for HL candidates, should you find it appropriate for what you want to create. You will need to bear in mind that if you choose this type of text (adding a chapter to a book for example, it has to be in the style of the original work of literature. It also has to respect the plot and the characters' traits. Not always easy but writing an alternative ending for a novel or a play studied can be a very interesting "***Travail Écrit***" task. If you decide to go for this type of creative writing task, there are a few things that you need to bear in mind:

- Your chapter / ending etc. must be in line with the original work of literature both in terms of plot and style.
- It must be meaningful (even if you add details) and **STRUCTURED**. Avoid letting your imagination run too wild (*again- it has to be in line with the book studied- it cannot be just an independent imaginative piece of writing*) or you risk losing the plot and the good will of the examiner too!
- When you write part of a story / chapter etc, it must be structured, it is important to use **link words**.
- You may also need to use structures to create suspense, or fear or tension (etc.) - if it is appropriate with the style of the original work and the aim of your "***travail Écrit***" - such as:
    - Punctuation marks (! // !! / ? / ...)
    - Expression of feelings: *Quelle horreur!! Je commençais à avoir peur etc.*
    - Questions to reinforce tension *: Y avait-il vraiment quelqu'un derrière cette porte ? Que risquait-il de se passer si je l'ouvrais ?*

It must be logical and / or chronological.

Let's practise !

Match each link word with its translation.

(answers for both pages on p. 184)

1. ensuite / puis	a. all of a sudden / suddenly
2. d'abord	b. after
3. un peu plus tard	c. from now on
4. avant	d. then
5. tout à coup / soudain	e. indeed
6. malheureusement	f. when
7. après	g. now
8. enfin	h. at last
9. dans un premier temps	i. before
10. c'est à ce moment précis que…	j. moreover
11. c'est alors que …	k. after a while
12. à présent	l. however
13. en effet	m. first of all
14. pourtant	n. unfortunately
15. de plus	o. firstly
16. au bout d'un moment	p. it is at this precise moment that
17. dorénavant	q. a little later
18. quand…	r. it is then that…

<u>Let's practise further</u> !

Now put into practice what you have just seen / revised.
Complete this mini-story by filling in the gaps with the link words that can be found underneath the text. Hopefully, this will also provide you with an example of how to create suspense and tension (should it be your intention) using the structures and devices mentioned previously. You will also be able to see for yourself that this can be achieved even with / from a basic starting story line and how to use link words to structure a "***récit***", whatever type it may be.

C'était au mois de décembre l'année dernière. J'étais dans ma chambre et je révisais ma grammaire car j'avais un examen de français le lendemain matin. Dehors il faisait froid. C'était la nuit.
J'étais seul à la maison ce soir-là car mes parents étaient sortis avec des amis.
............................***1***, j'ai entendu un bruit bizarre. Je me suis levé pour regarder par la fenêtre de ma chambre. Rien. Je me suis donc remis au travail sans me poser de questions. ....,***2*** il m'a semblé entendre quelqu'un frapper à la porte. Je suis ....***3*** descendu, ...***4*** j'ai ouvert la porte ....***5*** Il n'y avait personne. Bizarre... J'ai refermé la porte et je suis remonté dans ma chambre un peu perplexe... Avais-je vraiment entendu quelqu'un frapper à la porte ou était-ce le fruit de mon imagination ? Non, je devais sûrement être fatigué. Je décidais donc d'aller me coucher. Je venais de me mettre au lit ....***6*** un bruit étrange et angoissant se fit à nouveau entendre. Cette fois-ci j'en étais sûr. Je n'avais pas imaginé ce bruit. Mais de quoi s'agissait-il ? Y avait-il quelqu'un dans la maison ? Que faire ? Appeler mes parents ? Non, ce n'était pas la peine de les inquiéter et de leur gâcher leur soirée. ....,***7*** ils ne prennent jamais leur portable quand ils sortent. ....***8*** une idée aussi bizarre qu'extraordinaire m'a traversé l'esprit et si je ...

- puis - c'est alors que / qu' - tout à coup - de plus -

- d'abord - après quelques minutes - quand - mais -

A few more tips…

You should now feel a little more secure about the specific requirements attached to each and every single one of the types of texts that you need to master for Paper 2 SL and HL and / or the type of texts you may choose to use to create your "***Travail Écrit***". I must, again, mention that those are only examples and that provided that you make sure that you include the main elements mentioned in each specific section, there are possible variations in the general format of each type of text, be it in the use and choice of structures or sometimes even some visual variations (*an article, for example, does not necessarily have to be divided in columns*).

HOWEVER, it is important to mention again that sometimes, two types of texts, or the elements of two types of texts can be part of one question and you might have to combine elements of both types of texts and styles into your answer. This is why, again, it is important to devote a few minutes to understand the analysis of the questions and their requirements before starting. You will often need to "mix and match" and adapt.

Below are a few examples of types of texts that can appear together in one question.

film or book review and letter	You could be asked to write a letter to an author to criticise his / her latest book. → *You will therefore need to respect the format of the formal letter and use the language of the book review.*
guide and article	You could be asked to write a guide to give advice about something which will be published in a magazine.
summary and brochure	You could be asked to write a brochure about the opening of a new sports centre to advertise it and summarise the inaugural event of the preceding week.
personal diary and film / book review	You could be asked to write your impressions in your diary after the reading of a book or the viewing of a film.
article and internet page	You can be asked to write an article which will be published on the net. You will therefore need to think about the format and layout of each type of text and combine them.
speech and report	As part of a speech, you could be required to report on an action / an event etc. which has happened previously and is linked to the topic / purpose of your speech.

Let's practise!

Read each one of the following examples. Try and find out in which context(s) you could use them / what type(s) of text? What type of register do they belong to? *(you may wish to have a look at the section on registers first!)*

(answers p. 184)

EX: J'en ai marre ! *le journal intime / lettre à un ami*
(registre familier)

1) Il est important de bien dormir la veille des examens.

2) Veuillez agréer, Monsieur, l'expression de mes sentiments dévoués.

3) Pourquoi c'est toujours sur moi que ça retombe?

4) C'est donc à nous, chers confrères, de veiller à ce qu'un tel scandale ne se reproduise plus!!!

5) Je suis tout à fait insatisfait par le service fourni.

6) Gros bisous. A bientôt.

7) lundi 10 mai 2004

8) Sois attentif lors des réunions. C'est très important si tu veux progresser rapidement.

9) Cet incident se serait produit à 4h du matin, Place Bellecour.

10) Je vous remercie pour votre attention.

11) En conclusion, on peut dire que…

12) Bonne chance pour les examens!

13) Bon, il faut que j'aille manger…à tout à l'heure.

14) Ne restons pas ainsi! Agissons!!

15) Je trouve inadmissible que l'on permette aux élèves de sortir en ville le midi.

LES REGISTRES DE LANGUE

Depending on who you are talking to, you are going to use different words or expressions. The context in which you are will dictate which "*register of language*" you should use. Is it a ***formal situation*** or an ***informal one***? Surely you are not going to address your boss in a letter the same way as you would address your friend?!
Registers of language are important and you will need to indentify who your audience is before you can choose the appropriate level of language necessary to accomplish the task in hand. For example, your choice of vocabulary items and style will be different if your task is to write a speech about the environment which will be delivered in front of a group of children or a room full of experts and politicians!
HOWEVER, *be careful, familiar language does **NOT** mean that grammar has to suffer. Grammar is grammar whatever the context and needs to be used correctly. You must ensure that you use a wide variety of tenses and grammatical structures, regardless of the context!*

Le "vous" et le "tu"

Remember that in French, « ***tu*** » is used in ***informal*** situations (*when you are talking to a friend, one of your parents, someone younger than you*).
"***Vous***" is used either in ***informal*** context when addressing / referring to **several people**. "***Vous***" is also used in a ***formal*** context / situation. It is a mark of respect and deference (*when talking to your boss or someone older you do not know for example*).

Language registers

There are 3 (main) registers of language in French.

- Formal Language ***(langage soutenu)***
  This is the language used in formal situations / contexts (talking to a politician, your head teacher, your teachers, etc.).This is also the language of literature, especially classical literature such as Hugo or Zola.

- Everyday language / informal ***(langage courant)***
  This refers to the language used in everyday situations in less formal situation / context. (E.g. when talking to your parents or their friends)

- Colloquial language ***(langage familier)***
  This refers to the language used in familiar or "very familiar" context. (with your friends) CAREFUL...familiar language does not suggest that you can use rude or inappropriate words!

NB: When learning a new word, make sure you know to which register of language it belongs. Equally, if you can learn synonyms of a word in different registers, this could come handy on the day of the exam ***BUT*** don't panic if you can't find synonyms for a word in a different register! Not all words have synonyms in all registers! Sometimes, one word will do whatever the context.

Examples:

Registre soutenu	Registre courant	Registre familier
un ami	un copain	un pote
Ça me laisse indifférent	Ça m'est égal	Je m'en fous
Avoir un différend	se disputer	S'engueuler

Let's practise!

All the words in the left hand column belong to the "***registre courant***". Can you match them up with their equivalent from the "***registre familier***" and then write their translation into brackets?
Remember: a verb for a verb, an adjective for an adjective etc.

(answers p. 184)

1) une fille (---------------) ☐
2) comprendre (-------------) ☐
3) de l'argent (---------------) ☐
4) se disputer (--------------) ☐
5) un surveillant (--------------) ☐
6) un policier (-----------------) ☐
7) fou (------------------) ☐
8) mon frère (---------------) ☐
9) bizarre (-------------------) ☐
10) avoir de la chance (----------------) ☐
11) des vêtements (---------------------) ☐
12) se dépêcher (---------------------) ☐

a) dingue
b) des fringues
c) du fric
d) se magner
e) une nana
f) un flic
g) piger
h) louche
i) s'engueuler
j) avoir du pot / du bol
k) un pion
l) mon frangin

Same exercise but, this time, the words in the right hand column belong to the "***registre soutenu***".

1) écrire (----------------) ☐
2) avoir peur de (----------------) ☐
3) disputer quelqu'un (-----------------) ☐
4) être en colère (-------------------) ☐
5) fou (-----------------) ☐
6) abandonner (--------------------) ☐

a) aliéné / dément
b) réprimander
c) craindre
d) renoncer à
e) rédiger
f) être courroucé

Let's practise further!

As with most aspects of the language, the concept of "*registres de langue*" only truly takes its full meaning in context. Below is a task aimed at allowing you to both practice further and hopefully pick up a few more words too!

*Xavier is spending his holidays in the south of France with his parents, but things aren't going too well. He writes his feelings in his personal diary (*journal intime*). His mother finds Xavier's diary by accident and decides to read it. However, Xavier's use of familiar language is somewhat puzzling her. Could you help her by changing the words in bold with equivalent from the* "registre courant"*?*

(answers p.184)

le 12 juillet 2008

Cher journal,

J'en ai marre !! Ici c'est l'horreur ! Depuis que nous sommes arrivés dans ce **bled**1 **paumé**2 pour les vacances, rien ne va ! Il n'y a rien à faire ici ! Dimanche, il **a draché** 3 toute la journée ! Hier, je voulais aller en ville pour m'acheter des **fringues** 4 et des nouvelles **godasses**5, mais mes **vieux**6 ont refusé de me **filer**7 la **bagnole** 8! J'ai l'impression qu'ils ne me font pas confiance. Tous mes **potes**9 ont le droit de sortir quand ils veulent ! Pourquoi pas moi ?! C'est vraiment pas juste, mon cher journal !! En plus, mon petit frère m'énerve ! Il **a** toujours **la dalle** 10 et il demande sans arrêt à quelle heure on va **bouffer** 11! Il est vraiment pénible ! Si j'avais su que les vacances seraient aussi **galère**12 j'aurais cherché un **boulot**13 pour l'été comme ça au moins j'aurais **bossé** 14 et j'aurais gagné de la **tune**15 et en plus je n'aurais pas été obligé d'aller en vacances avec ma famille !! Ah ! Qu'est-ce que je m'ennuie ! , je viens de finir mon **bouquin**16.. Qu'est-ce que je vais faire aujourd'hui ? Mes parents veulent que je les accompagne au marché ce matin ! Certainement pas !J'ai pas envie de **me taper la honte** 17! J'en viendrais presque à regretter le **bahut**18...Tu te rends compte, journal !! Moi qui déteste l'école !! C'est vraiment **naze**19 ici et je sens que ces vacances vont être **loupées** 20!! ça me donnerait presque envie de **chialer** 21!! Enfin bref, il faut que je te quitte, mon cher journal, car je dois aller prendre mon petit- déjeuner (tu vois ; il n'y a même pas moyen de faire la **grasse mat**22 !). Alors à ce soir, journal.

1)....................
2)....................
3)....................
4)....................
5)....................
6)....................
7)....................
8)....................
9)....................
10)...................
11)...................
12)...................
13)...................
14)...................
15)...................
16)...................
17)...................
18)...................
19)...................
20)...................
21)...................
22)...................

A little bit of help...

nul / travaillé / parents

amis / pleurer / manger

travail / perdu / livre

prêter / ratées / godasses

être embarrassé / l'argent

village / grasse matinée

difficiles / lycée / voiture

a faim / a plu / vêtements

Even though the notion of ***"registres de langue*"** mostly applies / refers to your choice of vocabulary, there are a few other aspects that can be taken into account too.

- **Abbreviations of words / forms**

It is possible to use a shorten version of certain words in familiar contexts such as:

les ados	les adolescents
une pub	une publicité
Il est trop perso	personnel (= *selfish here*)
un appart	un appartement
Quelle cata !	Quelle catastrophe !
mon prof de géo	mon professeur de géographie

- **Negative forms with omissions of the "*ne...pas*"**

It is possible in familiar contexts, to drop the negative form in some expressions.

C'est pas facile	Ce **n**'est **pas** facile = *c'est difficile*
C'est pas vrai !	Ce **n**'est **pas** vrai ! = *c'est faux !*
C'est pas possible	Ce **n**'est **pas** possible = *C'est impossible*
Y'a pas photo	Il **n**'y a **pas** photo = *c'est évident / il n'y a aucun doute*

- **Use of adverbs**

It is possible to use adverbs such as "**trop**" / "**vachement**" or "**carrément**" in familiar contexts to insist on something or even exaggerate.

J'aime beaucoup ce film. Il est **trop** bien!
La meilleure amie de ma sœur est **vachement** canon ! (« canon » (fam) = pretty).
Eteins ta clope, c'est interdit de fumer ici. De toute façon, c'est **carrément** naze de fumer ! *(« clope » (fam) = cigarette / « naze » (fam) = nul)*

- **Use of words / verbs / adjectives in a different meaning**

It is possible to use words in familiar contexts but to use them in the opposite meaning to their usual meaning. It is a form of irony. It is also possible for some words / verbs / nouns (etc.) to take a totally different meaning in a familiar context.

Je rêve!	C'est incroyable! / je n'y crois pas!
Tu m'étonnes !	Tu ne m'étonnes pas du tout !
Génial ! Super!	*They can be used to mean « great! » but they can also be used to express the opposite.*
C'est mortel!	*Again, this expression can be used to mean « it is boring!" or "it is fantastic" or even "No chance"!*
Il est lourd / il est grave	Il est nul / ennuyeux / embêtant etc.
Ça craint !	C'est nul !

NB: Don't forget that some verb tenses such as the past historic will be out of place in familiar contexts.

LINK WORDS

All your pieces of written work, regardless of the type of texts required, MUST be **STRUCTURED**. As part of the markscheme for Paper 2, criteria B (*Cultural Interaction*) takes this requirement into account. Link words cannot just simply be used anywhere and anyhow. Some will prove to be useful tools for chronologically building an account or a story. Others will help you create suspense or will help you express the cause and / or consequences of actions etc.
Below is a list of these all important link words. Learn them and use them well! Try and avoid always using the same ones. Vary them and pay attention to the nuances they bring to the meaning of your sentences.

Note that they are in no particular order.
Bear in mind that this list is far from being exhaustive. Remember as well, that some work better in formal contexts than others and that most can be put at different places in your sentences.

CHRONOLOGY / TIME	
D'abord	First / firstly
Tout d'abord	First of all
après	after
avant	before
En premier lieu / en second lieu	Firstly / secondly
ensuite	afterwards / then
puis	then
enfin	at last
Dans un premier temps	In the first instance
En dernier lieu	Finally
Pour commencer	To start
Pour finir	To finish
Pour conclure / en conclusion	To conclude
Plus tôt / plus tard	Earlier / later
désormais	from now on
maintenant	now
à présent	nowadays
C'est à ce moment (précis) que ...	This is at that (precise) moment que
C'est alors que ...	This is when…
dès que...	as soon as
aussitôt que...	as soon as
Autrefois / jadis	A long time ago
Depuis	Since
Au cours de / pendant	During
soudain	suddenly
Tout à coup	All of a sudden

PRESENTATION OF ARGUMENTS / POINTS OF VIEW	
cependant	however
toutefois	however
néanmoins	nevertheless
D'une part ...d'autre part	On one side…on the other side
Par ailleurs	Besides
De plus	Moreover
Bien que + *subjunctive*	Although
En outre	Moreover
En revanche	On the other hand
mais	but
aussi	as well / equally
également	equally
non seulement...	not only ...

ILLUSTRATION OF ARGUMENTS / POINTS OF VIEW	
en effet	indeed
ainsi	thus
par exemple	for example
parce que	because
notamment	notably
soit ...	thus
donc	therefore
c'est-à-dire	That is to say
en d'autres termes	in other words

CAUSE	
parce que	because
puisque	because / as
car	because
en effet	indeed
à cause de…	because of
comme	as
c'est la raison pour laquelle...	this is the reason why…
d'autant plus que…	all the more than…
pour avoir / être + *past participle*	In order to have…..

CONSEQUENCE	
par conséquent	as a result
donc	therefore
ainsi	thus
alors	then
du coup *(fam)*	as a result
de ce fait	as a result
de sorte que + *indicatif*	as a result
si bien que + *subjunctive*	as a consequence

AIM / GOAL	
pour + *infinitive*	in order to
pour que + *subjunctive*	so that
dans le but de	with the intention of
afin de + *infinitive*	so that
afin que + *subjunctive*	So that
en vue de + *infinitive*	with a view to
de manière à	so
de manière à ce que / de sorte que + *subjunctive*	so that
de façon à	so that
de façon à ce que + *subjunctive*	so that

Making REFERENCES / GIVING OPINIONS	
à mon avis	in my opinion
selon	according to
en ce qui concerne…	as far as…is concerned
à ce sujet / à ce propos	on this topic
d'après	according to…
à cet égard	in that respect
dans le contexte / le domaine de …	in the context of…
dans ce cas	in this case
à ce niveau	at this level
à l'échelle de	at this level
dans cette optique,	In this vein,
en tant que	as / in my capacity as
dans le cadre de	in the context of

COMPARISON	
comme	as
plus / moins / autant / aussi que	more / less / as much / as many as
semblable à / similaire à / identique à pareil à	similar to

CONCLUSION	
(en) Bref *(oral)*	In brief
en un mot *(oral)*	in a word
En conclusion	In conclusion
Pour conclure	To conclude
en somme	overall
somme toute	overall / all in all
en résumé	to summarise

A few more	
grâce à	thanks to
sous prétexte que	under the pretext that
à condition que	on condition that
étant donné que	given that
malgré / malgré que	despite

Examples:

CHRONOLOGY / TIME:

- Il se versa ***d'abord*** un grand bol de café ***puis*** alla s'asseoir en silence dans le canapé.
- ***Maintenant*** que tu as réussi à mettre tes parents en colère, j'espère que tu es satisfait !
- ***Dès que*** j'aurai de nouvelles informations sur l'accident, je te téléphonerai pour te tenir au courant.

PRESENTATION OF ARGUMENTS :

- *La hausse du prix du pétrole est à l'origine d'une crise économique mondiale.* ***Par ailleurs****, si cette crise perdure, plus d'une entreprise se verra contrainte de fermer ses portes.*
- *La situation est* ***certes*** *grave,* ***néanmoins****, il ne faut pas désespérer.*

ILLUSTRATION OF ARGUMENTS :

- *Le réchauffement climatique est un problème d'actualité.* ***En effet,*** *la fonte de la banquise et l'augmentation de la pollution dans les villes nous montrent qu'il devient urgent de réagir.*

CAUSE / AIM / CONSEQUENCE:

- ***Comme*** *c'était son anniversaire, nous lui avons offert un cadeau.*
- *Personne n'est à l'abri du besoin,* ***c'est la raison pour laquelle*** *je vous demande de vous montrer généreux et de faire un don* ***pour*** *aider les plus démunis.*
- *Lisez les journaux* ***afin de*** *mieux vous rendre compte de l'ampleur des dégâts causés par l'ouragan.*
- *Il était toujours en retard, ne rendait jamais ses devoirs et se montrait souvent insolent envers les profs* ***de sorte qu'****il a été renvoyé de son établissement.*
- *Il était en voyage d'affaires en Chine.* ***Par conséquent****, il n'a pas pu assister aux obsèques de son beau-père.*

REFERENCES :

- *Le réchauffement climatique est un problème important* ***à l'échelle de*** *la planète.*

There are a few more link words, but as I have mentioned before, this guide does not pretend to be exhaustive. It is important to be able to use these link words (*and to actually use them!!*) in context in order to use them appropriately. There is often a question "fill in the blank" with link words in Paper 1 so it might help if you know what they mean and which ones are followed by a subjunctive / an infinitive or a noun for example.

Let's practise!

(answers p.184)

A) Without looking at the previous page, try and link each link word to its translation. Then complete the gap filling exercises.

1) soudain	a) although
2) tout à coup	b) then
3) quand	c) suddenly
4) cependant	d) moreover
5) pourtant	e) then / next
6) bien que	f) however / but
7) d'ailleurs	g) however
8) ensuite	h) all of a sudden
9) puis	i) when

B) Fill in the blanks using the appropriate linking words.

1. C'était un samedi après-midi, il n'y a pas si longtemps. Il faisait beau et je venais juste de rentrer du lycée. Comme j'avais faim, je décidai d'aller dans la cuisine pour me préparer un sandwich mais ------------------------- un phénomène bizarre se produisit.

2. Je n'arrivais pas à retrouver mon téléphone portable, ... j'étais sûr de l'avoir laissé sur la table du salon avant d'aller prendre ma douche. Je n'y comprenais rien ! J'étais ---------------- bien seul à la maison et un téléphone, ça ne peut pas disparaître tout seul !! Je commençais à prendre peur…

3. .... Paul soit arrivé tard à la soirée, il a réussi à se faire plein de nouveaux amis. Mais comment a-t-il fait ?

4. J'étais assis dans le jardin et je lisais un livre tranquillement. .... un cri horrible se fit entendre.

5. L'inspecteur est entré dans son bureau, il a enlevé son pardessus, il s'est servi un verre d'eau .... s'est assis à son bureau. ...., il a commencé à relire les témoignages des personnes présentes ce soir-là. Quelque chose ne collait pas.

6. Monsieur Laporte dormait à l'étage .... les cambrioleurs se sont introduits dans sa maison.

7. Elle était convaincue d'avoir fermé la porte avant de partir. ...., n'était-elle pas l'une des personnes les plus prudentes de sa famille ? Avait-elle jamais oublié de fermer la porte ?

8. Il avait enfin réussi à finir son travail. ...., il n'était pas satisfait.

C) Same exercise

There might be a few new ones in this exercise *(in addition to the ones listed on pages 59 and 60)*. This is in the hope that you will pick up some more and therefore have a more varied toolbox at your disposal.

- sous prétexte que – comme – à force de – en réponse à – étant donné que –

- sous l'emprise de – dès l'instant où – sous le coup de - grâce à – à défaut de –

1) .... que nous n'avons pas confiance en lui, nous avons refusé de le laisser partir seul en vacances.

2) J'ai réussi à finir mon devoir de français .... l'aide de mon ami François.

3) .... de la colère, il a quitté la salle subitement.

4) .... vouloir tout faire toute seule, elle a fini par craquer.

5) .... votre annonce parue dans le Monde, je me permets de postuler au poste d'ingénieur.

6) .... il était dans les mains d'un bon médecin, il a guéri rapidement.

7) Il est impossible de le raisonner quand il est .... l'alcool.

8) Il a refusé de nous accompagner au cinéma .... il avait un devoir d'anglais à terminer.

9) On va boire du café .... ne pas avoir de thé.

10) .... elle est arrivée, l'ambiance a changé.

General comments about Paper 2

That's it! That's Paper 2 covered now! This section should have refreshed your mind and hopefully reassured you about how to best tackle the questions. Don't forget that the specific requirements attached to each type of texts will come handy in the writing of the **Written Assignment**. Don't forget either that some structures covered for some types of texts can also be used judiciously in others.

In the box below, you can find a summary of all the essential points to remember along with a few more tips.

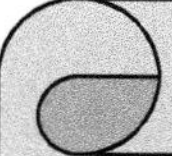

- Use the 5 minutes reading time at your disposal and use it well. Make sure you read **ALL** the questions and spend some time analysing the targeted audience, type(s) of text(s), topics etc.
- Make sure you respect the format and specific linguistic tools attached to each type of texts.
- Make sure that you answer ALL the aspects of the question if there is more than one.
- Mind your language: grammar and vocabulary... and "yes", accents do matter, they are part of the French language so don't neglect them!
- Consistent use of register please!
- STRUCTURE your work: use appropriate link words.
- Avoid at all cost reciting lists of idiomatic expressions. By all means, do use a few if you know how and if you are sure that they work well in the context in which you are working, but leave them well alone if you are not sure. If what you are doing is desperately trying to place them somewhere in the hope that this will impress the examiner...believe me, he / she will NOT be impressed if you have too many and / or if it is clear that you do not understand how and in which context they work.
- Make sure that you reach the minimum of words required (250 words for SL and HL section A and 150 for HL section B).
- Make good use of the time allocated.
- Mind the presentation of your work and if you are aware that your handwriting is not your best ally, try and make an extra effort on the day.
- Only use black or blue ink to write.
- Make sure you leave yourself enough time to check your work before getting rid once and for all of your precious piece of work.

Chapter 3 **Travail Écrit or Written Assignment** ***(receptive and productive skills)***

As the requirements vary for SL and HL, let's start with SL! (*note that these requirements are valid until the November 2014 session only as they will change slightly from 2015 onwards*)

The aim of the *Travail Écrit* is to test your "*lecture intertextelle*" skills and your productive skills at the same time. What does that mean?

- "***lecture intertextuelle***" means your ability to understand and process information from different sources (3 in this case) on a given topic and establish links between the texts (reading and comprehension skills)
- "**productive skills**" means your ability to produce a text of your own (based *on the ideas from the 3 sources given to you*)– (writing skills)

The "*Travail Écrit*" takes place at some point during the second year of your IB studies. It is a kind of coursework in a way and the dates will be set by your school.

It is externally assessed and counts for 20% of your final grade.

It is marked out of 25:

- 8 marks for language
- 10 marks for the content or message (*have you been able to use the information from the sources efficiently and in an organised way or not*)
- 4 points for presentation (*type of text: format and register*)
- 3 points for the rationale (*does it make direct reference to the sources / texts, is it organised and clear*).

So how does it (practically) work?

- you will have 3 to 4 supervised hours (*either in one sitting or on separate ones*) to complete this task
- you will be given 3 texts. Each text will contain between 300 and 400 words
- the 3 texts will be linked together by one "theme": they will be on one of the Core topics (*Relations sociales, Communication and médias, Questions mondiales*) that you have studied in class (*well - on one aspect of one of the Core Topics studied*)
- the 3 texts may be of a different type *(an article / a diary entry etc.)*
- You will not be told in advance on which exact topics of the Core that you have studied, your "*Travail Écrit*" will be on but you will probably be given pointers so that you can revise some items of vocabulary at least (*so no need to put pressure on your teacher to tell you! That would be unethical, disappointing coming from an IB student and simply against the spirit of the IB!*).
- the 3 texts will be based on topics you have covered, however, they will be completely new to you on the day you complete your "*Travail Écrit*". It will be the first time you see them.
- On the day(s) you complete your "travail Écrit", once you have read the texts and decided what you are going to do, you will need to agree your choice of task with your teacher. Once this is done, no further guidance can be given to you.
- Once you have completed your "*Travail Écrit*" (*including the 100 words rationale*) and completed the official coversheet that your teacher will give to you, your work, along with a copy of the 3 texts, will be sent to an external examiner. Your fate (*as far as the TE is concerned at least*) will then be sealed! You may wonder why the texts are sent to the examiner. The answer is simple: so that the examiner can judge how well you have been able to organise and use the ideas expressed in the 3 texts (**Not** how well you have managed to quote / copy from the texts… copying from the texts is not allowed).
- Your work will have to be handwritten.

➢ If your task is completed in several sittings, you will not be allowed to take the texts and / or your work home and once your task has been agreed, it should not be changed anyway!

What do I have to do then?

☑ read and understand the 3 texts
☑ make links / connections between the main ideas in the 3 texts
☑ choose the relevant pieces of information / ideas from each one of the 3 texts on which you are going to base your own text- Note that I did not say that you will be able to re-use the information from the texts as it is in the texts. Quoting from the texts is not allowed.
☑ decide on the text / task you are going to create:
  - type of text you are going to create *(letter / speech / diary entry etc.- see Chapter 2)*
  - targeted audience *(this will determine which register of language you are going to use)*
  - aim of the text you are going to write
☑ agree your task with your teacher
☑ handwrite your text which must be 300 to 400 words in length
☑ give your task a title
☑ write the 100 words rationale in French (*"préambule"*) to explain what you were aiming to do
☑ fill in the coversheet

Et voilà!

Will I be allowed to use any reference material?
The answer is "yes" and below is the list of what you can use:

☑ a dictionary (*bilingual or monolingual or both*!)
☑ a verb book (*like the "bescherelle" if you are familiar with that resource*)
☑ general guidelines on the format of the different types of texts
☑ the Written Assignment instructions and assessment criteria *(to be found in the Language B guide)*

To help you understand better what I mean by "create" your own text based on ideas expressed in the 3 text sources, below is an example:

TRONC COMMUN : Communication et médias **<u>SOURCES</u>**: - one article about the dangers of internet - an interview with a victim of cyber-bullying - extract of a parental guide designed to give advice to parents to help them protect their children against the dangers associated with internet use

The link between the 3 texts would clearly be: dangers associated with the use of the internet / safe use of the internet by young people

Examples of possible tasks / texts you could create:
Note that I am giving you several examples of tasks here but you only write one task.

Task 1: - diary page of a parent of a victim of cyber-bullying	Aim: Express emotions and reflect on child's and own experience	Targeted audience: The person who is writing the diary entry	**Possible title:** *Pourquoi est-ce que ça m'est arrivé à moi ?*

⇩

Task 2: - speech to inform about the dangers of the internet	Aim: Inform about the dangers of the internet and give advice to protect oneself	Targeted audience: A group a young people	**Possible title:** *Internet: Attention danger!*

⇩

Task 3: - letter from a parent to his / her child who has been the victim of cyber-bullying	Aim: Express emotions and regrets and explain how it could have been avoided	Targeted audience: The child	**Possible title:** *Si seulement j'avais su te protéger !*

⇩

Task 4: - " Guide de recommendations"	Aim: Inform teenagers about dangers of internet and give advice to stay safe on line	Targeted audience: teenagers	**Possible title:** *Pour une utilisation intelligente et sans danger de l'internet*

NB : Note that it is possible to choose for your written task the same format as one of the type of texts handed to you in the first place. For example here, task 4 is a "guide de recommadations" (brochure) yet one of the texts from which you are getting the ideas is also a "guide de recommandations". This is fine as the original is for adults and yours is aimed at teenagers.

What about the rationale or « Préambule"?

- ✓ It is a compulsory element of the Written Assignment and carries 3 marks out of the potential 25 marks available in total
- ✓ 100 words (*written in French too*)
- ✓ handwritten
- ✓ must make clear references to the texts / establish a clear link with the 3 sources
- ✓ must explain clearly your choice of task : aim(s) / type of text / why? how?

***NB**: It can be written before or after the task. However, even if you decide to write it after, you should have a clear idea in your head of what you are trying to achieve before you start writing your "travail écrit".*

Example based on task 1:

Les textes parlent des dangers liés à l'utilisation d'internet. Dans l'extrait du guide, des conseils sont donnés aux parents pour protéger leurs enfants. L'interview et l'article expliquent ce qui peut se passer lorsque l'on n'est pas prudent. J'ai décidé d'écrire la page du journal intime d'un parent d'une victime de cyber-intimidation car j'ai trouvé intéressant de pouvoir exprimer les émotions (les parents souffrent de voir leurs enfants souffrir) et surtout les sentiments de culpabilité et impuissance éprouvés par un proche. Si ce parent avait été plus informé, plus attentif, il aurait pu conseiller son fils et peut-être éviter la situation.

100 mots

⇒ clear references / links to texts / sources
⇒ presentation of choice of type of text and of who is writing
⇒ aim of task (and here it also kind of justifies why the diary entry)

100 words is not a lot so you need to be concise and precise.
Your "*préambule*" must be clear and organised.
It is meant to help your examiner understand what your aims were and how you went about your writing.

Take a look at this second example fictionally based on task 2.

Les textes parlent des dangers liés à l'utilisation d'internet. Dans l'extrait du guide, des conseils sont donnés aux parents pour protéger leurs enfants. L'interview et l'article expliquent ce qui peut se passer lorsque l'on n'est pas prudent. Mon but est de donner conseils aux jeunes pour les prévenir des dangers potentiels d'internet et de leurs donner des conseils pratiques pour se protéger. J'ai donc choisi un discours car ça permet de s'adresser directement à son public donc c'est plus efficace. Comme c'est un public de mon âge, je peux utiliser le langage familier.

93 mots

Let's look at an example!

Below are 3 texts which are linked by a common theme.

TEXTE A

L'esclavage domestique en France

Au 21ème siècle, l'esclavage domestique existe en France. Il touche des enfants, des jeunes filles et des femmes, et plus rarement de jeunes garçons ou des hommes. Le Comité contre l'esclavage moderne a aidé des centaines de personnes à sortir de situations d'asservissement. Ces victimes viennent en général de l'étranger, d'Asie et d'Afrique principalement, espérant trouver en France une vie meilleure. Il est très difficile d'estimer le nombre de victimes dans l'Hexagone, car les faits se déroulent dans le huis clos des domiciles. Contrairement aux idées reçues, ces drames existent dans tous les milieux sociaux. Le mot « esclavage domestique » fait souvent penser aux diplomates. C'est largement inexact : si 20% des victimes aidées par le Comité contre l'esclavage moderne ont été asservies dans le monde diplomatique ou les beaux quartiers, ces drames sont aussi présents dans les pavillons de banlieue ou les grands ensembles des quartiers défavorisés.

Il s'agit d'une population vulnérable et clandestine, ignorant souvent la langue française et les droits fondamentaux garantis dans notre pays. Ces personnes sont des proies faciles pour des individus sans scrupules. Le scénario est souvent le même. Soit « embauchée » à l'étranger par des «maîtres» qui s'installent en France, soit recrutée par un truchement pseudo familial, la jeune fille se retrouve très rapidement sous l'emprise totale de ses exploiteurs. Comment ? Papiers d'identité confisqués, menacée, affamée, isolée, en manque de sommeil, apeurée, elle perd rapidement tous ses repères. Insultée, voire frappée, elle exécute les ordres et enchaîne les heures de travail parfois 15 à 16 heures par jour. Epuisée, humiliée, peu ou pas rémunérée, elle semble se résigner à son sort et perd peu à peu toute confiance en elle même et dans la vie.

Ce sont le plus souvent des voisins qui signalent ces situations d'esclavage domestique. Ils ont remarqué la détresse ou la très grande maigreur d'une jeune femme aperçue descendant les poubelles ou enfermée sur un balcon un soir d'hiver.

323 mots

Extrait reproduit avec l'aimable autorisation du Comité contre l'esclavage (http://www.esclavagemoderne.org)

TEXTE B

Premier procès pour "esclavage domestique" en France

La justice française a examiné pour la première fois jeudi à Lyon un cas présumé d'"esclavage domestique et traite des êtres humains", une qualification prévue depuis trois ans par le Code pénal. Le procureur du tribunal de grande instance de Lyon a requis deux ans de prison avec sursis pour un couple accusé d'avoir employé durant douze ans en France une Sénégalaise en la rémunérant très faiblement.

Il a également requis deux ans de mise à l'épreuve. L'avocat de la plaignante a réclamé de son côté 60.000 euros de retard de salaires, de droits à la retraite et de préjudice moral pour sa cliente. Fatou, aujourd'hui âgée de 58 ans, s'est enfuie de chez ses employeurs en juin 2009 après trente ans au service de cette famille d'expatriés, d'abord au Sénégal, puis en Côte d'Ivoire, en Espagne et enfin en France.

Elle a dit qu'elle était payée environ 120 euros par mois pour 16 heures de travail par jour, sans jour de repos ni congés. Son travail consistait à préparer les repas de ses employeurs, sortir les chiens, s'occuper de la maison et d'une grand-mère placée en maison de retraite.

Le Comité contre l'esclavage moderne, vers qui elle s'est tournée avant de porter plainte, s'est porté partie civile à ses côtés.

"Toutoune", comme l'appellent ses anciens employeurs, était habillée avec les vieux vêtements de sa patronne. Elle n'avait pas de papiers, n'était pas déclarée et ne bénéficiait d'aucune protection sociale. Elle possédait un compte bancaire dont le couple avait une procuration. Ils ont dit lui avoir versé 20.000 euros au Sénégal pour l'achat d'un terrain où elle devait se faire construire une maison.

Le couple, aujourd'hui à la retraite, a dit voir "beaucoup d'exagération" dans ses propos. "*Elle faisait partie de la famille et partageait ses peines et ses problèmes, et nous avons tenté à quatre ou cinq reprises de régulariser sa situation mais nous avons échoué*", a expliqué Daniel Chaumier, âgé de 66 ans.
Son épouse Jeanine a dit ne l'avoir jamais déclarée aux organismes sociaux "*par ignorance*". C'est ce qui l'a toujours empêchée d'obtenir des papiers.

Après sa fuite, Fatou a été accueillie à Bordeaux par une famille française connue au Sénégal. Elle a dit avoir aujourd'hui des papiers en règle et un emploi rémunéré.
Le jugement a été mis en délibéré au 16 décembre.

394 mots

Catherine Lagrange, édité par Clément Guillou - http://www.rmc.fr/editorial/131561/premier-proces-pour-esclavage-domestique-en-france/

TEXTE C

Moi, Rania, esclave en France de mes 10 ans à mes 20 ans

23 juin 2007

Témoignage de Rania, une Marocaine de 24 ans, arrivée en France à 8 ans.

"Mon vrai prénom est Aïcha, mais je ne veux plus en entendre parler ; c'est le prénom de la sorcière qui m'a exploitée pendant dix ans. J'avais 8 ans quand cette femme a proposé à mon père, seul depuis la mort de ma mère, de m'emmener avec elle en France. A l'époque, nous vivions à Agadir. C'était la fille d'un de ses plus vieux amis, alors il a accepté. La première année s'est bien passée. J'étais scolarisée comme une enfant normale. C'est ensuite que l'enfer a commencé. Aïcha m'a envoyée travailler dans une famille, elle aussi d'origine marocaine, et m'a retirée de l'école. Je gardais toute la journée deux enfants d'un an et 4 ans, je cuisinais, je repassais, je faisais le ménage. Et le week-end, quand je rentrais chez Aïcha, je devais de nouveau m'occuper des enfants et faire toutes les tâches ménagères. Je me couchais rarement avant minuit, j'étais épuisée. J'avais alors 10 ans.

Un jour, la femme chez qui je travaillais m'a demandé de faire les carreaux. J'ai refusé parce que j'avais peur de monter sur l'escabeau. Elle m'a frappée et insultée. J'ai prévenu Aïcha, mais elle n'a rien fait. Au contraire, elles se sont mises d'accord pour me sanctionner dès que je travaillais mal. Elles trouvaient toujours quelque chose à redire, un prétexte pour me gifler, m'injurier, m'humilier. Aïcha m'a même menacée avec un couteau parce que je ne voulais pas faire le ramadan. Elle insultait sans cesse mes parents, ce qui me faisait beaucoup souffrir. Elle m'a emmenée au Maroc l'été de mes 11 ans. J'ai vu mon père quelques heures, mais je ne lui ai rien dit. Je crois que je ne voulais pas lui faire de peine. Pendant toutes ces années, je n'ai pas été payée.

C'est Aïcha qui percevait directement l'argent de mes employeurs. Par la suite, j'ai travaillé chez elle. Cela a duré presque trois ans avant que je m'enfuie. Elle me faisait peur, tellement peur. J'étais son objet, sa chose. Je ne pouvais pas sortir, je ne pouvais fréquenter personne, je ne pouvais pas étudier à la maison (je le faisais en cachette la nuit), je devais être sans arrêt disponible pour elle et j'étais astreinte à d'interminables corvées. Elle n'avait entrepris aucune démarche pour que mes papiers soient en règle. Je ne comprends toujours pas comment mes voisins ont pu se taire pendant tant d'années, vivre comme si de rien n'était.

432 mots

http://www.bladi.net/esclavage-moderne-maroc-france.html - reproduit avec permission –

Task :	Aim:	Targeted audience:	**Possible title:**
- " tract"	Inform general public about slavery in their own country and appeal for action	General public	*Ça se passe ici et aujourd'hui !*

Préambule:

Read these two potential Rationales.
Which ones do you think is the best one for this task / the most efficient and why?
Could you improve the one which you think is not as good and re-write it?

A)

Je viens de lire trois textes qui traitent du thème de l'esclavage moderne en France. Le premier est un article qui donne des informations sur la situation générale, le deuxième parle du procès intenté par une ancienne victime à ses « employeurs » et décrit ses conditions de travail. Le troisième et le témoignage d'une ancienne victime. Je trouve cette situation choquante : comment des gens peuvent-ils être encore esclave s aujourd'hui en France ? J'ai décidé d'écrire un tract pour choquer et faire réagir tout le monde. Le tract permet d'être direct et d'utiliser un langage persuasif pour convaincre.

100 mots

B)

Je viens de lire trois textes qui traitent du thème de l'esclavage moderne en France. Le premier est un article qui donne des informations sur la situation générale, le deuxième parle du procès intenté par une ancienne victime à ses « employeurs » et décrit ses conditions de travail. Le troisième et le témoignage d'une ancienne victime. Je veux faire réagir les gens et donner des informations sur ce sujet. J'ai donc choisi de rédiger un tract.

77 mots

....

....

....

....

....

....

....

....

....

Exemple de travail écrit :

Lorsque vous entendez le mot **ESCLAVAGE**; à quoi, à qui pensez –vous ?

À l'Afrique ? À l'Asie ? Aux pays en voie de développement ?

Eh bien NON ! L'esclavage ; ça se passe aussi **ICI** en France et **AUJOURD'HUI** !

Le saviez-vous ?

Les enfants, les filles et les femmes en sont le plus souvent les victimes.

Le saviez-vous ?

Ces esclaves modernes travaillent parfois jusqu'à 16 heures par jour, n'ont pas de vacances et ne sont souvent pas ou très peu payées.

Le saviez-vous ?

Leurs conditions de vie sont souvent inacceptables. Ces esclaves modernes n'ont souvent aucune possession, sont contraints de porter les vêtements usagés de leurs « employeurs ». Elles vivent dans des conditions indécentes souvent battues et mal traitées. Elles souffrent derrière les portes fermées des pavillons de banlieue, des appartements des grandes villes et parfois même dans les HLM des zones défavorisées, dans l'indifférence générale.

Le saviez-vous ?

Leurs « employeurs » ont généralement confisqué leurs papiers et ces victimes vivent dans la clandestinité, sans protection sociale, sans aide, sans espoir d'échapper à leur triste sort. Les jeunes filles ne sont pas scolarisées et deviennent des bonnes à tout faire.

Ça suffit !

Majoritairement venues de l'étranger, exploitées par des gens sans scrupules, trompées par des amis ou membres de la famille affirmant emmener les jeunes filles vers un avenir meilleur, parfois injuriées, humiliées, menacées, ces personnes sont vulnérables.

Tous ensemble il faut que nous agissions pour mettre fin à l'esclavage !

Arrêtons d'être complices ! Ouvrons les yeux et aidons les victimes d'esclavage à sortir de leur calvaire.

Aidons la justice à continuer à punir les coupables et rendre leur liberté et dignité aux victimes de l'esclavage. Si vous savez que derrière les murs du pavillon de vos voisins une femme, un enfant, une personne est exploitée, accomplissez votre devoir civique et parlez.

Aidez à redonner une voix à ces victimes pour que l'esclavage ça ne soit plus ici ni aujourd'hui !

Si vous voulez en savoir plus, rendez-vous sur le site www.comitécontrelesclavage.fr
Venez aussi écouter le témoignage de Rania, ancienne victime, qui a vécu 10 ans prisonnière d'une femme mal intentionnée.

clear references to text A (*without copying sentences from text)*

clear references to text B

clear references to text C

More specific to HL students…

At HL, the « travail écrit » is based on one of the two works of literature that you have formally studied during the course of your IB studies. It can therefore be based on a specific novel, short story, play or poem. Your teacher will choose which works of literature you study.

NB: Studying literature is great and essential as it gives you an insight into francophone culture and helps you further develop both your vocabulary and general language skills. It should be enjoyable. It is not about literary analysis however. It is more about understanding the characters, story line, themes etc.

As for SL students, the aim of the *Travail Écrit* is to test your receptive skills and your productive skills at the same time. What does that mean?

- "***receptive skills***" means your ability to understand and process information from a text – a literary text to be more precise here – (reading skills)
- "**productive skills**" means your ability to produce a text of your own based on the chosen (out of the two formally studied) original work of literature – (writing skills)

The "*Travail Écrit*" takes place at some point during the second year of your IB studies. It is a kind of coursework in a way and the dates will be set by your school.
It is externally assessed and counts for 20% of your final grade.
It is marked out of 25:

- 8 marks for language
- 10 marks for the content or message (*have you understood the literary work and made clear and relevant connections with it without simply summarising it? Have you managed to organise your ideas clearly?*)
- 4 points for presentation (*type of text: format and register*)
- 3 points for the rationale (*does it make direct reference to the sources / texts, is it organised and clear*).

As advised before, get your hands on the marking criteria!

So how does it (practically) work?

- you will have 3 to 4 supervised hours (*either in one sitting or on separate ones*) to complete this task
- you will have to choose the literary work on which you want to base your creative writing piece.
- On the day(s) you complete your "travail Écrit", you will agree your choice of task with your teacher. Once this is done, no further guidance can be given to you. Bear in mind that you probably ought to have thought about it as you were / are reading the book, play etc. There is nothing stopping you from thinking about it at all!
- Once you have completed your "*Travail Écrit*" (*including the 150 words rationale*) and completed the official coversheet (*which will contain details of the work of literature you have chosen*) that your teacher will give to you, your work will be sent to an external examiner. Your fate (*as far as the TE is concerned at least*) will then be sealed! You may wonder what may happen if your examiner has not read the specific text that you have chosen as a starting point / background for your written assignment. The answer is simple: as details of the work of literature are sent with your task, even if the examiner has not read the book, he or she will be able to understand the context and assess whether or not the references and connections that you have made with the original text are superficial or meaningful. (Word of advice: copying from the texts is not allowed *so it is not what the examiner will be looking for!*). Reassured now?
- Your work will have to be handwritten.

If your task is completed in several sittings, you will not be allowed to take the texts and / or your work home and once your task has been agreed, it should not be changed any more.

What do I have to do then?

- ☑ re-read / revise the piece of literary work you have chosen to base your Written Assignment on. Each teacher chooses which pieces of literature they wish to study so it will be different for each one of you- even if you are in the same school.
- ☑ make sure you are familiar with the story line, understand the characters, the themes etc.
- ☑ choose the relevant pieces of information / ideas from the original work of literature on which you are going to base your own text- Note that I did not say that you will be able to re-use the information from the text as it is in the text. Quoting from the text is not allowed.
  It is not about summarising the information from the text either and recounting the story! It is about being creative and giving you the opportunity to show a deeper understanding of the work of literature. So it is about re-using / making references to specific details / events etc. from the original text in an original way which is adapted to a chosen type of text. For example, if you choose to write the diary page of a character at a specific moment in the book in order to show the character's feeling about a specific event, you need to understand the character and the feelings he / she may have / display or even hide about the specific event in the first place. Equally, if you are writing the diary page of an eighteenth century character, the tone of your diary entry should be slightly different from the tone of a more modern diary entry. While being creative and unique, your work needs to be in tune with the original work. You therefore need to decide which type of text may be the most appropriate in accordance to what you want to achieve.
- ☑ decide on the text / task you are going to create:
  - type of text you are going to create *(letter / speech / diary entry etc.- see Chapter 2)*
  - targeted audience *(this will determine which register of language you are going to use)*
  - aim of the text you are going to write
- ☑ agree your task with your teacher
- ☑ handwrite your text which must be 500 to 600 words in length
- ☑ give your task a title
- ☑ write the 150 words rationale in French ("*préambule*") to explain what you were aiming to do. Don't forget to establish a clear link with the original text.
- ☑ fill in the coversheet

Et voilà!

Will I be allowed to use any reference material?
The answer is "yes" and below is the list of what you can use:

- ☑ a dictionary (*bilingual or monolingual or both*!)
- ☑ a verb book (*like the "bescherelle" if you are familiar with that resource*)
- ☑ general guidelines on the format of the different types of texts
- ☑ the Written Assignment instructions and assessment criteria *(to be found in the Language B guide)*

You can have a non annotated copy of your original text too.

To help you understand better what I mean by "create" your own text based on a work of literature, below are a few generic examples:

- ✓ Letter from one character to another to express his / her feelings about an event
- ✓ Letter to the author or one character to react to a character's behaviour for example
- ✓ diary entry of a character at a specific moment in the work
- ✓ speech from one character
- ✓ interview with one of the characters to try and understand his / her behaviour or reactions to specific events
- ✓ extra chapter
- ✓ alternative ending

Those are only a few examples. If you are inspired by the books / short stories etc. that you have read, then you should have no trouble coming up with a creative idea.

What about the rationale or « Préambule"?

- ✓ It is a compulsory element of the Written Assignment and carries 3 marks out of the potential 25 marks available in total
- ✓ 150 words (*written in French too*)
- ✓ handwritten
- ✓ must make clear references to the text
- ✓ must state clearly the part of the literary in the book / play etc. your work is linked too specifically (for example: *J'ai choisi d'écrire la page de journal intime de l'officier* ***après son séjour à Paris*** *car je voulais montrer comment ses sentiments ont changé…)*
- ✓ must explain clearly your choice of tasks : aim(s) / type of text / why? how?

***NB**: It can be written before or after the task. However, even if you decide to write it after, you should have a clear idea in your head of what you are trying to achieve before you start writing your "travail écrit".*

Let's look at an example based on the well-known novel ***L'Étranger*** d'Albert Camus.

Just in case you are not familiar with this book, below is a brief summary of the story line:

> *The scene is set in Alger. Meursault, an office clark who has just learnt of his mother's death and not shown any emotion, kills an Arab on the beach. His motive? Well…"il faisait chaud"… Sentenced to death, Meursault remains "impassible"; an outsider to the world and himself.*

The example below is linked to a very specific passage in the book. Meursault is being judged and he is in court. He relates what the prosecution lawyer has just said in his concluding speech before the jury retires to deliberate and reach a conclusion.

Task:	Aim:	Targeted audience:	**Possible title:**
- speech Réquisitoire de l'avocat de l'accusation	Prove / convince the jury of Meursault's culpability	The jury (before retiring to decide on a verdict) and the judge	*Cet homme est un monstre !*

Préambule:

This is only one example. Bear in mind that your examiner will read it before reading your Written Assignment so it must be clear and convincing.

Mon discours a pour point de départ le livre intitulé L'Étranger d'Albert Camus que j'ai étudié en classe. Dans ce livre, Meursault, le personnage principal, tue un homme sur une plage à Alger peu de temps après la mort de sa mère. Il ne semble avoir aucun motif et n'exprime aucune émotion. Mon discours est en fait le réquisitoire de l'avocat de l'accusation et est basé plus spécifiquement sur l'épisode du procès dans le livre. Dans ce passage, Meursault « raconte » le déroulement de son procès à la troisième personne. J'ai voulu donner une voix à l'avocat de l'accusation qui essaie de peindre Meursault comme un monstre dépourvu de sentiments humains. J'ai utilisé un vocabulaire fort car le but est de convaincre les jurés de la culpabilité de Meursault ; cet homme est inhumain et n'a aucune circonstance atténuante. J'ai voulu donner vie au procès en faisant parler l'avocat.

150 mots

clear link / reference to original text

reference to the specific part of the literary work the WA is based on

choice of text / aim of the task / how

Exemple de Travail Écrit:

Regular and precise references to passages / events from the story

\+

Use of the information from the trial without copying the original text

Monsieur le Juge, Mesdames et Messieurs les Jurés,

Cet homme ici présent devant vous, si tant est qu'on puisse l'appeler un homme, est ici parce qu'il a tué un homme, un Arabe, parce qu'il a pris la vie d'un homme innocent.

Il a tué cet homme sur la plage, en plein jour et aux yeux de tous. Son motif ? La chaleur et le soleil ! Insensé ! Un meurtre, car il s'agit bien d'un meurtre de sang froid sans aucune circonstance atténuante, un meurtre qui défie les lois les plus élémentaires de notre société.

Je le répète, aucune circonstance atténuante ne peut être retenue. Pourquoi ? Tout simplement parce que cet homme au visage impassible qui à aucun moment lors de ce procès n'a exprimé un quelconque sentiment de regret, remords ou peine, cet homme qui se tient devant vous est sain mentalement. C'est un homme intelligent, capable de répondre aux questions qui lui ont été posées, parfaitement conscient des faits retenus contre lui. Il n'a pas agi sur un coup de tête. Il s'agit d'un acte réfléchi, calculé et prémédité.

Structured speech

+

appropriate and effective use of rhetorical devices

easy to identify type of text created

Permettez-moi en effet de le répéter clairement. Le meurtre terrible que nous considérons aujourd'hui n'était pas un accident ou le résultat d'un coup de colère inattendu. C'était bel et bien un acte violent, gratuit et réfléchi !

J'utilise le terme « homme » pour le désigner, mais en réalité, c'est un monstre que vous avez ici devant vous ! Certes, il s'agit d'un monstre au visage humain, mais un monstre tout de même. Pas un homme ! Un homme a un cœur. Un homme est capable d'exprimer des remords, des regrets et de montrer des sentiments. Ce monstre sans cœur n'a montré aucune émotion ; que ce soit dans ce tribunal, au moment du rappel des faits ou encore lors de la mort et enterrement de sa propre mère. Comment un être humain digne de ce nom peut-il rester de marbre devant tant d'abominables actions et événements ?

Je voudrais donc finir aujourd'hui avec une phrase, une seule phrase dont j'espère vous vous souviendrez quand vous déciderez du jugement de cet homme : C'est un monstre, pas un être humain ! C'est un monstre incapable d'amour et de compassion. Un criminel, un danger pour notre société ! Ce monstre n'est pas un danger pour notre société parce qu'il est brutal, mais au contraire parce qu'il est à la fois intelligent et incapable d'émotions ! Il n'a pas d'âme ! C'est l'archétype même de la personne contre laquelle nous essayons de protéger notre société.

Accurate and effective use of specific vocabulary (justice / crime)

Ma tâche aujourd'hui est lourde de conséquences mais je l'accepte pleinement. Pourquoi ?

Tout simplement parce que ce monstre au visage humain mais au cœur vide de toute émotion n'a pas sa place dans notre société ! Il n'en connait aucune des règles les plus basiques. C'est un danger dont il faut nous débarrasser !

De toute ma carrière, jamais jugement n'a été plus clair qu'aujourd'hui et peine plus évidente à demander.

Je demande donc à ce que justice soit faite et à ce que notre société soit enfin protégée et réclame aujourd'hui que l'accusé, dont la culpabilité ne fait aucun doute, soit condamné à la peine capitale.

Merci.

534 mots

NB: Forthcoming changes from May 2015 to be aware of if applicable

Please be aware that if you are using this guide to prepare for your exam in May 2015, the Written Assignment requirements will be slightly different from the ones stated above.

What is / will be different from May 2015 onwards?

General changes:

- Not handwritten any longer but **word processed** (still all in target language)
- Not under supervised exam conditions any longer but **in your own time** (still with guidance from your teacher)
- There will only be **3 assessment criteria** instead of 4: Rationale and task / message and Language. The Written assignment will be marked out of 24.

Specific to SL students:

- The rationale will be longer and increased in length from 100 words to **150 words**.
- **You** will be **responsible** for **choosing your own topic** (still based on the core) and you will also need to **choose 3 to 4 texts** as your starting point (again in consultation with your teacher who will guide you)

Specific to HL students:

- The word count for the **rationale** will be between **150 to 250** words (instead of the 150 words maximum)
- It will be possible to base your Written Assignment on not just one but two pieces of literary work studied in class if suitable.

Chapter 4: **THE ORAL**

As you already know, the oral component of the exam is divided into two: the individual oral and the interactive oral. You might not need to spend much time on these pages as at this stage of your revision, you have probably already done your oral. However, just in case you are getting ahead of yourself and using this guide in an early stage of the process, below are some details about the orals and a few tips to help you be ready on the day.

General comments:

- The individual oral takes / will take place at some stage during the second year of your IB studies (*generally between February and March*). It will be linked to one of the options you have studied.

- You will do several group (or interactive) orals during the course of the two years, but more specifically in the second year of your IB studies. The group orals will take place in class and you will be marked individually on your participation and interaction in a group situation on a given topic linked to one of the core topics. Your marks will be recorded. At the end of the process, your teacher will select your best mark but you will be kept in the dark!

- The exact dates will be decided between you and the teacher who takes your oral.

- As far as the individual oral is concerned, you will not be given the provisional mark awarded to you by your teacher / examiner as a sample of your school individual oral work (*and maybe your oral!*) will be submitted to the IB for external moderation. So there is no need to harass your teacher to try and find out how you might have done!

- The marks submitted to the IB will be the sum between the individual oral mark (out of 20) awarded by your teacher and your group oral mark (out of 10) .

- Like with any of the exam components, it is essential that you familiarise yourself with the marking criteria for the internal assessment so that you know what is expected of you. Just ask your teacher to provide you with a copy of these criteria.

- The sum of your oral scores is out of 30 and accounts for 30% of your final IB grade. It constitutes therefore a substantial part of your exam and one that is worth not neglecting!!

So, now that you have a clear / clearer idea of the general procedure for the oral, let's concentrate on each type of oral!

A) The individual oral

- ✓ Based on one of the two options (*Santé / Loisirs / Diversité culturelle / Coutumes et Traditions / Sciences et technologies*) that you have studied formally.
- ✓ Marked out of 20 (*10 marks for language and how you use it / 10 marks for content: can you express and defend ideas and opinions clearly? Can you follow and actively take part in a conversation?)*
- ✓ Prepared, organised, conducted and recorded by your teacher.
- ✓ Mark awarded by your teacher but submitted for external moderation.

So how does it actually work?

The photo

- The individual oral is based on an unseen photo chosen by your teacher.

- This photo will be related to one of the options you have studied.

- When you arrive to take your exam, you will be given:
- a photo (*with an accompanying caption*)
- 15 minutes preparation time.

You are allowed to take notes during the preparation time. Those notes should be limited to 10 brief bullet points to avoid the temptation of simply reading your notes!.

Note that at SL, you have a choice between 2 unseen photos. You will choose only one.

No choice at HL, I am afraid!

- Each photo will have a caption. The aim of the caption is to guide you but you can / should go beyond the direction the caption might be suggesting and not limit your interpretation in any way.

NB: You may not be told the exact topics / sub-topics your oral might be on (*and you cannot demand it from your teacher*!), however, I am sure that your teacher will narrow down the choice of topics and let you know what to concentrate on.

A few more details about the type of photo:

- More likely to be a colour photo but could be in black and white too
- Previously unseen
- Linked to one of the options
- Accompanied by a caption
- Linked to an aspect of Francophone culture
- May contain text in French
- Should be a scene so that you have enough to describe
- Up to 4 other candidates may get the same picture as me but they will be given a different caption each time

How about the oral itself?

It will last between 8 and 10 minutes.

It will be divided into two parts:

Presentation	3 – 4 minutes	You must: - Describe the photo - give your personal interpretation of this photo (*remember: the caption is there to help you / guide you but not restrict or limit your interpretation of the photo*) - go further than what is shown on the on photo / relate more widely to the option studied - give opinions Your presentation must be STRUCTURED. Your teacher will not interrupt you.
Discussion	5- 6 minutes	You will be asked further questions about the photograph, the issue it may be raising, and more generally about the option it is linked to. The aim is for you to demonstrate that you can hold a conversation in French and that you can express ideas and opinions. It is both your productive (speaking) skills and your receptive (listening) skills that are being assessed. NB: If you run out of things to say on the topic, your teacher may then ask you questions on another aspect of the option in question or even on one aspect of your second option.

How can I prepare for it? What is the best thing to do to be well-prepared?

Well…hopefully it is not too late and you have contributed in class and spoken as much French as possible during your IB years (and before!). However, knowing both generic vocabulary to describe a photo, present ideas and express opinions will be crucial. Examples are given in this chapter but it is a non-exhaustive list. You will also know on which sub-topics your oral will be on so you must revise specific items of vocabulary linked to this / these option(s). Remember that vocabulary is always best revised in context so re-read articles related to the topics so that you will not only revise your vocabulary but you will also refresh your memories with various ideas, opinions and views on the topic.

Un peu de vocabulaire pour se préparer…

Below are a few expressions that you may want to use either to describe or express opinions. There are other expressions that you can use of course. Those are only examples.

Pour décrire une image

- **sur cette photo il y a / on peut voir…***on this picture, there is / one can see…*
- **En regardant cette photo…** - *looking at this picture*
- **Sur cette photo, il s'agit de…** *this photo is about*
- **au premier plan** – *in the foreground*
- **à l'arrière plan** – *in the background*
- **à gauche / à droite**
- **en haut / en bas**
- **dans le coin** – *in the corner*
- **dans le coin en haut à gauche** – *in the top left hand corner*
- **au centre / au milieu** – *in the middle*
- **derrière / devant / à côté / entre / en face de / au-dessus / en dessous / près de etc.**

- Utilisez des ***adjectifs*** pour décrire les personnes etc.
- Attention ***à l'accord*** des adjectifs**…**

Faire un lien

- **Cette photo est liée au thème de**– *this photo is linked to the topic of*
- **Ça montre** … *it shows*
- **Il est évident qu'il s'agit du thème de-** *it is obvious that the topic is*
- **La légende suggère que …** ***the caption suggests that***

Exprimer des opinions

- **à mon avis / selon moi** – *in my opinion*
- **je pense que**
- **cela suggère que…** - *it suggests that …*
- **on peut en déduire que …** - *one can guess / deduct that …*
- **on peut imaginer que…** - *one can imagine that*
- **je suis d'accord / je ne suis pas d'accord** – *I agree / disagree*
- **je partage votre avis / opinion** – *I share yopur point of view*
- **il est évident que …** - *it is obvious that*
- **cela me fait penser à** – *it makes me think of*
- **Il est possible de dire que** … - *one can say that*

Let's look at a couple of examples!

Exemple 1 : **les loisirs**

©reuters

Une rencontre agressive

La photo dont je vais parler est liée au thème du sport et de la violence.

La scène se passe sur un terrain de sport, un terrain de rugby pour être plus précis(e) lors d'un match de rugby. ***En effet***, sur cette image on peut voir 2 joueurs de rugby et un arbitre. Le joueur qui est au premier plan porte un maillot vert et jaune. On ne voit pas son visage. Le joueur qui est au deuxième plan porte un maillot bleu foncé. On peut voir son visage. Il n'a pas l'air content. Il a l'air agressif comme le suggère la légende. Il essaie de donner un coup de poing à l'autre joueur. Sur la photo, on peut ***aussi*** voir l'arbitre qui se trouve au milieu des deux joueurs. Il essaie de les empêcher de se battre et de les séparer.
On sait qu'il s'agit de l'arbitre ***car*** il porte un maillot rayé blanc, bleu et vert qui est différent des maillots des deux autres joueurs et on peut aussi voir le sifflet qu'il tient dans sa main droite. On ne sait pas ce qui vient de se passer ***mais*** on peut peut-être en déduire que l'un des joueurs a essayé de tricher ce qui a mis l'autre joueur en colère.

description

J'en déduis que le thème de la violence dans le sport est le thème qui est inspiré par cette image. Ce thème est relié à l'option Loisirs que j'ai étudiée en classe.
Je pense que l'un des buts du sport et de développer l'esprit d'équipe et la coopération. Il y a toujours un élément de compétition dans le sport. Je trouve que c'est essentiel ***d'ailleurs*** car ça encourage les joueurs en général et ça les motive à améliorer leurs performances. Ça contribue ***aussi*** à la beauté du jeu. ***Cependant***, la violence détruit l'image du sport. Les sportifs devraient, **selon moi**, montrer l'exemple surtout pour les jeunes générations. Ils sont bien payés en général et devraient se comporter civilement sur un terrain. Ils ont une responsabilité et en tant que rôles modèles. Il est essentiel qu'ils montrent l'exemple et gardent leur sang-froid et leur « *fair play* » en toute circonstance. C'est **aussi** une question de respect selon moi. Respecter son adversaire est dans l'esprit du sport. Il est vrai que si l'autre joueur a essayé de tricher, il a aussi manqué de respect à l'autre équipe et à son équipe aussi, mais la violence ne résout rien. En se montrant violent envers un adversaire, ce n'est pas seulement à l'adversaire que l'on manque de respect mais à soi-même et à son équipe. Un sportif doit être discipliné et savoir se contrôler. Le sport est un spectacle où, à mon avis, la violence n'a pas sa place.

interprétation personnelle

\+

opinions

NB: *the photo that you will be given will be linked to an aspect of francophone culture. It is just an example here to practise.*

Thèmes qui pourraient être abordés dans la deuxième partie de l'oral :

- le sport et le dopage
- le sport et l'argent
- le sport et le handicap
- le sport à la télé
- Les responsabilités des sportifs de haut niveau et sportifs célèbres / professionnels *(déjà abordé dans la première partie mais on pourrait creuser davantage ce thème dans la deuxième partie)*

Quelques exemples de questions possibles pour la deuxième partie de l'oral :

Le sport et le dopage

- Que penses-tu des sportifs qui se dopent ?
- Y-a-t-il trop de pression exercée sur les sportifs de haut niveau aujourd'hui ?
- Le dopage est souvent associé au Tour de France. Penses-tu que le tour de France soit encore un événement crédible aujourd'hui ? Devrait-on l'arrêter ?

Le sport et l'argent

- Les sportifs sont-ils trop payés selon toi ?
- Le sport c'est assez futile comme activité. Les salaires de certains sportifs ne sont-ils pas exagérés selon toi en comparaison aux salaires des docteurs ou chirurgiens qui sauvent des vies tous les jours par exemple ?
- L'argent ternit-il l'image du sport selon toi ?

Le sport à la télé

- Se déclarer supporteur de tel ou tel sport ou de telle ou telle équipe mais ne pas pratiquer ce sport et / ou ne jamais aller supporter son équipe fétiche quand elle joue, est-ce vraiment être fan de sport ?
- Peut-on vraiment « vivre un match » en le regardant à la télé ?
- Le sport féminin est-il assez représenté sur nos écrans selon toi?

A few generic comments:

- Bear in mind that your examiner, although he or she will be prepared, will not have a list of pre-prepared questions that he / she will exclusively stick to. He or she will react to what you say and engage in a "real" discussion (*as far as is possible in an exam situation*). You therefore have an opportunity to lead the discussion and stir it in the direction that you are more comfortable with.
- Develop your answers as much as possible. Give / express your opinions even if you have not explicitly been asked for it.
- Don't panic if you have not understood a question; simply ask for it to be repeated.

Exemple 2: **diversité culturelle**

Rondes et belles ! C'est ça la vraie beauté.

http://missrondes.blogspot.co.uk/ - ©Christphoto – photo reproduite avec l'aimable autorisation du studio Cristphoto

La scène représentée sur cette photo se passe lors d'un concours de beauté. Il s'agit plus précisément de l'élection de Miss Ronde 2011 comme on peut le voir sur les banderoles que les jeunes femmes portent.
Sur cette photo on peut voir six jeunes femmes de type européen d'une vingtaine d'années peut-être qui sont sur un podium. Derrière elles, il y a un rideau noir. Elles portent toutes une robe de soirée et des chaussures à talon. Elles sont bien habillées. Trois d'entre elles portent une robe noire, les deux autres portent des robes d'une couleur différente. Celle qui se trouve à gauche sur la photo porte une longue robe bleue. On dirait que cette robe est en soie. Celle qui se trouve à droite porte une longue robe rouge. La jeune femme au milieu porte un diadème blanc dans ses cheveux qui ressemble à une couronne. On peut donc en déduire que c'est la gagnante du concours et que les autres femmes sont ses dauphines. Elles tiennent toutes un bouquet de fleurs et un sac et elles sont toutes souriantes.

description

J'en déduis qu'il s'agit ici du thème des concepts de la beauté humaine. Ce concours se passe en France ou dans un pays francophone puisque les inscriptions sur les banderoles sont toutes en français. On est plus habitués à des concours du style Miss France ou Miss Monde où les jeunes femmes en compétition sont toutes minces, voire très minces. **Je trouve** rafraichissant et encourageant de me rendre compte qu'il existe d'autres types de concours de beauté surtout dans nos sociétés où l'idéal de beauté représenté par les médias et en général trop souvent celui de l'ultra minceur. **Comme la légende le suggère** « *Rondes et belles ! C'est ça la vraie beauté.* ». Je suis d'accord avec cette légende et je pense que l'on devrait téléviser davantage ce genre de concours de beauté **car** cela montrerait aux jeunes filles que l'on peut être belle même si on a quelques rondeurs ou autres traits physiques trop souvent considérés comme défauts. La beauté est un concept suggestif de toute façon. En général, **je ne suis pas forcément en faveur** des concours de beauté car je trouve ce genre de concours superficiel, **mais** si ces concours étaient basés sur des critères plus réalistes, peut-être que je changerais mon opinion. En tout cas, **il me semble important** de médiatiser ce type de concours pour faire concurrence aux images traditionnelles de l'homme ou de la femme parfait/e médiatisées par les concours style Miss France qui sont, **selon moi**, en partie responsable de la pression exercée sur les adolescentes influençables et qui sont parfois responsables du développement de maladies comme l'anorexie chez certaines jeunes filles.

réference explicite à la légende

interprétation personnelle

\+

opinions

Thèmes qui pourraient être abordés ou développés dans la deuxième partie de l'oral :

- Le concept de la beauté dans d'autres sociétés
- L'idéal de beauté
- L'image de la femme projetée par ce type de concours
- Les concours de beauté réservés aux enfants
- Les autres types de concours comme Monsieur Muscles ou l'homme le plus fort
- Les conséquences que peuvent avoir ce genre de concours

Quelques exemples de questions possibles pour la deuxième partie de l'oral :

L'image de la femme

- Tu dis que tu ne suis généralement ce genre de concours. Pourquoi ?
- Est-ce que tu trouves humiliant que des femmes défilent en maillots de bains ou petite tenue et soient jugées sur de prétendus critères de beauté ?
- Pourquoi vouloir devenir Miss France ou Miss Monde selon toi ?

Le concept de la beauté

- Est-il possible de définir la beauté selon toi ?
- Crois-tu vraiment que ce genre de concours influence les jeunes filles ? Les jeunes filles ne laissent-elles pas davantage influencer par les images des mannequins et autres stars publiées dans les magazines ?
- Les concours de beauté sont-ils ringards d'après toi ? Ont-ils encore leur place dans nos sociétés aujourd'hui ?

Les concours de beauté réservés aux enfants

- Inscrirais-tu ta fille à un concours de mini Miss ? Pourquoi ? Pourquoi pas ?
- Trouves-tu honteux que ce genre de concours puisse exister ?
- Qu'est-ce que ce genre de concours peut encourager chez les jeunes enfants ?

Remember :

- Develop your ideas
- Give opinions
- Try and lead the conversation as much as possible
- Vary your vocabulary and grammatical structures
- Show off!

Let's practise!

Look at the photo below and try and prepare a structured presentation.

description

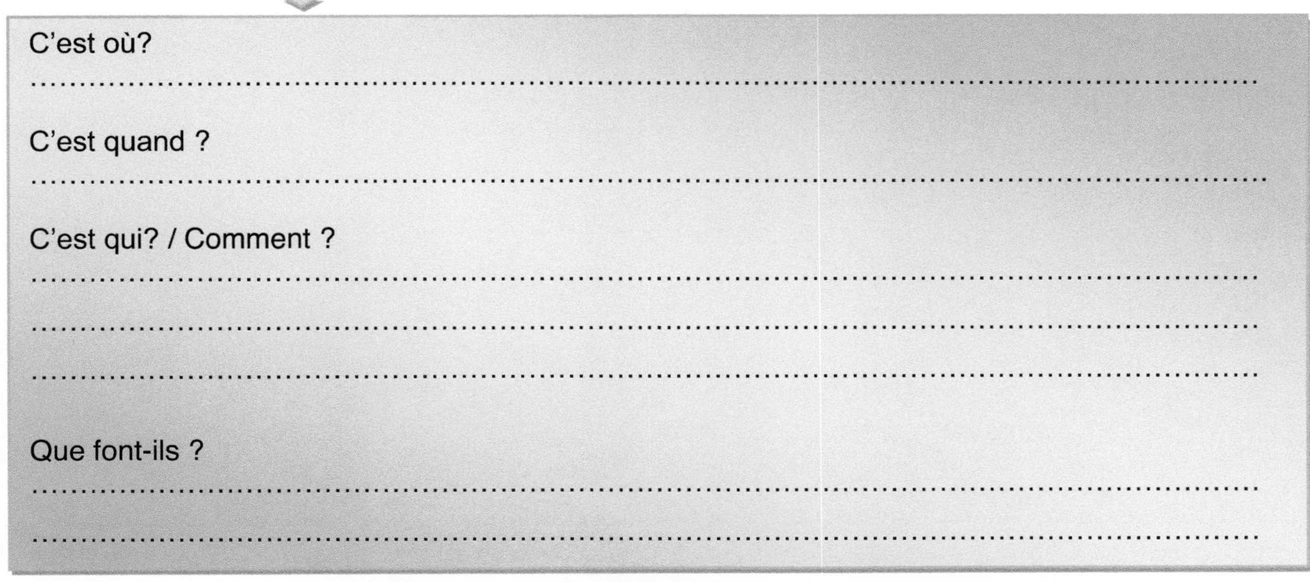

C'est où?

C'est quand ?

C'est qui? / Comment ?

Que font-ils ?

Thème / option

On a tous passé des super vacances !

Interprétation et opinions

Let's practise further !

description

C'est où?

……

C'est quand ?

……

C'est qui? / Comment ?

……

……

……

Que font-ils ?

……

……

***Thème /* option**

Interprétation et opinions

Quand le progrès nous simplifie la vie

©www.kempf.fr

……

……

……

……

……

……

……

A few things to be aware of / bear in mind....

- You can only do your individual oral once...so make sure that you are well-prepared (*you can revise some specific vocabulary beforehand and perhaps re-read some of the articles studies in class as part of the appropriate option topics to give you some ideas*)!
- Use your preparation time productively.
- Make sure you know your candidate number before entering the room and why not give it in French on the recording? It is a French exam after all!
- The conversation must sound as natural as possible so forget the recording device, look at your examiner and engage with her or him. Your individual oral will be recorded. Make sure that you speak clearly.
- You are allowed to take a few brief notes with you in the examination room. These notes cannot be longer than 10 lines and you must at all costs avoid reading them!
- It is not a recitation contest and again, your delivery of your photo description and interpretation must sound as natural as possible.
- Remember to use the correct register of language when addressing your examiner. The exam is a formal situation and you must use the "***vous***" form all the way through!

So to summarise below are your essential lists of Dos and Don'ts in preparation for the exam:

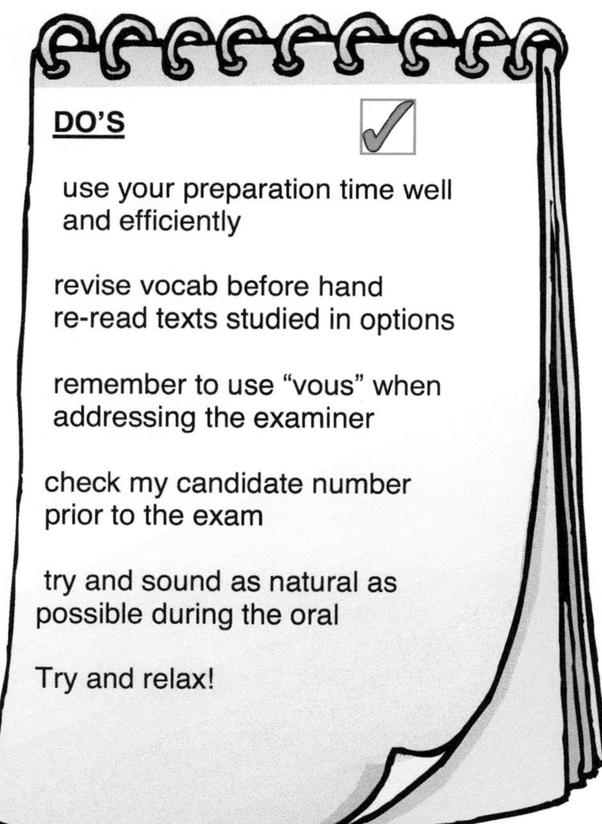

DO'S
use your preparation time well and efficiently
revise vocab before hand
re-read texts studied in options
remember to use "vous" when addressing the examiner
check my candidate number prior to the exam
try and sound as natural as possible during the oral
Try and relax!

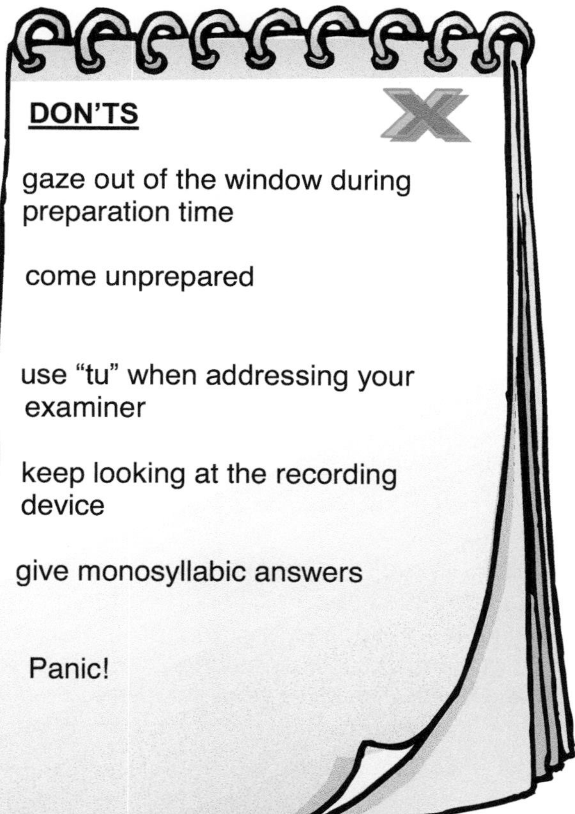

DON'TS
gaze out of the window during preparation time
come unprepared
use "tu" when addressing your examiner
keep looking at the recording device
give monosyllabic answers
Panic!

B) Interactive oral or "*oral de groupe*" ou *« activité orale interactive »*

During the course of your two years of your IB studies, you have to do a few interactive orals (*and a minimum of 3*). Those are the orals that take place in the classroom and they can and might have taken different forms. I do not intend to dwell on it here as they are probably done and dusted for most of you by now. So this is just a few pieces of information to help you just in case you still have some coming your way....

- You are being assessed on your individual performance within the group.
- The he same criteria are different from the individual oral assessment criteria. A maximum of 5 points are awarded to your productive skills (*clarity, correctness and variety of language used*) and a maximum of 5 points to your interactive and receptive skills (*can you express ideas? Are these ideas clearly and convincingly expressed? Do you interact readily? Are you fully engaged in the discussion?*)
- The marks of 3 of these orals will be recorded on a form but your teacher will probably take the mark for your best performance to be sent to the exam board.
- One of these activities will have an audio document (*song / extract of film / TV programme etc...*) as a starting point.
- These orals can take different forms: debate / "role plays" / presentations and they will all be based on one of the topics that you have studies as part of the **CORE** (*relations sociales / communication et médias / questions mondiales*)

So...how to best prepare for it and optimise my performance on the day(s)?

Beforehand:

- Get into the habit of joining in during lessons
- Learn expression to express your opinions
- Prepare specific vocabulary related to the given topic
- Think of arguments pro and against the issues debated / discussed... beforehand

During the oral(s):

- Don't insist on reading notes that you might have prepared beforehand! Make eyes contact with others
- Don't just sit there waiting for someone to address you or invite you in...be proactive.
- Equally don't keep interrupting others
- Express and defend your opinions when appropriate

Remember as well that even if there is no formal listening assessment in the exam, listening is an essential communication skill so keep tuning into the radio / TV etc...This will help you for the orals and you will pick up vocabulary and grammar without realising! In addition, to help you practice your pronunciation and clear speaking, below are a few tongue twisters for you to have fun with! (*You can even try and repeat them with a pencil between your teeth!!*)

- *Un chasseur sachant chasser doit savoir chasser sans son chien.*
- *Les chaussettes de l'archiduchesse sont-elles sèches, archi-sèches ?*
- *Sache que la mousse tache la moustache car la mousse tacha la moustache de Sacha.*
- *Ma sœur est maire, mon père est frère, ma mère est sœur, mon frère est masseur.*

Pour vous aider…

Donner son opinion

Selon moi…
D'après moi…

Je crois que….

A mon avis…

Personnellement…

En ce qui me concerne,….

Je trouve que…

Pour ma part, je pense que…

Je considère que…

Il est vrai que…..mais……

Je pense que + indicative
*Je pense qu'il **est** nécessaire de réagir*

Je ne pense pas que + subjonctif
*Je ne pense pas qu'il **soit** nécessaire d'agir*

Permettez-moi de dire que…

Pour dire qu'on est d'accord / pas d'accord

Je (ne) suis (pas) d'accord avec vous.

Je ne suis pas du tout d'accord.

Je (ne) partage (pas) votre avis.

Absolument!
Tout à fait!

Je suis entièrement d'accord avec vous.

Ce n'est pas toujours **vrai**…

Oui, mais…

Pas du tout!
C'est complètement faux!

Vous plaisantez! (*langue parlée)*

Vous n'êtes pas sérieux!

Comment osez-vous dire / affirmez une chose pareille? C'est absurde !

Prendre……….. et…….. donner la parole

Excusez-moi…

Désolé(e) de vous interrompre, mais…

Si je peux me permettre une remarque…

Je peux continuer….?

Je voudrais dire que….

Pourriez-vous répéter votre argument ?

Allez-y!

Quel est votre argument?

Qu'est-ce que vous en pensez?

Partagez-vous cette opinion?

Etes-vous du même avis?

Vous avez la parole.

<u>Let's practise</u>!

Here is an example of a speech that you might have to prepare, either as a written or as an oral exercise in class, so you can practice with environmental specific vocabulary as well as perfecting the specific techniques for a speech. Of course, you would not have any of the grammar suggestions in the question (*these are not exhaustive in any case*) but I have put them there so that you remember to vary your structures. Hopefully this will also help you revise the grammar. In class, as an interactive oral activity, you would have questions afterwards or it could be part of a debate in which you would have a specific role to play.

Vous voulez inciter vos camarades à agir au quotidien pour protéger l'environnement. Préparez un "mini" discours pour leur faire prendre conscience de l'urgence et l'importance d'agir.

Dans votre discours, vous devez utiliser :

- le présent / l'imparfait / le passé – composé / le futur / le conditionnel et le subjonctif au moins une fois.
- au moins 2 pronoms relatifs simples (qui / que / dont / où / ce qui / ce que ou ce dont)
- au moins 2 pronoms relatifs composés (lequel, laquelle… auquel... duquel…)
- 2 verbes suivis de la préposition **à**
- 2 verbes suivis de la préposition **de**

Bon courage !

....

....

....

....

....

....

....

....

....

....

....

....

Chapter 5

GRAMMAR

Whether you like it or not, grammar is an essential part of language learning; it provides the framework and foundation for communication and so it has to be accurate. At both standard and higher levels, criterion A (Language) in Paper 2 counts for 10 marks towards the overall mark and it counts for 8 marks in the written task. Better not neglect it then!

It is therefore important to revise and work on your grammar before the exam. What follows is only a refresher that should complement your work with other sources. It is not exhaustive! However, it should (hopefully) point you in the right direction.

Here is a list of some of the grammar points covered in this section:

+ a brief revision of useful structures

There are of course many other grammar points that you need to master such as the *possessive adjectives*, how to make *comparisons*; *tout vs tous*, c'est *vs s'est*...etc...
Some are mentioned briefly in this section.

All answers to the grammar exercises can be found on pages 185 and 186

NB: *This guide is not a grammar revision guide and as such and it only tries to help you with the basics.* Therefore, do use a more exhaustive grammar if you feel you need it as only the bare essentials have been covered in this guide.
There are many specific grammar books that you can use if you are desperate. See the reference lists *section for suggestions.*

LE PRÉSENT

Le Présent is one of the most basic tenses in the French language and the first tense learnt by any learner. You have probably been studying it for years and hopefully, you will not need to use the next few pages of this guide. However, if you think you might have forgotten it, you'd better revise them for not only is the present tense essential for forming some other tenses such as *the imperfect*, *the imperative or the subjunctive*, it is also not a good idea to try and fill your essay with all the nice structures and tenses that you have learnt if you can't master the present tense!
So, let's get started!

1) -er verbs

To put an "–er verb" in the present, all you have to do is to take the infinitive of the verb, get rid of the *"–er"* part of the verb and add the correct endings.

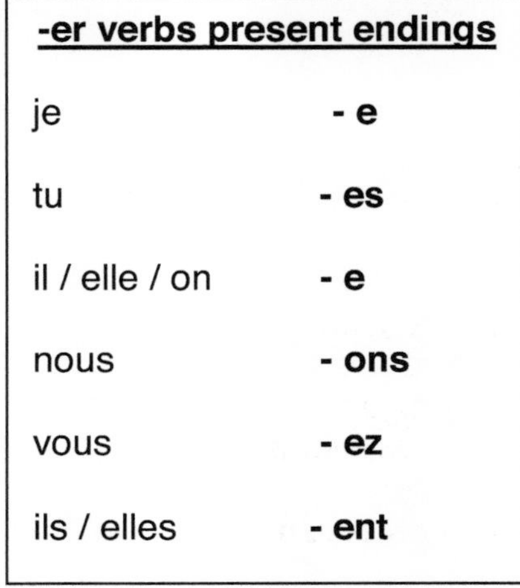

-er verbs present endings	
je	**- e**
tu	**- es**
il / elle / on	**- e**
nous	**- ons**
vous	**- ez**
ils / elles	**- ent**

Eg.

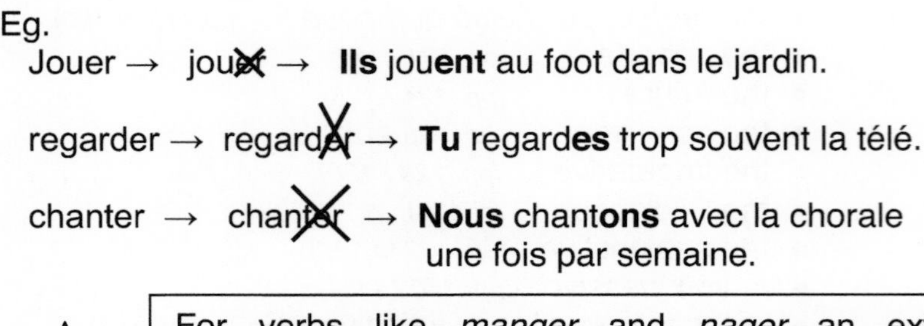

Jouer → jouer → **Ils** jou**ent** au foot dans le jardin.

regarder → regarder → **Tu** regard**es** trop souvent la télé.

chanter → chanter → **Nous** chant**ons** avec la chorale une fois par semaine.

For verbs like *manger* and *nager* an extra "**e**" needs to be added for the ***nous*** form. *This is for pronunciation reasons.*
Eg.:
Nous nag***eons*** / **nous** mang***eons***

ALLER is irregular and needs to be learnt!

Je	**vais**	nous	**allons**
Tu	**vas**	vous	**allez**
Il / elle / on	**va**	ils / elles	**vont**

For verbs like ***acheter***, ***se lever***, you need to add an accent on the 1st "*e*" for the je / tu / il / elle / on / ils and elles forms.
Eg. J'ach**è**te // Elles ach**è**tent

Some *–eler* verbs such as ***appeler*** and some ***–eter*** verbs such as **jeter,** double the "**l**" or "**t**" in the *je, tu, il, elle, on, ils and elles* forms.
Eg. Je t'appe**ll**e
Il je**tt**e toujours ses papiers pas terre!

2) "regular" - ir verbs

Not all the *"–ir verbs"* form their present tense the same way and at the end of the day, the best thing to do is to revise lists of verbs. However, below are a few examples.

Verbs like : **finir / choisir / réfléchir / réussir / maigrir / grossir / vieillir / rougir**

	finir	**réussir**
Je	fin**is**	réuss**is**
Tu	fin**is**	réuss**is**
Il / elle / on	fin**it**	réuss**it**
Nous	fin**issons**	réuss**issons**
Vous	fin**issez**	réuss**issez**
Ils / elles	fin**issent**	réuss**issent**

3) «irregular» -ir / -re / -oir verbs

Again, verbs take different forms in the present and the best way to go about it is to revise / learn them from a verb list. Below are a few examples of verbs for each category; just to refresh your memory!

- ir verbs

such as *partir / dormir*

je	par**s**	dor**s**
tu	par**s**	dor**s**
il / elle / on	par**t**	dor**t**
nous	part**ons**	dorm**ons**
vous	part**ez**	dorm**ez**
ils / elles	part**ent**	dorm**ent**

-ir verbs

such as *venir / revenir / devenir*

je	**viens**
tu	**viens**
il /elle /on	**vient**
nous	**venons**
vous	**venez**
ils / elles	**viennent**

-re verbs

such as *prendre / comprendre / apprendre surprendre* etc…

je	pren**ds**
tu	pren**ds**
il / elle / on	pren**d**
nous	***prenons***
vous	***prenez***
ils / elles	***prennent***

- oir verbs

such as *voir / recevoir*

je	voi**s**	reçoi**s**
tu	voi**s**	reçoi**s**
il / elle / on	voi**t**	reçoi**t**
nous	**voyons**	***recevons***
vous	***voyez***	***recevez***
ils / elles	***voient***	***reçoivent***

As you can see, there is not really a rule as such and you simply need to know your verbs.
Here are a few more essential verbs:

	faire	dire	lire	écrire	vendre / entendre	boire	avoir
Je / j'	fais	**dis**	lis	**écris**	vends	**bois**	ai
Tu	fais	**dis**	lis	**écris**	vends	**bois**	as
Il / elle/ on	fais	**dit**	lit	**écris**	vend	**boit**	a
Nous	faisons	**disons**	lisons	**écrivons**	vendons	**buvons**	avons
vous	faites	**dites**	lisez	**écrivez**	vendez	**buvez**	avez
Ils / elles	font	**disent**	lisent	**écrivent**	vendent	**boivent**	ont

	être	pouvoir / vouloir	devoir	savoir	conduire / produire	ouvrir / offrir	mettre
Je / j'	suis	**peux**	dois	**sais**	conduis	**ouvre**	mets
Tu	es	**peux**	dois	**sais**	conduis	**ouvres**	mets
Il / elle/ on	est	**peut**	doit	**sait**	conduit	**ouvre**	met
Nous	sommes	**pouvons**	devons	**savons**	conduisons	**ouvrons**	mettons
vous	êtes	**pouvez**	devez	**savez**	conduisez	**ouvrez**	mettez
Ils / elles	sont	**peuvent**	d**oi**vent	**savent**	conduisent	**ouvrent**	mettent

Let's practise!

Complete the blanks with the right forms of the verbs in the present. Try not to look back on the previous pages and / or try to not use any grammar help.

1) Les médias .... de plus en plus d'influence sur les jeunes. ***(avoir)***

2) Papa et maman ne .... pas comprendre que je ne suis plus un bébé ! Ça m'.................. ***(vouloir / énerver)***

3) Pourquoi tu .... toujours les sujets les plus difficiles ? ***(choisir)***

4) Je ne .... pas pourquoi elle .... toujours la même chose alors qu'elle .... plein de vêtements dans son armoire ! ***(comprendre / mettre / avoir)***

5) Les déchets que nous .... la planète. ***(produire / polluer)***

6) Nous .... trop de sucreries. Nous .... beaucoup. ***(manger / grossir)***

7) Vous .... du sport régulièrement ? ***(faire)***

8) Mon frère .... 18 ans alors il .... voter. ***(avoir / pouvoir)***

9) La violence dans les banlieues .... d'augmenter malgré les nouvelles mesures mises en place par le gouvernement. ***(continuer)***

10) Le nombre de sans-abris ne .... qu'augmenter dans les grandes villes. ***(faire)***

11) Ma mère .... toujours ses crêpes. ***(réussir)***

12) Mes amis et moi .... en vacances ensemble sans nos parents cette année. ***(partir)***

13) Il ne .... pas travailler sous pression. Il .... à toutes les interrogations. ***(savoir / échouer)***

14) Je vous .... cette lettre dans l'espoir de vous faire entendre raison. ***(écrire)***

15) Pourquoi .... -vous tout le temps ? ***(mentir)***

16) Mon mari et moi .... à nos enfants de passer trop de temps devant la télé. (***interdire)***

LE PASSÉ COMPOSÉ

As you probably know, le ***passé composé*** is one of the past tenses. Again, it is one of the basic French tenses and one that is very commonly used. It is essential that you know how to use it well and therefore revise it!
You will need to use the *Passé composé* for completed actions in the past.

Example :

Présent

Je **joue** au rugby tous les jours.
(I play rugby every day)

Passé composé

J'**ai joué** au rugby hier.
(I played rugby yesterday)

- It is formed :

avoir or **être** in the present		**past participle** of the verb

NB : " *avoir*" et "*être*" are called « ***auxiliaires*** » (= auxiliary verbs or helping verbs)

Examples :

J' ai mangé un sandwich au fromage.

Je suis allé à la piscine .

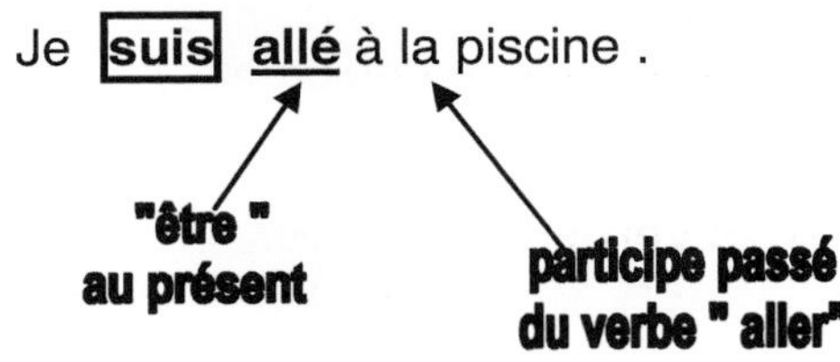

a) Passé composé with *avoir* :

Most verbs form their *passé composé* with " *avoir*".

avoir + participe passé du verbe

avoir *(present)*

j'	**ai**
tu	**as**
il / elle /on	**a**
nous	**avons**
vous	**avez**
ils / elles	**ont**

Past participle of " -er " verbs...

- take off the "**r** "
- add and accent on the " **é** "

eg :

manger	→	mang**é**
chanter	→	chant**é**
regarder	→	regard**é**

Past participle of a few irregular verbs :

faire → ***fait***	*voir* → ***vu***	*savoir* → ***su***
dire → ***dit***	*prendre* → ***pris***	*entendre*→ ***entendu***
finir → ***fini***	*vouloir* → ***voulu***	*pouvoir* → ***pu***
écrire → ***écrit***	*lire* → ***lu***	*devoir* → ***dû***
dormir → ***dormi***	*apprendre* → ***appris***	*connaitre* → **connu**
boire → ***bu***	*mettre* → ***mis***	*recevoir* → ***reçu***
conduire → ***conduit***	*avoir* → ***eu***	*être* → ***été***

Examples:

J'**ai bu** un verre d'eau
I drank a glass of water

Il **a perdu** son portefeuille hier.
yesterday, he lost his wallet

Nous **avons réussi** notre examen.
We have passed our exam.

Ils **ont dormi** chez moi samedi soir.
They slept at mine last Saturday night.

NB : With" *avoir* **", the past participle does not agree with the subject. So even if the subject is feminine or plural, no extra "e" / "s" or "es" are added to the past participle.**

b) **Passé composé with *être* :**

Some verbs form their *passé composé* with "*être* ". Once you know which verbs they are; then you should always be able to decide which auxiliary verb to use.

- **Reflexive verbs :** ***se** lever*
  ***se** laver*
  ***se** coiffer*
  ***s'**habiller*
  etc…

Je me *suis habillé* **.**
Il s'*est coiffé* avant d'aller à l'école.

- **+ the following verbs :**

(re)	M	**monter**
	R	**rester**
(re)	S	**sortir**
(de /re)	V	**venir**
	A	**arriver**
	N	**naître**
(re)	D	**descendre**
(r)	E	**entrer**
(re)	T	**tomber**
	R	**retourner**
	A	**aller**
	M	**mourir**
	P	**partir**
		(repartir)

Verb :	*translation:*	***past participle:***
aller	*to go*	***allé***
venir	*to come*	***venu***
entrer	*to go in*	***entré***
sortir	*to go out*	***sorti***
arriver	*to arrive*	***arrivé***
partir	*to leave*	***parti***
descendre	*to go down*	***descendu***
monter	*to go up*	***monté***
rester	*to stay*	***resté***
tomber	*to fall*	***tombé***

+		
retourner	*to return*	***retourné***
naître	*to be born*	***né***
mourir	*to die*	***mort***

All those forms form their **passé composé** with **"être"** as follows:

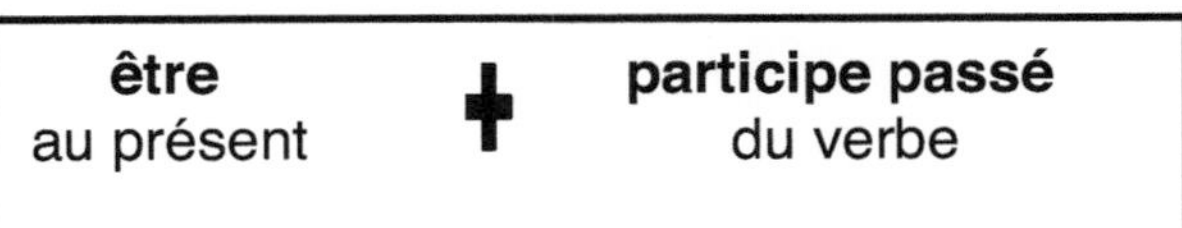

<u>**être**</u> *(present)*

je	**suis**
tu	**es**
il /elle / on	**est**
nous	**sommes**
vous	**êtes**
ils /elles	**sont**

NB : Note that although « on » Is grammatically singular, it can have a plural meaning. Therefore, the agreement is possible.

On est sorti**s** hier soir.

<u>Examples</u> :

Je ***suis allé*** au parc ce week-end.
Mon frère ***est sorti*** en boite Samedi soir.

Elles **sont descendu***es* .
Ils **sont parti***s* .

Avec "être", the past participle agrees with both the gender and the number of the subject.

- ***<u>Conclusion</u> :***

Le passé composé, it's relatively easy.
<u>Before putting a verb in the *passé composé*</u>**:**

1) **Décide if you need to use "** *avoir"* **or "*être".***
2) **Conjugate "** *avoir* **" or** "être " **in the present.**
3) **Find the** *past participle* **of the verb**.
4) **If you are dealing with an *être verb*, don't forget the agreement.**

NB : Remember that in the *passé composé*, the negative form goes around the auxilary part of the verb!

Marie **n'**est **pas** sortie hier soir.
Ils **n'**ont **pas** regardé la télévision cet après-midi.
Nous **n'**avons **jamais** triché* à une interro.

*tricher = *to cheat*

Let's practise!

1) Le mois dernier, les professeurs ....la grève* en France. ***(faire)***

2) Marie .... lors de la dernière élection présidentielle. Elle .... sa carte d'électeur. ***(ne pas voter / perdre)***

3) Greenpeace .... les électeurs à voter pour le candidat du parti écologique. ***(appeler)***

4) Lors des émeutes** dans les banlieues en France, les gens .... très peur. ***(avoir)***

5) Hier, mon père .... la voiture au garage. ***(conduire)***

6) Le 10 juin dernier, Rafael Nadal .... le tournoi de tennis de Roland Garros pour la troisième fois. ***(remporter)***

7) L'année dernière, mes copains et moi .... en vacances en France. Nous .... dans un hôtel au bord de la mer. ***(aller / rester)***

8) Hier, un accident .... sur l'autoroute du soleil. Une voiture .... la rambarde de sécurité. Une vitesse excessive semble être à l'origine de l'accident. ***(se produire / heurter)***

9) Je .... avec mes parents parce que je suis rentrée tard hier soir. ***(se disputer)***

10) Est-ce que tu .... le dernier Harry Potter ? ***(lire)***

* ***faire la grève*** = *to go on strike*
** ***une émeute*** = *a riot*

Some special rules to know about the *passé composé*.......

a) *Passé composé* with "*avoir*" and the preceding direct object :

When a verb forms its *passé composé* with "*avoir*" the past participle NEVER agrees with the SUBJECT. However, the past participle can agree with the DIRECT OBJECT if and when the direct object is placed in front of the verb.
This will mainly happen when the direct object is replaced by a pronoun or in the relative clauses constructions.

Eg:

1) J'ai mangé *la pomme.*
direct object

Je l' ai mangé***e***

In this example, "***je***" is the **subject** of the verb as "j***e***" did the action of eating the apple.
"***la pomme***" is the direct object as the action expressed by the verb has been done to it "*directly*".
In the second sentence, "***la pomme***" has been replaced by its equivalent direct object pronoun "l***a***" ("***l'*** *here as it is in front of a vowel).* As a pronoun is always placed in front of the verb, this means that now the direct object is in front of the verb in the *passé composé* with *avoir.* The past participle now needs to bear the mark of the gender and number of this direct object.

2) C'est la robe que j'ai acheté**e** hier.

preceding direct object

In example 2, "***je***" is the **subject** as ""***je***" has done the action expressed by the verb; "***je***" has bought the dress.
"***la robe***" is the **direct object** as the action expressed by the verb has been done to it : the dress has been bought by the subject "***je***".
As "***la robe***" is the **direct object** and "***la robe***" is placed **in front of the verb** conjugated in the *passé composé* with *avoir*, the past participle has to agree with "*la robe*" and must therefore bear the mark of the feminine singular.

NB: The sentence contains a relative clause.

PS : *If you can't quite remember what the direct object pronouns are or what a relative clause is, don't panic, just turn the pages to page 111.*

b) Exceptions to the passé composé with "être" rules:

- Some of the verbs which normally form their *passé composé* with *être* such as ***sortir ou (r)entrer / descendre ou monter***, can sometimes use *avoir* to form their *passé composé* when they are followed by a direct object.

You will therefore say: Je suis sorti **BUT** J'AI SORTI les poubelles.
direct object

In the first sentence, "j***e***" went out BUT in the second sentence. "j***e***" ***took something out*** : the bins. As ***sortir***, is here followed by a direct object, ***sortir*** now has to be conjugated in the *passé composé* using the auxiliary verb ***avoir***. All of the the *passé compose rules* with *avoir* must now be applied. Therefore, if "***les poubelles***" is replaced by its direct pronoun equivalent "***les***" and so preceeds the verb, the previous agreement rule has to be followed:

Je ***les*** ai sorti***es***

- The ***reflexive verbs*** *always* form their *passé composé* with *être* therefore, the past participle agrees with the subject.
Eg:

Elles *se sont lavé**es***

HOWEVER, if a **reflexive verb** is followed by a **direct object**, "*être*" is still used **BUT** the ***agreement disappears***.

Elles *se sont lav**é*** les cheveux.

In the example, the reflexive verb "***se laver***" is in the ***passé composé*** using "***être***" but as it is followed by a **direct object** to which the action is being done : "***les cheveux***", the **past participle does not agree** any longer with the **subject**.
However, if "***les cheveux***" is replaced by its equivalent direct pronoun, the past participle will then have to agree with the direct object as follows:

Elles se ***les*** *sont lav**és***

Let's practise !

Le week-end dernier, toute ma famille .... ***(se réunir)****1* pour fêter l'anniversaire de ma grand-mère. Nous .... ***(offrir)****2* des cadeaux à ma grand-mère. Elle les .... ***(ouvrir)****3.* Elle .... ***(avoir)****4* des nouvelles chaussures qu'elle .... ***(mettre)****5* tout de suite.
Après le repas, mon père, mon grand-père et mon oncle .... ***(jouer)****6* aux cartes et ils .... ***(bien s'amuser)****7.* Ma mère, ma grand-mère et ma tante .... ***(ne pas vouloir)****8* jouer. Ma mère .... ***(sortir)****9* les albums de photo de famille et elles les .... ***(regarder)****10.* Mes cousins et moi .... ***(aller)****11* faire du skate dans le parc. Malheureusement, je .... ***(tomber)****12* et .... ***(se casser)****13* la jambe.
A l'hôpital, le médecin m' .... ***(prêter)****14* des béquilles* mais je les .... ***(oublier)****15* chez ma grand-mère !

****une béquille*** *= a crutch*

L'IMPARFAIT

L'imparfait is one of the past tenses. It is used for:

- ***a description in the past*** *(description of place / people / emotions / weather etc…)*

→ C'***était*** un jour de semaine ordinaire. Il ***pleuvait***. L'homme ***portait*** un chapeau noir et un imperméable gris. Il ***souriait***. Il ***avait*** l'air heureux.

- ***an action / an habit that "used to" happen in the past but does not anymore***

→ Quand il ***avait*** dix ans, il ne ***sortait*** jamais seul le soir. (*Here, we are implying that he now goes out on his own in the evenings*)

- ***an unfinished action in the past and / or an action which was "in progress" in the past when it was interrupted by another shorter action.***

→ Je ***faisais*** mes devoirs quand le téléphone a sonné. (*The action of doing the homework was interrupted by the phone ringing which is a short completed action in the past.*)

So, how is the imperfect or ***imparfait*** formed?
To be able to conjugate a verb in the imperfect, it is essential that you learn / revise the "***nous***" form of the verbs in the **present.** Why? Well simply because to conjugate a verb in the imperfect, you need to:

- Take the "***nous***" form of the verb in the ***present*** tense
→ ***nous regardons / nous finissons / nous prenons***

- ***Take off*** the « ***nous*** » and the « ***-ons*** » ending
→ ***regard / fais / pren***

- Add the correct imperfect ending :
ais - ais - ait - ions - iez - aient

⇨ ***je*** regard***ais*** / ***vous*** faisi***ez*** / ***elles*** pren***aient***

The good thing about the imperfect is that not only it is an easy tense to form so long as you know the « nous » form of your verbs in the present, but also, there is only one exception.

⚠ **Etre**

J'	**étais**
Tu	**étais**
Il / elle / on	**était**
Nous	**étions**
Vous	**étiez**
Ils / elles	**étaient**

NB: don't forget that the verbs such as ***nager / ranger or manger*** keep the "***e***" after the "***g***" and in front of the "a".

Je rang*eais*	*nous* rang*ions*
Tu rang*eais*	*vous* rang*iez*
Il rang*eait*	*ils* rang*eaient*

Let's practise !

1) Quand il .... jeune, mon grand-père .... dans une ferme. ***(être / habiter)***

2) Avant, ma sœur .... toujours sa chambre. Maintenant, sa chambre est toujours en désordre. ***(ranger)***

3) La femme qui .... un martini ....préoccupée. ***(boire / sembler)***

4) Ce matin là, il .... et il .... froid. ***(neiger / faire)***

5) Avant, vous .... toujours le métro pour aller au travail. Pourquoi avez-vous changé soudainement ? ***(prendre)***

6) Les filles .... à sortir quand leur père est rentré. ***(s'apprêter*)***

****s'apprêter à =***

LE PLUS-QUE-PARFAIT

The pluperfect is used to refer to actions in the past which took place in the past and were completed in the past before other actions (also in the past) took place. *(I think that you have gathered that "past" is the key word here!).*
Its English translation is "*had*".

J'**avais fini** mes devoirs quand ma mère <u>*est rentrée*</u>.

plus-que-parfait (J'avais fini) — *passé composé* (est rentrée)

→ I had finished my homework when my mother came back – *Here, the action of "finishing the homework" was completed before the return of the mother, the pluperfect is therefore used to convey this idea of anteriority in the past.*

How is it formed?
Well, if you know how to put a verb in the ***passé composé*** and ***know the imperfect forms of "avoir" and "être"***, you should then find the ***plus-que parfait*** relatively easy as...

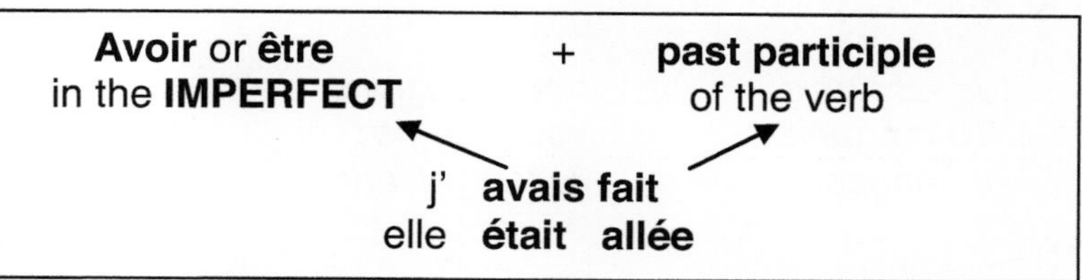

Avoir or **être** in the **IMPERFECT**
+
past participle of the verb
j' **avais fait**
elle **était allée**

NB:
All the rules of the ***passé composé*** apply to the ***plus- que- parfait***.

<u>Let's practise</u> !

PASSÉ COMPOSÉ, IMPARFAIT ou PLUS-QUE-PARFAIT?

1) Lundi dernier, nous...................... (***aller***) à la plage. Il .... (***faire***) beau et chaud.

2) Je .... (*ne jamais* ***comprendre***) pourquoi ils .... (***partir***) aussi tôt ce soir-là.

3) Autrefois, mes grands-parents......................... (***ne pas pouvoir***) regarder la télé. Ça .... (*ne pas* ***exister***) !

4) L'accident qui .... (***se produire***) hier à 20h30 .... (***faire***) un mort et deux blessés graves. Une jeune mère de famille et ses deux enfants .... (***traverser***) la rue quand un automobiliste ivre les .... (***heurter***) de plein fouet.

5) Dimanche dernier, toute la famille .... (***se rassembler***) chez mes grands-parents. Mes cousins .... (déjà ***installer***) devant la console de jeux vidéo quand nous .... (***arriver***).
Nous .... (***jouer***) pendant deux heures et mon frère et moi nous les .... (***battre***).
Les adultes .... (***rester***) dans le salon toute la journée. Ma tante et ma mère .... (***regarder***) les vieilles photos de famille que ma grand-mère....................... (***sortir***) pendant que mon père et mon oncle .... (***discuter***) football.

6) Comment ....-ils .... (***croire***) à une histoire pareille ?

7) Comme j'.......................... (***réviser***) pour mon bac de français, j'....................... (***obtenir***) de bons résultats.

8) ....vous .... (***remarquer***) quelques chose d'anormal ou d'inhabituel quand vous .... (***entrer***) dans la pièce ?

9) Il .... (***boire***) quand il................. (***prendre***) le volant de son cabriolet ; c'est pourquoi je ne suis pas surprise qu'il ait eu un accident !

10) Cette histoire .... (***être***) de plus en plus étrange. Pourquoi le professeur .... -il .... (***monter***) dans cette voiture noire ? Pourquoi .... –il.................... (***refuser***) mon aide avant de s'engouffrer dans la voiture malgré ses blessures apparentes ? Qui .... (***être***) les deux hommes qui .... (***se trouver***) à l'arrière du véhicule ?

LE FUTUR

The future tense is used to refer to actions which will take place at a later date / in the future or which are about to happen. The future tense is all about **certainty.** *If you use it it is because what you are saying has been planned and will take place for sure at some stage in in the future,*

Nous ***irons*** *en France l'été prochain.*

- next Summer-

Futur it is planned and will happen for sure.

There are two future tenses in French: le futur proche *et* le futur simple.

Tu réussiras tes examens et tu auras un avenir brillant.

Le futur proche (going to / about to)

Le futur proche *is mainly used to refer to actions which are about to happen.*

Je **vais partir** dans 5 minutes / *I am going to leave in 5 minutes*

To form the near future, it is very easy. Here is the formula:

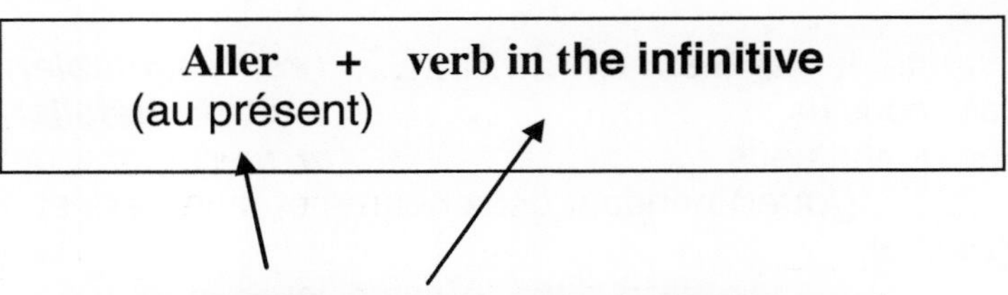

E.g.:

Nous ***allons sortir*** *avec des amis ce soir.*

NB *:* Although knowing the *futur proche* tense is important, this tense is considered as very easy. You can use it; no problem BUT you must aim to demonstrate that you can use the other future with ease too!

Le futur simple (will)

This should be the most commonly used of the two futures and the one that you should mainly aim to use in your work.

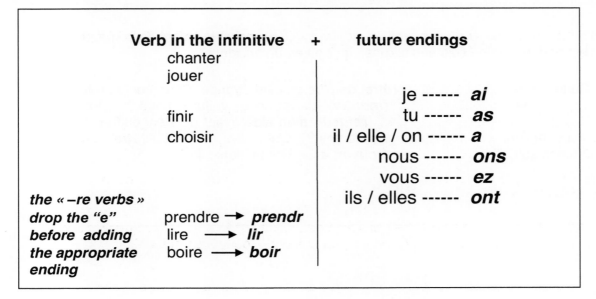

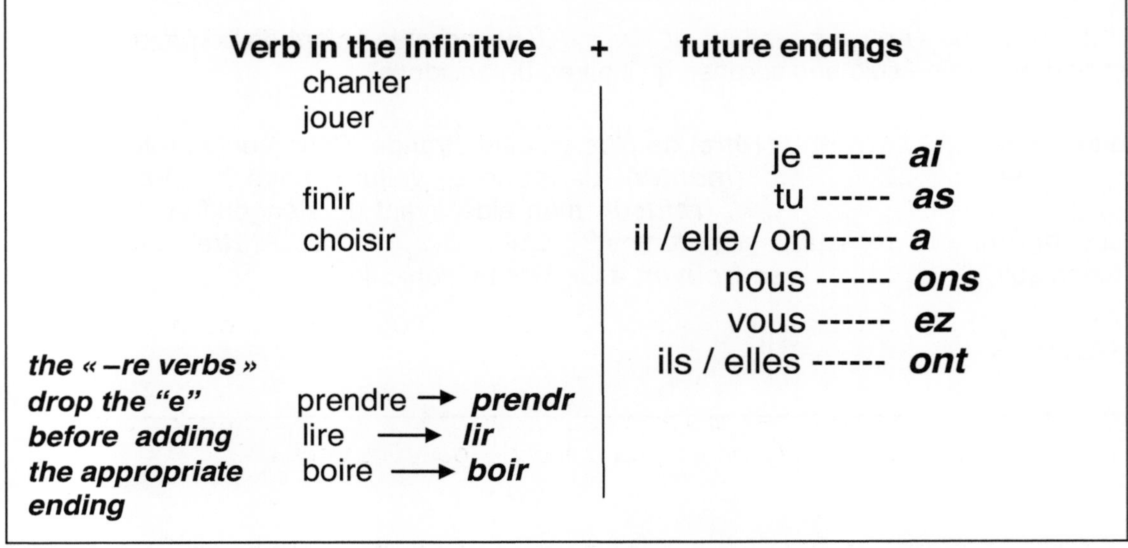

E.g.: *Je **regarder**ai* / *tu **choisir**as* / *il **achèter**a* / *nous **vendr**ons*

vous rir**ez** / **elles** apprendr**ont**

As always, there are exceptions and as you can guess, these exceptions need to be learnt !!
Below is the list of the main ones *(I am only giving you the "je" forms, except for the impersonal verbs- once you know that form, all is left for you to do is change the ending to the appropriate one)*

INFINITIF	FUTUR
aller	***J'irai***
avoir	***J'aurai***
devoir	***Je devrai***
envoyer	***J'enverrai***
être	***Je serai***
faire	***Je ferai***
falloir (il faut)	***Il faudra***
mourir	***Je mourrai***

INFINITIF	FUTUR
pleuvoir	***Il pleuvra***
pouvoir	***Je pourrai***
savoir	***Je saurai***
tenir	***Je tiendrai***
valoir (il vaut)	***Il vaudra***
venir	***Je viendrai***
voir	***Je verrai***
vouloir	***Je voudrai***

Let's practise!

1) Le gouvernement .... ***(annoncer)*** demain le nouveau projet de loi qui vise à l'interdiction de fumer dans les lieux publics.

2) Mon frère et ma sœur .... (***aller***) au concert samedi prochain.

3) Est-ce que vous .... (***venir***) me voir lorsque j'aurai déménagé ?

4) Ne t'inquiète pas... ils .... (***finir***) bien par avouer la vérité.

5) Je suis sûre que pendant les vacances, il .... (***se lever***) à 11 heures comme d'habitude !

6) Dès que je .... (***savoir***) ce qui s'est passé , je vous ....(***écrire***) une lettre ou je vous .... (***envoyer***) un message pour vous prévenir.

LE CONDITIONNEL *(présent)*

If the future tense is about actions which will definitely happen, whenever there is **a doubt** the *conditionnel* is used. Indeed, the conditional tense is used to translate ***may / might / could / would or should***.

E.g: Le suspect ***travaillerait*** dans la même entreprise que la victime.
The suspect may be working in the same firm as the victim

(Here, the information has not been confirmed. It is very likely that it is the case but there is a possibility that this information is wrong. The conditional expresses this doubt.)

The conditional can also be used in formal circumstances / contexts, as a form of politeness.

E.g: ***Pourrais***-tu me prêter ton téléphone, s'il te plaît ?

(in this example, you are asking a friend a favour but by using the conditional you are leaving him/ her the choice of doing the action or not- this is more polite)

How is it formed?
Well, it is quite easy provided you know how to form the future tense of your verbs....

Future stem	+	**Imperfect endings**
(For most verbs, the stem is the ***infinitive*** of the verb. Don't forget that the "-re" verbs drop the "e". And, good news.....***all*** the irregular stems in the future are the same in the conditional!! (faire – *fer* / *aller –ir etc.....*) *(refer back to section on the future tense)*		Je ----- ***ais*** tu ------- ***ais*** Il / elle / on ------- ***ait*** nous ------- ***ions*** vous ------ ***iez*** Ils / elles --------***aient***

Examples :

je jouer***ais*** / ***tu*** lir***ais*** / ***elle pourrait*** / ***nous*** dormir***ions***

vous sauriez / ***ils*** téléphoner***aient***

Let's practise!

Que .... (***faiere***)*1* –vous si la télé n'existait pas ?
Nous avons posé cette question à plusieurs personnes et voici les réponses qui nous ont été données :

2) Je .... (***passer***) plus de temps avec mes enfants.

3) Nous .... (***lire***) plus souvent.

4) J'.................. (***envoyer***) mes enfants chez leurs grands-parents tous les week-ends.

5) Les jeunes .... (*ne plus* ***avoir***) rien à faire et le nombre de délinquants juvéniles .... (***augmenter***).

FUTUR ou CONDITIONNEL ?

Now that you know how to form the future and conditional tenses and that you are also aware in which contexts you can use each one, the exercise below should be a piece of cake for you!

Let's practise !

1) La semaine prochaine, nous .... (*aller*) au concert de Charles Aznavour.

2) Non, je ne .... (**regarder**) pas cette émission. Je déteste l'animateur !

3) Si tu gagnais ou loto, que .... (**faire**)-tu ?

4) .... (**pouvoir**) –vous me passer le sel, s'il vous plaît ?

5) .... (***vouloir***) –tu lui dire de se taire, s'il te plaît ? Elle commence à m'agacer !

6) Ils .... (***venir***) ce soir, ils me l'ont promis.

7) Si tu réussis tes examens, tu .... (***avoir***) la permission de sortir en boite avec tes amis.

8) Est-ce que tu me .... (***dire***) la vérité ? ...j'ai des doutes...

9) Si seulement mes parents m'écoutaient ! Ma vie .... (***être***) beaucoup plus simple !

10) Je le connais, il .... (*ne jamais* ***accepter***) de m'accompagner au théâtre demain soir !

11) Si mes parents le laissaient faire, mon frère .... (***boire***) de l'alcool à chaque repas !

12) D'après les prédictions météorologiques, il .... (***pleuvoir***) toute la journée demain.

LE FUTUR ANTÉRIEUR

In the same way as the « *passé composé*" and "*plus-que-parfait*" exist, there is also what we call a "***futur antérieur***" tense in French. This tense is used to refer to future contexts. However, it is used to refer to actions in the future which *will have happened* and *will be finished* by the time another action other actions take(s) place (in the future!). If you feel lost and wonder what this really means, look at the example below, this should help you.

Lundi prochain, il ***aura fini*** tout son travail quand tu *rentreras*

futur antérieur — futur.

The action of finishing one's work will be completed by the time you come back. The action of finishing the work takes place before the other action, but both will take place in a future context (next Monday).

How is it formed?
Same as for the other compound tenses really:

Avoir or **être** in the **FUTUR**
+
past participle of the verb
j' **aurai fait**
elle **sera allée**

NB:
All the rules of the ***passé composé*** apply to the ***futur antérieur***.

LE CONDITIONNEL PASSÉ

The past conditional is also a very commonly used tense. It is mainly used to express **regret** or **remorse**. Something might / could and perhaps even should have happened but did not...and now it is too late!

*J'**aurais dû** la prévenir que le cours était annulé. Elle ne **serait** pas **venue** pour rien.*

conditionnel passé

I should have warned her that the lesson was cancelled. She would not have come for nothing.
Here, you did not warn her and therefore, she came for nothing. By using the past conditional, you are implying that really you could and should have warned her to avoid her wasting her time and you are regretting not doing it...but it is too late!

How is it formed?
You have probably guessed by now...

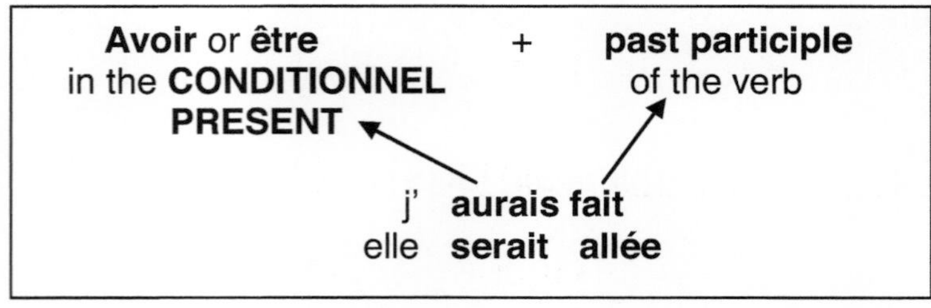

Avoir or **être** in the **CONDITIONNEL PRESENT**
+
past participle of the verb
j' **aurais fait**
elle **serait allée**

NB:
All the rules of the ***passé composé*** apply to the ***conditionnel passé***.

L'IMPÉRATIF

The imperative *is used when one wants to give someone an order, make suggestions or give advice. This will come in useful in many different contexts, including:*

- Guide de recommandation
- Discours
- Lettre de réclamation
- Etc....

To put a verb in the imperative...

To put a verb in the imperative, you only need to use 3 forms of that verb: ***tu*** , ***nous***, ***vous.***
Put the verb in the present tense, remove *tu*, *nous* and *vous* and you now have the impérative!

EX :	**Présent**	**impératif**
REGARDER :	tu regardes nous regardons vous regarder	**regarde** ! **regardons** ! **regardez** !
FINIR :	tu finis nous finissons vous finissez	**finis** ! **finissons** ! **finissez** !
PRENDRE	tu prends nous prenons vous prenez	**prends** ! **prenons** ! **prenez** !

NB: For all of the "**–er verbs"** (*chanter, pleurer, jouer* etc..) , you need to take off the "***S"*** ending of the ***tu*** form of the verb.
The same rule applies for the verb **aller**:
Va tout droit!

However, there are certain occasions when you will need to keep the "**S**" for **pronunciation** reasons (ie-in front of a vowel)

Mange**s-e**n! (eat some!)
Va**s-y**! (go!)

Allons au cinéma ce soir !
Let's go to the ciné tonight !

Range ta chambre !
Tidy your bedroom

Buvez un verre d'eau !
Have glass of water !

negative form

The negative form is placed around the verb.

Ne parle **pas** en cours ! *Don't speak in lessons*!

Ne jetez **pas** vos papiers par terre! *Don't throw your rubbish on the floor!*

ATTENTION....Verbes Irréguliers !!

Être	**Avoir**	**Savoir**
Sois !	Aie !	Sache !
Soyons !	Ayons !	Sachons !
Soyez !	Ayez !	Sachez !

Reflexive verbs and the imperative

The same rules as previously apply but you need to remember the reflexive pronoun and place it **after** the verb. Note as well that the reflexive pronoun "***te"*** becomes "***toi".***

Ex :
SE TAIRE :

Présent	impératif	
Tu te tais	tais **–toi !**	*Be quiet !*
Nous nous taisons	taisons-**nous !**	*Let's be quiet !*
Vous vous taisez	taisez-**vous !**	*Be quiet !*

NB: Note the use of the **hyphen** between the verbs and the pronouns

Negative form

The negative form comes around the verbs and the **pronoun** which remains **in front of the verb**!! In the negative form, the pronoun "***te"*** is being used again!!

Ne te couche **pas** tard! *Don't go to bed late!*

Ne vous habillez **pas** comme un clochard! *Don't dress like a tramp!*

Let's practise… !

Put the verbs in brackets in the imperative

EX : être gentils avec ses grands-parents (vous) :
Soyez gentils avec vos grands-parents !

1) **Se comporter** en adultes responsables (*Vous*)
2) **Faire** ses devoirs (*tu*)
3) **Rendre** ses devoirs à l'heure (*tu*)
4) **Aller** au cinéma (*nous*)
5) **Ecrire** une lettre au ministre (*nous*)
6) **Eviter** de marcher sur les pelouses (*tu*)
7) **S'abonner** à un magazine français (*nous*)
8) **Prendre** soin de la faune et la flore (*vous*)
9) **Ranger** ses affaires (*tu*)
10) **Se mettre** au régime (*nous*)
11) **Partir** maintenant (*tu*)
12) **Ne pas avoir** honte (*tu*)
13) **se dépêcher** (*vous*)
14) **Choisir** une activité adaptée à ses besoins (*tu*)
15) **Se battre** pour défendre ses convictions (*vous*)

SI CLAUSES

There are 3 types of Si Clauses.

1) Si + PRESENT , FUTUR

EX : Si je ***peux,*** *je* ***viendrai*** *te voir demain.*

présent **futur**

Si je n'avais pas révisé,
je n'aurais pas eu une
bonne note.

2) Si + IMPARFAIT , CONDITIONNEL PRÉSENT

*EX : Si j'****étais*** *riche, j'****achèterais*** *une grande maison.*

Imparfait **conditionnel présent**

3) Si + PLUS-QUE-PARFAIT , CONDITIONNEL PASSÉ

EX : Si ***j'avais su****,* ***j'aurais revisé*** *pour mon contrôle de français.*

Plus-que- parfait Conditionnel passé

NB: *il est important de réviser tes temps !!*

Let's practise!

1) **If I had time, I would go to France.**

2) **If I win the lottery, I will stop working.**

3) **If I see you, I will give you the money.**

4) **If I had finished earlier, I would have come to see you.**

5) **If I had gone to the toilets before the exam, I would not have had to leave the room.**

6) **If I was a politician, I would ban Saturday school!**

<u>LE SUBJONCTIF</u> (présent)

Le subjonctif is often dreaded by students as they (*and my guess is that you are probably one of them*) have a tendency to think that it is very complicated to use. Well, it is like everything else, if you know how to form it and when to use it, it becomes easy! So instead of trying to ignore the issue, get started with the notes and practice below for after all, you do need to be able to use it correctly in the exam!

First of all, the subjunctive is NOT a tense. It is what we call in French "*un mode*". There is no need to go into too much detail about this grammatical subtlety here, but what this implies (*and you do need to remember this*) is that the subjunctive can therefore be used in present / past / future or conditional contexts. The subjunctive remains the subjunctive and it is the preceding verb which will indicate if the action is taking place in a present / past or future context.

<u>Examples</u>:

Il ***faut*** que je **révise** pour mon examen de français.

présent (faut) — *subjonctif* (révise)

Il ***faudrait*** que je **révise** pour mon examen de français.

conditionnel présent (faudrait) — *subjonctif* (révise)

So, how is it formed??

A) To form the "***je / tu / il / elle / on / ils et elles***" forms of the verb in the subjunctive :

- Take the "**ils**" form of the verb in the **present tense**

  Ils achètent / ils finissent / ils boivent / ils comprennent

- Get rid of the « ***ils*** » and « ***ent*** » ending
- Add the appropriate **subjunctive ending** to the stem

Je -----------	**e**
Tu-----------	**es**
Il / elle / on ----------	**e**
Nous ---------	**ions**
Vous ---------	**iez**
Ils / elles ---------	**ent**

<u>Examples:</u>

- Il est tard. Il faut que <u>tu</u> ***dorm<u>es</u>*** m*ai*ntenant.
- J'aimerais que <u>les filles</u> ***dis<u>ent</u>*** la vérité.
- Il faudra qu'<u>ils</u> ***particip<u>ent</u>*** pendant la réunion la semaine prochaine.
- Il a souhaité que <u>je</u> lui ***racont<u>e</u>*** tout.

As you have noticed, I have given you the subjunctive endings for the "***nous***" and "***vous***" forms of the verbs, but I have not included these two forms in the previous explanations. So you are probably wondering why this is? Well, in most cases, you can follow the same rules as for the other forms and you will have no problem. However, some verbs, as you know, have a different "*nous*" (*and "vous"*) form in the present and this will also be the case in the subjunctive ("***nous prenons***" but "***ils prennent***"). Therefore, if you get into the habit of making a distinction between the "***nous***" and "***vous***" forms and the other forms, you should avoid unnecessary mistakes.

B) To form the "***nous***" and "***vous***" forms of the verbs in the subjunctive :

- Take the "***nous***" form of the verb in the present

  nous achetons / nous finissons / nous buvons / nous comprenons

- Get rid of the « ***ons*** » ending »

- Add the appropriate subjunctive endings for the "*nous*" or "*vous*" forms

Examples:

- Il faut que nous ***achetions*** une nouvelle voiture car la nôtre tombe sans arrêt en panne.
- j'aimerais que vous ***finissiez*** votre devoir pour demain matin.
- Il est essentiel que vous ***buviez*** au moins deux litres d'eau par jour.

Let's practise !

1) Il est urgent que nous .... (***prendre***) conscience de nos actions et de leurs effets négatifs sur l'environnement.

2) J'ai bien peur qu'elle ne .... (***rentrer***) pas à l'heure ce soir.

3) Si vous étudiez le français au niveau supérieur, il est essentiel que vous .... (***lire***) beaucoup de livres en français.

4) Comme les employés de la SNCF étaient en grève, il a fallu que nous .... (***réserver***) un taxi.

5) Ton père souhaiterait que tu lui .... (***écrire***) deux fois par mois afin de le tenir au courant de tes progrès.

6) Bien que je la .... (***connaitre***) de puis longtemps, je redoute toujours ses réactions.

7) J'aurais aimé qu'il m'.............. (***aider***) à faire mon exposé d'histoire mais il a refusé.

8) J'ai peur que ma mère .... (***se mettre***) en colère si je lui demande la permission de sortir avec mes amies samedi soir.

Irregular verbs

Of course, as you have probably guessed, there are a few exceptions to the rule. Some verbs are irregular and the only way of knowing their subjunctive forms is to learn them!
Below are the essential ones.

aller	avoir	être	faire
Il faut que...			
J' **aille**	**aie**	**sois**	**fasse**
Tu **ailles**	**aies**	**sois**	**fasses**
Il / elle / on **aille**	**ait**	**soit**	**fasse**
Nous **allions**	**ayons**	**soyons**	**fassions**
Vous **alliez**	**ayez**	**soyez**	**fassiez**
Ils / elles **aillent**	**aient**	**soient**	**fassent**

pouvoir	savoir	vouloir	valoir
Il faut que...			
Je **puisse**	**sache**	**veuille**	**vaille**
Tu **puisses**	**saches**	**veuilles**	**vailles**
Il / elle / on **puisse**	**sache**	**veuille**	**vaille**
Nous **puissions**	**sachions**	**voulions**	**valions**
Vous **puissiez**	**sachiez**	**vouliez**	**valiez**
Ils / elles **puissent**	**sachent**	**veuillent**	**vaillent**

Don't forget the two following structures which can only be used in the « ***il*** » form:

- Il pleut ⟶ qu'il ***pleuve***
- Il faut ⟶ qu'il ***faille***

NB: **Le subjonctif passé**

The past subjunctive is formed by using the ***subjunctive*** form of ***avoir*** or ***être*** + the ***past participle of the verb***. *(it follows all the rules for the verbs in the "**passé composé**")*

... qu'il ***ait mangé*** / que nous ***ayons pris*** / que vous ***soyez arrivés***
Tu ne les rencontreras pas ce soir car j'ai bien peur qu'elles ne ***soient*** déjà ***parties***.

*« avoir peur que » + subjunctive. Here the action of the verb "partir" has already happened. The verb therefore needs to be in the **past** subjunctive.*

⟶ You will not meet them tonight as I am afraid they are already gone / they have already left.

When do we use the subjunctive ?
You now know how to put a verb in the subjunctive form, but the main question remains to be answered yet: ***when do we use it***?

The subjunctive is used **AFTER** certain verbs / expressions or conjunctions. If you know those verbs / expressions or conjunctions, then it should be easy to use the subjunctive! Here is a list of the essential ones for you to revise / learn. ***The subjunctive is used....***

...**after** verbs which express **will / preference / need or necessity**	
aimer que	*to like*
demander que	*to ask for /require*
désirer que	*to desire*
permettre que	*to allow*
souhaiter que	*to wish*
vouloir que	*to want*
aimer mieux que	*to prefer*
préférer que	*to prefer*
suggérer que	*to suggest*
recommander que	*to recommend*
empêcher que	*to prevent*
exiger que	*to demand*
ordonner que	*to order*
avoir besoin que	*to need*

...**after** verbs which express **emotions and surprise / fear / doubt**	
être étonné que	*to be surprised*
être en colère	*to be angry*
être heureux que	*to be happy*
avoir honte	*to be ashamed*
être ravi que	*to be delighted*
être satisfait que	*to be satisfied*
être surpris que	*to be surprised*
être triste que	*to be sad*
(etc....)	
se plaindre que	*to complain*
regretter que	*to regret*
se réjouir que	*to rejoice*
avoir peur que	*to be afraid*
craindre que	*to fear*
redouter que	*to fear*
douter que	*to doubt*

...after impersonal expressions	
il / c'est bizarre que	*it is strange that*
il est curieux que	*it is peculiar*
il est essentiel que	*it is essential*
il faut que	*one must*
il est impensable que	*it is unthinkable*
il est important que	*it is important*
il est impossible que	*it is impossible*
il est indispensable que	*it is indispensable*
il est inutile que	*it is not necessary to*
il est nécessaire que	*it is necessary to*
il est possible que	*it is impossible*
il est primordial que	*it is essential*
il est regrettable que	*it is regrettable*
il est souhaitable que	*it is to wish that*
il est utile que	*it is useful that*
il suffit que (il **suffit qu**'il parle pour que tout le monde se taise)	He needs only to open his mouth and everyone stops talking
il n'y a pas de danger que	*there is no risk / danger of...*

...after some verbs expressing opinions	
accepter que ***approuver que*** ***convenir que***	*to accept* *to approve* *to agree that*

...after some conjunctions	
à condition que **afin que** **à moins que** **avant que** **bien que** **de crainte que** **de peur que** **jusqu'à ce que** **pour que** **pourvu que** **quoique** **sans que**	*provided that* *so that* *unless* *before* *although* *by fear of* *by fear of* *until* *so that* *provided that* *although* *without*
NB : Note that ***après que*** is **NOT** followed by the subjunctive.	example: ***Après qu'***il rentrera, nous regarderons un film.

Note that the subjunctive is also used in relative clauses (*refer back to this notion)* which:

a) are dependent on an adjective in the superlative:

C'est *la meilleure* amie que j'***aie***.
superlative *subjunctive*

b) refer to an idea / wish expressed by the subject which has not realised itself yet:

Je voudrais réserver une chambre qui ne ***soit*** pas trop bruyante.

→ *Here, the person would like to have a quiet room and expresses this wish but at this stage, does not know whether it is possible or not. Once it is confirmed that the room is a quiet one, the indicative mood (present / past etc...) is used:*

*J'ai une chambre qui n'**est** pas bruyante.*

However, you need to be careful for not all verbs expressing opinions are followed by the subjunctive. It depends on whether they are "objective" verbs (***constater que / affirmer que / supposer que / remarquer que / déclarer que***) or not (*opposite of emotional verbs*).

Indeed, the following verbs, when they are in the ***affirmative form***, are **NOT** followed by the subjunctive but by the indicative mood: *present, past, future or conditional tenses* depending on the context.

Je crois que....

Je pense que....

Je trouve que...

Examples :

Je crois qu'il ***est*** malade.
↗ *présent*

Elle pense que nous ***pourrons*** venir ce soir.
↑ *futur*

BUT

If and when those verbs are either in the ***negative*** or i***nterrogative*** forms, then they are followed by a verb in the ***subjunctive*** form.

Je ***ne*** crois ***pas*** qu'il ***soit*** malade.
↗ *Subjunctive* ↘

Penses-tu que nous ***puissions*** venir ce soir ***?***

Let's practise !

Look at the sentences below. For each one, decide whether the verb in bold is in the subjunctive mood (*subj)* or the indicative mood *(ind)*. Tick the appropriate box. If the verb is in the indicative, indicate the tense (*present / imperfect / perfect / future / conditional etc...*) in which it is conjugated on the line provided.

	Ind		subj
1. La consommation des ménages reprendra à condition que les prix ***baissent***.	☐	....	☐
2. Je pense que les jeunes ***regardent*** trop souvent la télévision.	☐	....	☐
3. Les profs exigent que tu ***rendes*** tes devoirs à l'heure.	☐	....	☐
4. Crois-tu qu'elle ***soit*** déjà ***arrivée*** ?	☐	....	☐
5. J'espère qu'il ne ***mentira*** pas à ses parents.	☐	....	☐
6. Je voudrais que vous ***soyez*** heureux.	☐	....	☐

Let's practise further !

Put the verbs into brackets into the subjunctive.

1) Les grèves persisteront jusqu'à ce que les ouvriers .... (***obtenir***) gain de cause.

2) Je souhaite que vous .... (***réussir***) vos examens.

3) Il faut prendre des mesures efficaces pour lutter contre la pollution avant qu'il ne .... (***être***) trop tard.

4) Le juge a ordonné que la famille de l'accusé .... (***quitter***) la salle.

5) La meilleure blague que je .... (***connaitre***) est une blague belge.

6) Il est indispensable que tu .... (***dormir***) au moins 8 heures par nuit si tu veux être en forme.

More specific to HL students…

LE PASSÉ SIMPLE

If you are studying French at Standard level, you do not need to worry about this tense. However, if you are a Higher Level candidate, it might be a good idea to have a look at the notes below.

"*Le Passé simple*" or past historic is a ....past tense. It is often referred to as a literary tense as it is mainly used in literature context. This is why it might therefore be helpful / useful to be able to at least recognise it as there is always a literary extract in paper 1 at Higher Level. It can also be used in your imaginative type stories.

The past historic is used when describing **short / brief** completed **actions** in the past.

*Soudain, la porte s'**ouvrit** avec fracas et il **apparut** dans la pièce.*

It is formed :

a) **The –er verbs** :

- Take off the "–er" ending of the infinitive form
- Add the appropriate "***passé simple***" endings for the –er verbs:

ai - as - a - âmes - âtes - èrent

Cet après-midi là, je ***nageai*** dans la rivière avec mes cousins. Ma sœur ***chanta*** pour nos invités. A la fin de la journée, les garçons ***allèrent*** en ville. Nous ***passâmes*** tous un très bon dimanche.

b) **Verbs such as : *finir / choisir / grandir / rougir / haïr / sentir / dormir / fuir***

- Take off the "–ir" ending from the infinitive form
- Add the appropriate endings for those verbs :

is - is - it - îmes - îtes - irent

Some verbs also use the above endings but their stem varies. Here is a list of the most common ones at the "*je*" form (*all is left for you to do is change the endings according to "who" is the subject of the verb)*:

verbs	Passé simple	verbs	Passé simple
(s') asseoir	*Je m'**assis***	prendre	Je ***pris***
dire	Je ***dis***	ouvrir	J' ***ouvris***
écrire	J' ***écrivis***	rejoindre	Je ***rejoignis***
faire	Je ***fis***	répondre	Je ***répondis***
mettre	Je ***mis***	rire	Je ***ris***
peindre	Je ***peignis***	voir	Je ***vis***

Les enfants ***choisirent*** un livre et ***se mirent*** à lire en silence.
Cette année-là, il ***grandit*** beaucoup en peu de temps.
Après son départ, nous lui ***écrivîmes*** souvent mais ne le ***vîmes*** que rarement.

c) **All the other / remaining verbs such as** : ***lire / boire / courir / mourir / recevoir / savoir / devoir / pouvoir / vouloir / connaître / croire / vivre***

- use the following endings :

us / us / ut / ûmes / ûtes / urent

Their stems, however, may vary and below is a table of the "*je*" form of those verbs:

verbs	Passé simple	verbs	Passé simple
apparaître	J'***apparus***	lire	Je ***lus***
boire	Je ***bus***	mourir	Je ***mourus***
connaître	Je ***connus***	pouvoir	Je ***pus***
courir	Je ***courus***	recevoir	Je ***reçus***
croire	Je ***crus***	savoir	Je ***sus***
devoir	Je ***dus***	vivre	Je ***vécus***
disparaître	Je ***disparus***	vouloir	Je **voulus**

Il était une fois une jolie princesse qui vivait seule dans une forêt enchantée. Un jour, un beau prince ***apparut*** sur son cheval. Il *s'arrêta* devant le logis de la princesse et *frappa* à sa porte. La princesse *ouvrit* sa porte et ***reçut*** le prince chez elle. Depuis ce jour, ils ne *se quittèrent* plus et ***vécurent*** heureux jusqu'à la fin de leurs jours.

As always, they are a few exceptions and all you need to do is learn them.

Avoir	
J'	***eus***
Tu	***eus***
Il / elle / on	***eut***
Nous	***eûmes***
Vous	***eûtes***
Ils / elles	***eurent***

Être	
Je	***fus***
Tu	***fus***
Il / elle / on	***fut***
Nous	***fûmes***
Vous	***fûtes***
Ils / elles	***furent***

venir	
Je	***vins***
Tu	***vins***
Il / elle / on	***vint***
Nous	***vînmes***
Vous	***vîntes***
Ils / elles	***vinrent***

Same for :

- tenir - je ***tins***
- obtenir : j'***obtins***

NB:
Note that for all the verbs, there is ***always*** an "***accent circonflexe***" (**^**) on the vowel in the "***nous***" and "***vous***" forms.
However, there is ***never*** such an accent on the "***il***" form.

More specific to HL students…

LA VOIX PASSIVE

The passive is commonly used in French. The passive is used when the grammatical subject of the verb in the sentence is not the active subject of the verb. A bit confusing at first glance admittedly but it really is not as complicated as it sounds. Take a look at the examples below. The first one is in the "***voix active***" and the second one in the "***voix passive***".

→ *Le chien a mordu le garçon.*

grammatical and active subject

In this example, the verb is in the « voix active » and not in the passive as the « *chien* » who is the grammatical subject of the verb « *a mordu* » is also the active subject- It is indeed the dog who has bitten the boy.

→ *Le garçon a été mordu par le chien.*

grammatical subject — *« real subject » or « **complément d'agent**" as it is called in French.*

However, in this second example, « *le garçon* » is the grammatical subject of the verb but he is not the active subject as he is not the one who has bitten; he is the one who has been bitten. The boy has therefore been on the receiving hand of the action performed by the dog even though the boy is grammatically the subject of the verb in the sentence. This is the **PASSIVE**.

So, how do you put a verb in the "*voix passive*"?
It is relatively easy if you follow the recipe given below:

Always use "**être**" in the appropriate tense *(the tense in which the verb is / would be conjugated when the sentence is in the "voix active")*	**+**	PAST PARTICIPLE of the verb

Examples:

VOIX ACTIVE:

*Le directeur **a renvoyé** Julien.*
passé composé

VOIX PASSIVE :

*Julien **a été renvoyé par** le directeur.*

« être » au passé composé + participe passé du verbe « renvoyer »

NB : As you are using "**être**", don't forget to make the past participle agree with the subject if and when necessary!

VOIX ACTIVE :

*En 2025, les scientifiques **découvriront** une nouvelle thérapie contre le sida.*
futur

VOIX PASSIVE :

*En 2025, une nouvelle thérapie contre le sida **sera découverte par** les scientifiques.*

« être » au futur + participe passé du verbe « découvrir » + agreement with the grammatical subject.

NB : "*par*" is used to introduce the "***complément d'agent***" in the sentence in the "*voix passive*" when there is one.

When is the passive used?

The passive can be used in different contexts. It can, for example, be used when the intention is to emphasise the person / object who is the recipient of the action. Placing the recipient first, by using it as the grammatical subject of the sentence, stresses its importance.

→ *Cette pièce de théâtre* ***a été écrite*** *par Molière.*

It can also be used when the focus is not on who has really done / will really do the action but the action itself. The "real subject" is unimportant and will as such remain unidentified.

→ *Il faut que la lumière* ***soit faite*** *sur cette affaire.*
Here, it does not matter who finds the truth about the affair, what is important is that the truth is being found out.

NB: *Note that the "voix passive" in French is often used in formal / literary contexts. Therefore, if you are / have been studying French at Higher Level, you will undoubtedly have stumbled across it in some of your more literary pieces of reading.*
It is important to be able to recognise it and use it too. If you know your tenses, this will obviously help you form the "voix passive".

Let's practise!

Transform the sentences from the "*voix active*" into the "*voix passive*".

1) L'agence immobilière ***loue*** cet appartement.
   ....
2) Des milliers de téléspectateurs ***suivaient*** cette émission tous les mois.
   ....
3) Il faut que la loi ***protège*** mieux les enfants défavorisés.
   ....
4) Le gouvernement ***prendra*** des mesures efficaces pour lutter contre l'inflation.
   ....
5) Des hommes cagoulés ***auraient menacé*** la caissière du magasin.
   ....
6) Sébastien Lirique ***a écrit*** les paroles de cette nouvelle chanson.
   ....
7) Le plus grand chirurgien de Paris m'***a opéré*** de l'appendicite.
   ....
8) Les chercheurs ***ont retrouvé*** des ossements humains sur ce site archéologique.
   ....

<u>Les verbes suivis de la préposition de + *infinitif*</u>

These lists are not exhaustive.

• **s'abstenir de**	to refrain from
• **accepter de**	to agree to
• **s'arrêter de**	to stop
• **avoir l'intention de**	to intend to
• **avoir peur de**	to be afraid of
• **avoir raison de**	to be right to
• **avoir tort de**	to be wrong to
• **brûler d'envie / d'impatience de**	to be burning to
• **mourir d'envie / d'impatience de**	to be dying to
• **se charger de**	to make sure of
• **choisir de**	to choose to
• **craindre de**	to fear
• **décider de**	to decide to
• **se dépêcher de**	to hurry to
• **s'empêcher de**	to refrain from
• **s'empresser de**	to rush to (eg. do something)
• **essayer de**	to try to
• **s'étonner de**	to marvel at
• **éviter de**	to avoid
• **s'excuser de**	to apologise for
• **finir de**	to finish
• **se flatter de**	to claim to
• **mériter de**	to deserve to
• **parler de**	to talk about
• **promettre de**	to promise to
• **se proposer de**	to offer to (do something)
• **regretter de**	to regret
• **risquer de**	to run the risk of
• **oublier de**	to forget to

<u>Examples</u> :

- Olivier **a promis de** *réviser* pour l'examen de français de vendredi.
- Elle **s'est empressée de** *raconter* cette histoire à tout le monde.
- Je **me chargerai de** *préparer* le repas pour tout le monde.
- Le prof **n'acceptera pas de** nous *donner* moins de devoirs !
- Il **a essayé de** *contacter* Cloé, mais il n'a pas réussi.
- Je **regrette de ne pas** *avoir* été présent au bon moment.
- Nous **avons eu raison de** *refuser* leur proposition.
- Tu **as fini d'***utiliser* l'ordinateur ?

NB: *Be careful- Some of these verbs can sometimes be used without the preposition.*
Eg.- ***mériter***
Il mérite vraiment cette récompense.

Les verbes suivis de la préposition à *+ infinitif*

• **réussir à**	to succeed in
• **s'amuser à**	to take pleasure in
• **apprendre à**	to learn to
• **arriver à**	to manage to
• **s'attendre à**	to expect to
• **chercher à**	to try to
• **commencer à**	to begin to
• **se consacrer à**	to devote oneself to
• **consentir à**	to consent to
• **continuer à**	to continue to
• **se décider à**	to make up one's mind to
• **s'ennuyer à**	to be bored / to get bored
• **s'exercer à / s'entrainer à**	to practice
• **s'habituer à**	to get used to
• **hésiter à**	to hesitate to
• **s'intéresser à**	to be interested in
• **se mettre à**	to begin to
• **s'obstiner à**	to persist stubbornly in
• **parvenir à**	to manage to / to succeed in
• **passer son temps à**	to spend one's time doing
• **penser à**	to be thinking of (doing something)
• **se préparer à**	to get ready to
• **se résigner à**	to resign one self to
• **songer à**	to be thinking of (doing something)
• **tendre à**	to tend to
• **tenir à**	to insist on

Examples :

- Je **songe à** *acheter* une maison au Canada.
- Je **passe mon temps à** *travailler* pour mes examens.
- Julie **a commencé à** *réviser* pour son examen de français.
- Elle **s'exerce à** *parler* français devant son miroir pour améliorer sa prononciation.
- Il **s'est enfin décidé à** *acheter* une nouvelle voiture !
- Nous **avons réussi à** le *faire* changer d'avis.
- Ils **n'ont pas hésité à** *téléphoner* aux gendarmes.
- Je **tiens à vous** *dédommager* pour les dégâts.

NB : Some verbs are always followed by the preposition **"à"** but are not necessarily followed by an infinitive.
Eg:

- **échouer à** *(to fail)* - Olivier **a échoué à** son examen de français. Il **n'avait pas pensé à réviser** !!
- **répondre à** *(to reply to)* – Il a répondu à ma lettre.

Be careful, some of these verbs can also be used without the preposition.
Eg- **chercher** *: Je cherche mon stylo.*

Let's practise!

Verbs followed by a preposition.

Try and translate the sentences without referring back to the above lists.

1) This speech is aimed at teenagers.

....

2) The politicians are beginning to realise the importance of protecting the planet.

....

3) The doctors will try to clone more and more people and animals.

....

4) If the sports centre was open, we would benefit from a range of activities.

....

5) It is difficult to understand why terrorists kill women and children too.

....

6) It is essential to stop children watching violent programs on T.V.

....

7) He needs to persuade his parents to let him go on holiday with his friends.

....

8) Pupils must get used to working with computers.

....

9) Advertisement encourages people to buy too many useless things.

....

10) She insists on choosing clothes which are expensive but they never suit her.

....

ADJECTIVAL AGREEMENT

It is important to remember that in French, nouns have different genders. Nouns can be masculine or feminine. There is only one way of knowing the gender of a noun: *learn the gender when you learn the noun*!
Adjectives are words used in conjunction with nouns. They give specific information about the nouns. They describe nouns. Adjectives have to "agree" in gender and number with the noun that they are describing. They have to bear the mark of the gender or / and the plural.
Adjectival agreement may seem easy to you as you have been learning them for a while. However, as with the present, past or future tenses, they must not be ignored for they constitute basic grammatical knowledge and if you don't get them right, you will give a bad impression.

A few general rules*:*
Most adjectives form their feminine form simply by adding an extra "***e***" at the end of the adjective: grand ⟶ grand***e*** petit ⟶ petit***e*** fatigue ⟶ fatigué***e***
Some adjectives already end in "e" when they are in the masculine form. As they already end in "e", you don't need to add an extra one in the femine form. Just leave them as they are. They have the same masculine and femine forms: simple ⟶ *simple* sensible ⟶ *sensible* rapide ⟶ *rapide*
For some adjectives which end in « ***l*** » / « ***n*** » or « ***s*** », you need to ***double the end consonant*** before adding the "***e***": actuel ⟶ actue***lle*** bon ⟶ bo***nne*** gros ⟶ gro***sse***
Some special agreement rules
Adjectives which end in « ***er*** » form their femine forms in « ***ère***": amer ⟶ am***ère*** cher ⟶ ch***ère*** fier ⟶ fi***ère***
Adjectives which end in « ***eux*** » form their femine form in « ***euse*** » : courageux ⟶ courag***euse*** frileux ⟶ fril***euse*** sérieux ⟶ séri***euse***
Adjectives which end in « ***eur*** » also form their femine form in « ***euse*** » : rêveur ⟶ rêv***euse*** rieur ⟶ ri***euse*** travailleur ⟶ travaill***euse***
Adjectives which end in « ***c*** » in the masculine form their femine form in « ***che*** » : blanc ⟶ blan***che*** franc ⟶ fran***che*** sec ⟶ s***èche***
Adjectives which end in "***if"*** in the masculine form their feminine form in "***ive***": chétif ⟶ chét***ive*** craintif ⟶ craint***ive*** plaintif ⟶ plaint***ive***

NB: To put the above adjectives in the plural, most of the time, all you need to do is add an extra « **s** » to the masculine or feminine endings. However, the adjective in "***eux***" keep the same "***eux***" ending in the masculine plural form.

As always with French grammar, you can guess that there are a few exceptions that you need to know. Below is a list of some of the most common.

beau	**belle**
doux	**douce**
faux	**fausse**
frais	**fraiche**
fou	**folle**
grec	**grecque**

NB: "***beau***" becomes "***beaux***" in the plural- same for "***nouveau***".

If an adjective already ends in "**s**" in the masculine singular ("***gris***") or in "**x**" ("***doux***"), then its masculine plural form is the same.

jaloux	**jalouse**
long	**longue**
mou	**molle**
nouveau	**nouvelle**
roux	**rousse**
vieux	**vieille**

*When using: "**c'est + adjectif**", the adjective always stays in the masculine singular form: La France, c'est **beau**!*

<u>Let's practise</u> !

Look at the sentences below. Some adjective endings might need completeting or even changing all together!

1) Il faut manger une alimentation équilibré__ et mener une vie sain__.
2) Il y a de plus en plus de familles monoparentale__.
3) Les drogues doux___ seraient moins nocif___ pour la santé que les drogues dure___.
4) C'est la fille la plus gentil___ et la plus mignon__ que je connaisse.
5) Certains établissements scolaires sont très sélectif__.
6) La précarité est injuste__. La vie quotidien__ des personnes dans le besoin devient un combat difficile__.
7) Cet homme politique a mauvais__ réputation, Je ne voterai pas pour lui aux prochain__ élections.
8) C'est une personne très sympathique__.

Comparatives and superlatives – a brief reminder -

To compare one person to another / one thing to another / one group of people to another etc...all you need to do is to use the **<u>COMPARATIVE</u>** form of the adjective:

plus............que
*mon cousin est **plus** <u>petit</u> **que** moi.*

moins.........que
*Ma sœur est **moins** <u>grande</u> **que** toi.*

aussi..........que
*Nous sommes **aussi** <u>grands</u> **qu**'eux.*

autant.......que

Il y a **autant** de <u>filles</u> **que** de garçons dans la classe.
*Here, with this structure, we are not using an adjective but a **NOUN.***

<u>EXCEPTIONS</u>:

bon → **meilleur .....que**

\+ mal (*adv*) → **pire.........que**
bien (*adv*) → **mieux....que**

LES PRONOMS

There are different types of pronouns. A pronoun is a grammatical word **used to replace a noun**. It is often used in an attempt to avoid repetition of a noun. Pronouns are therefore very useful grammatical tools as they will help you improve your style of writing, making it sound more fluid and fluent.
Below is an explanation of different types of pronouns. Don't get scared by what they are called and make the effort to carry on reading!

Different types of pronouns:

a. **pronoms personnels sujets**:
Those are the pronouns that you use all the time without knowing that they are pronouns. They are used instead of a subject noun / as a subject.

je - tu - il - elle - on - nous - vous - ils – elles

Marie révise pour son bac de français. ⟶ ***Elle*** révise pour son bac de français.

b. **pronoms réfléchis / pronominaux** :
Those are the pronouns that accompany reflexive verbs. They cannot be ignored. Remember that not all verbs are reflexive and that some reflexive verbs also exist in a non-reflexive form (***laver** and **se laver***). Whatever tense (*with maybe a slight exception in the imperative*) the reflexive verb is conjugated in, the reflexive pronouns always remain
the same.

je	**me** ⟶	Je **me** lève tôt le matin.
tu	**te** ⟶	Tu **t'**es bien amusé hier à la soirée ?
il / elle / on	**se** ⟶	Il **se** disputait souvent avec ses parents l'an passé.
nous	**nous** ⟶	Nous ne **nous** étions pas vus depuis 10 ans.
vous	**vous** ⟶	Il faut que vous **vous** prépariez pour votre voyage.
ils / elles	**se** ⟶	Ses parents **se** sont séparés en début d'année.

c. **Pronoms compléments d'objet direct** :

The direct object pronouns are used to replace nouns which are used as direct objects in a sentence. Ok; but what is a direct object? One way of finding out if there is a direct object in a sentence is:

- ask yourself the following question after the verb: "qui?" or "quoi?" (*who? or what?*). If you can find a direct answer for it in the sentence (*i.e. without having to use a preposition between the verb and the complement*), then this is a direct object.

E.g.:

⟶ *Il mange une pomme.*

Il mange (quoi?) = ***une pomme*** (*direct answer, no preposition in front of it*) - "***pomme"*** is therefore a ***direct object***.

⟶ Il parle de Paul

Il parle (qui?) – **de Paul** (*preposition*)- therefore « Paul » is not used as a direct object here.

I hope that it makes sense. Keep practising as it is one of the best ways to improve!

The direct object pronouns are:

1st person singular	**me**
2nd person singular	**te**
3rd person singular masculine	**le**
3rd person singular feminine	**la**
1st person plural	**nous**
2nd person plural	**vous**
3rd person plural masculine or feminine	**les**

Ex:

Je lis ***le journal***. → Je ***le*** lis. (*3rd person singular masculine*)
Nous écoutons ***la radio***. → Nous ***l'***écoutons. (*3rd person singular femine*)
Tu sortiras **les poubelles**. → Tu ***les*** sortiras. (*3rd person plural- feminine here*)

NB1: Remember that when the verb in the "*passé composé*", certain rules need to be followed (*refer back to section on "passé composé"*)

NB2: remember that the pronouns always go **BEFORE the verb** to which they are "related".

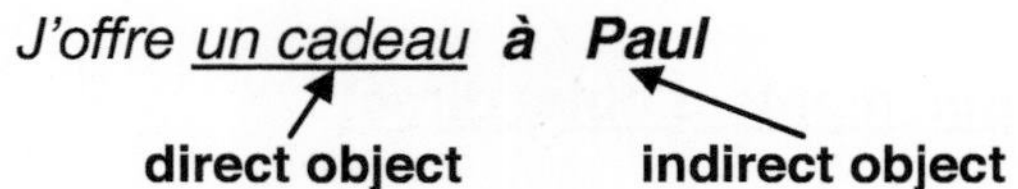
→ Nous devons lire ***ce livre*** pendant les vacances.
Nous devons ***le*** *lire pendant les vacances.*

a. **Pronoms complément d'objet indirect :**

The indirect object pronouns are replacing nouns that hold the function of indirect object in the sentence. Unlike the direct object nouns, you might have guessed that they are the ones which are separated from the verbs by a **preposition**.

J'offre un cadeau ***à Paul***

direct object (un cadeau) — **indirect object** (Paul)

The indirect object pronouns are:

1st person singular	**me**
2nd person singular	**te**
3rd person singular masculine	**lui**
3rd person singular feminine	**lui**
1st person plural	**nous**
2nd person plural	**vous**
3rd person plural masculine or feminine	**leur**

Ex:

J'offre un cadeau ***à Paul et Virginie***.
→ Je **leur** offre un cadeau.

Mes parlent ne parlent jamais **à notre voisine**.
→ Ils ne **lui** parlent jamais.

As you know, pronouns go in front of the verbs. When, in a sentence, you need / want to replace several nouns of different functions by their appropriate pronouns, below is the order in which they should be used:

subject pronouns / direct object pronouns / indirect object pronouns

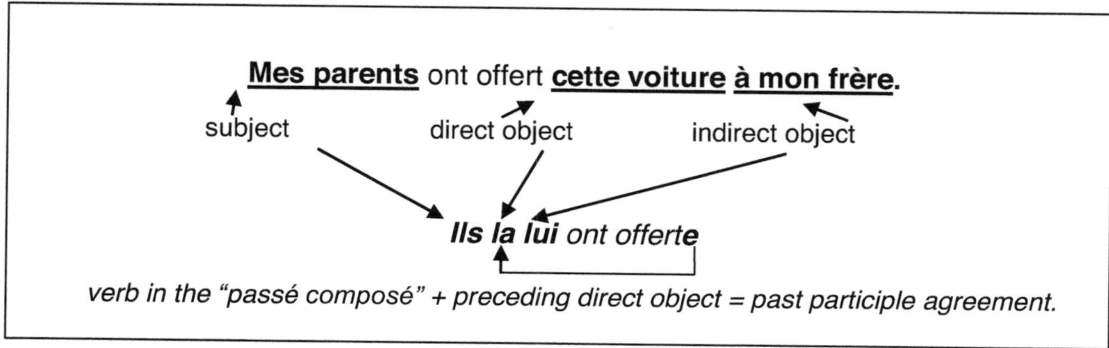

a. **"y" and "en" pronouns:**

1. **"Y"**:

- The pronoun "y" is used to replace **a place**:

*Je vais **à l'école*** → *j'**y** vais.*

Nous passons nos vacances **en Italie** → Nous **y** passons nos vacances.

- It is also used to replace **a concept / an idea** expressed by a **verb followed by** the preposition "**à**":

*Je pense **à l'amour*** → *j'**y** pense.*

*Je crois **à son histoire*** → *j'**y** crois.*

2. **« EN »** :

- The pronoun « en » is used to replace expressions / nouns when there is a notion of quantity (*whether this notion of quantity is precise or not*). It therefore replaces expressions preceded by the quantitative **du / de la / de l' / des / de or beaucoup de / trop de / pas assez de etc.... :**

*Je mange beaucoup **de sucreries.*** → *J'**en** mange beaucoup.*

*N'hésitez-pas à reprendre **du gâteau.*** → *N'hésitez pas à **en** reprendre.*

- It also replaces expressions preceded by **un / deux / trois / dix** etc.....
Note that when a precise number is present, this number is repeated at the end of the sentence even when the pronoun « en » has been used :

Il a acheté **trois ordinateurs.** → Il **en** a acheté **trois.**

*N'hésitez pas à reprendre **un morceau de gâteau.*** → *N'hésitez pas à **en** reprendre **un morceau.***

- It is also used to replace an **idea / a concept** expressed by a *verb followed* by the preposition « **de** »:

*Il doute **de ses compétences.*** → *Il **en** doute.*

*Elle a peur **de ses sentiments.*** → *Elle **en** a peur.*

Let's practise !

Replace the nouns in bold with the appropriate pronoun(s).

1) **Mes parents et moi** sommes allés **en France** l'été dernier.

....

2) Le prof a demandé **aux élèves** de se taire.

....

3) Il faudrait que j'achète **une nouvelle veste à Xavier**.

....

4) Ils ont regardé **la télé** très tard hier soir.

....

5) Il s'est acheté **trois nouveaux CDs** aujourd'hui.

....

6) Tu as revendu **ta voiture à ta collègue** ?

....

7) Le conseil d'orientation donne toujours de bons conseils **aux jeunes**.

....

8) Demande **à ton père** de te prêter **de l'argent** !

....

9) Il croit en **l'honnêteté et la franchise**. Pas toi ?

....

10) Je connais **son frère et sa cousine**.

....

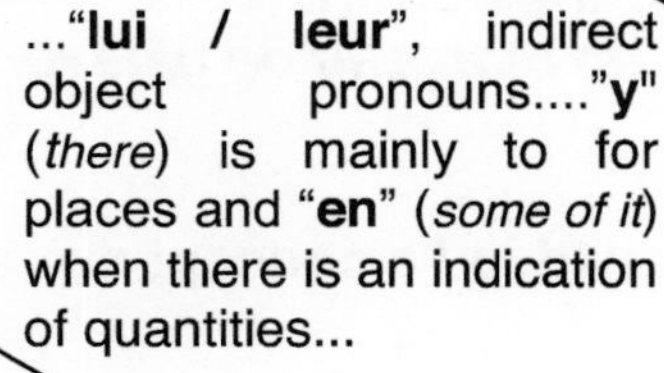

Alors...si j'ai bien compris... « ***le / la / les*** » are direct object pronouns…
..."**lui / leur**", indirect object pronouns...."**y**" (*there*) is mainly to for places and "**en**" (*some of it*) when there is an indication of quantities...
*C'est assez facile...je finirai bien par m'**y** habituer.*

LES PRONOMS RELATIFS

Relative pronouns, like any other pronouns, replace nouns in sentences. Their main function is to **link sentences** together in order to **avoid repetition(s)** of a noun already mentioned.

*J'ai regardé **une émission** à la télé hier soir. C'était **une émission** sur la violence dans les banlieues.*

→ ***L'émission*** **que** *j'ai regardée à la télé hier soir était sur la violence dans les banlieues.*

NB: *The first two sentences are grammatically correct and convey the message clearly. However, the noun "emission" is repeated twice. In the second example, the two sentences have been combined together to avoid that repetition. It is a more complex, more sophisticated, better style of writing.*

Relative pronouns are extremely useful tools when it comes to improving your style of writing as they allow you to write better, well-structured, more sophisticated sentences. You can understand now why it is important that you devote some time to revising them.

a. Pronoms relatifs simples

There are 4 main relative pronouns: **QUI / QUE / DONT / OÙ**

- « **QUI** » is used to replace a noun which is the **subject** of the verb in the sentence *(of the verb which follows the pronoun)*.

→ *Elle est mariée à **un homme**. **Cet homme** travaille pour le Quai d'Orsay.*

sujet du verbe « travaille »

Elle est mariée à un homme **qui** *travaille pour le Quai d'Orsay.*

sujet du verbe « travaille »

- « **QUE** » is used to replace a noun which is a **direct object** (*of the verb which follows the pronoun*) in the sentence.

→ *J'ai rencontré **une fille** la semaine dernière. **Cette fille** est allemande.*

direct object

La fille **que** *j'ai rencontrée la semaine dernière est allemande.*

direct object

NB: the past participle "*rencontrée*" has a feminine ending as the verb is in the "passé composé" and the direct object is preceding the verb....Just a reminder!

NB: It is possible to contract "**QUE**" when it is followed by a vowel. However, followed or not by a vowel, "**QUI**" cannot be contracted.

*Paris est la ville française **qui a**ttire le plus de touristes.*

*Le film **qu'i**l a regardé hier soir est très connu.*

- « **DONT** » **:** is used to avoid the repetition of a noun which is the complement of a verb followed by the preposition « **de** » *(see list on page …)*.

→ *Je n'aime pas **l'école**. Je ne parle jamais de **l'école** à mes parents.* **(parler de)**

*L'école est un sujet **dont** je ne parle jamais à mes parents.*

« **DONT** » is also used when there is a sense of belonging to someone or something.

→ *Il est le compositeur de **cette musique**. **Cette musique** est magnifique.*

Here, the music belongs to the composer as he is the one who has created it. Therefore, "dont" will be used to transform these two sentences into one.

La musique **dont** il est le compositeur est magnifique.

- « **Où** » is used to avoid the repetition of **a place** ...

→ *Nous allons en vacances dans **cette région** depuis 20 ans. C'est une **région** tranquille.*

*La région **où** nous allons en vacances depuis 20 ans est très tranquille.*

… it is also used to avoid the repetition of **a time / period** etc…

→ *Il a emménagé il y a plusieurs années. C'était l'année où Juliette est née.*

*Il a emménagé l'année **où** Juliette est née.*

"CE QUI" / "CE QUE" and « CE DONT »

« Ce qui", « ce que » and "ce dont" can also be used. Like "qui"," que" and "dont" :

- "**ce qui**" will replace a noun which is **subject**
- "**ce que**" will replace a **direct object**
- "**ce dont**" will replace the complement of a **verb followed** by the preposition "**de**"

So what is the difference?
They will be used when the noun that they are replacing is a concept / an idea / a "thing" which is not very precise or concrete or tangible.

Let's look at some examples to make sense of it...

*Elle mange seulement **ce qui** est naturel.*

subject of the verb

We don't know exactly what she eats, but whatever it is, it is always natural.

*Elle comprend tout **ce que** je dis.*

direct object of the verb

It does not matter what I say, whatever it is, she understands it.

*Il sait **ce dont** j'ai besoin. (avoir besoin **de**)*

Whatever I need, he knows what it is.

b. <u>les pronoms relatifs composés</u>

There are 3 main categories of "*pronoms relatifs composés*". They serve the same purpose as the "*pronoms relatifs simples*", this means that they are used to avoid repetition and link several sentences together harmoniously.

- "**AUQUEL / À LAQUELLE / AUXQUELLES / AUXQUELLES** " are used to avoid the repetition of a noun in conjunction with the **verb followed** by the preposition "**à**" (see list page ...)

→ *La solution **à laquelle** il a pensé n'est pas viable. (penser **à**)*

*Le livre **auquel** le prof a fait référence pendant le cours se trouve à la bibliothèque. (faire référence **à**)*

- "**DUQUEL / DE LAQUELLE / DESQUELS / DESQUELLES** " are used with verbs followed by a **preposition + « de »** such as :
  *habiter **près de** / vivre **à côté de***

→ *La villa **à côté de laquelle** nous habitons appartient à une actrice célèbre.*

« villa » is a femine word so « de laquelle » is being used.

- " **LEQUEL / LAQUELLE / LESQUELS / LESQUELLES**" are used with any other preposition *(avec / sans / sur / pour / grâce à etc...)*

→ *Je sors **avec des amis** samedi soir. **Ces amis** habitent à Paris.*

*Les amis **avec lesquels** je sors samedi soir habitent à Paris.*

*Ils se battent **pour une cause**. **Cette cause** en vaut la peine.*

*La cause **pour laquelle** ils se battent en vaut la peine.*

NB: It is worth mentioning that for people, "***qui***" is often used instead of "***lequel / laquelle*** etc...", but both versions are correct.

→ *Le patron **pour lequel** je travaille est compréhensif.*

*Le patron **pour qui** je travaille est compréhensif.*

*Les collègues **auxquels** je pense sont tous à temps complet.*

*Les collègues **à qui** je pense sont tous à temps complet.*

NB: *Note that these relative pronouns change according to the gender and number of the noun they are referring to.*

Let's practise!

Let's see if you've got it...Complete the sentences below with the right "***pronom relatif***".

1) Les amis .... je t'ai parlé sont originaires du sud de la France.
2) Ma sœur réussit toujours à avoir tout .... elle veut ! C'est pas juste !
3) La question .... je vous pose aujourd'hui, mes chers collègues, est la suivante : les associations .... nous travaillons ont-elles le droit de nous manipuler de la sorte ?
4) Arrête de croire .... il te raconte ! C'est un menteur.
5) La fille .... est assise à la table au fond à gauche est ma meilleure amie.
6) Le garçon .... elle est assise est mon frère.
7) La crise alimentaire .... menace les pays défavorisés est inquiétante.
8) Les vacances .... nous avons passées ensemble l'an dernier étaient géniales.
9) L'entreprise .... mon père travaille est connue mondialement.
10) .... est intéressant de retenir de cette histoire finalement, c'est que le mensonge ne sert à rien !
11) Le courage .... il a su faire preuve est un exemple pour tous.
12) Malheureusement, la vie ....il rêvait ne s'est jamais concrétisée.
13) Tu ne devineras jamais .... s'est passé ensuite !
14) Le Louvre est un musée .... j'aime beaucoup aller.
15) L'incident .... il a fait référence dans son discours s'est produit l'été dernier.
16) J'ai horreur de la manière .... il parle. C'est très vulgaire.
17) .... est incroyable, c'est que le cambrioleur soit revenu sur le lieu du crime après le passage de la police.
18) C'est l'amie .... j'ai pu obtenir ce poste. Elle m'a pistonnée.
19) Le concert .... nous avons assisté samedi soir était organisé par la municipalité.
20) Les conseils .... je te donne sont efficaces, mais libre à toi de les ignorer si tu préfères échouer !

A brief revision list of useful structures to use and further grammar points

1) Avant de + infinitif :

EX: Avant de quitter la maison, je prends mon petit-déjeuner car c'est le repas le plus important de la journée.
Avant d'aller me coucher, je regarde mon émission préférée **à** la télé.
Il a fait le plein d'essence **avant de venir.**

---

2) Après avoir + participe passé / Après être + participe passé:

EX : Après avoir regardé la télé, je vais me coucher parce que je suis fatigué.
Après avoir pris mon petit-déjeuner, je suis allé voir mon copain Antoine.
Après être allées au concert, les filles sont rentrées à la maison.

---

3) En train de + infinitif : *(although the use of the imperfect on its own is as effective)*

EX: J'étais en train de faire mes devoirs quand le téléphone a sonné.
Ma mère était en train de passer l'aspirateur quand je suis rentré de l'école ce soir là / ma mère ***passait*** l'aspirateur quand je suis rentré.

---

4) venir de + infinitif:

EX: Je viens de finir mes devoirs, **maintenant** je peux sortir avec mes amis.
Il venait de sortir de chez lui, quand **soudain,** le drame s'est produit.

---

5) EN + participe présent :
En **cuisin**ant / en **fais**ant / en **tomb**ant

EX : Ma sœur s'est brûl**ée en** fais**ant** la cuisine.
Elle s'est cass**é le** pied **en** tomb**ant** dans l'escalier.

---

6) J'ai dû + infinitif: (I had to)

EX: Après le voyage, j'étais tellement fatigué que **j'ai dû aller** me coucher.

---

7) Comme....décider de + infinitif :

EX: Comme il pleuvait averse, **nous avons décidé d'aller** au cinéma **pour voir** le dernier film de James Bond **car j'aime beaucoup l'intrigue de ses films.**

8) La négation:

- **ne .....pas :** Je **n'**ai **pas** regardé l'émission sur ma chanteuse préférée **hier soir à** la télé **parce que j'ai dû aller** rendre visite à ma grand-mère.
  (not)

- **ne .....plus : Avant** j'allais au cinéma tous les samedis **mais maintenant** je **n'**y vais **plus** car j'ai trop de devoirs.
  (not anymore)
  (no longer / none left)

- **ne...jamais :** Je **ne** suis **jamais** allé en vacances en Australie **parce que** c'est trop cher, mais j'aimerais y aller bientôt.
  (never)

- **ne...rien** : Il **ne** fait **rien** pour arranger les choses.
  (nothing)

- **ne... ni...ni :** Quand je vais en vacances avec ma famille, nous **ne** restons **ni** dans un camping, **ni** dans un gîte. Nous préférons rester à l'hôtel car c'est plus confortable.
  (neither...nor)

- **ne ......que** : Il **n'**y a **que** lui qui puisse nous aider.
  (only)

- **ne....aucun/e** : C'est bizarre...je **n'**entends **aucun** bruit. Pourtant je suis sûr qu'ils sont là.
  Il a voulu s'inscrire à ce concours mais il **n'**a **aucune** chance de gagner. Je lui ai dit mais il ne veut pas m'écouter.
  (none)

- **personne ne / ne ...personne : Personne n'est** d'accord avec toi.
  Personne ne peut **plus rien** y faire à présent.
  Il **n'**y avait **personne** à la maison ce soir là.
  (noone)

+ **ne.... pas encore :** Il **n'**a **pas encore** fini ses devoirs pourtant ça fait deux heures qu'il travaille dessus !
  (noy yet)

---

9) Les mots de liaison : adverbes et conjonctions : *(see chapter 2 for more details)*

D'abord, ensuite, puis, soudain, de plus
Cependant, pourtant, néanmoins, malgré cela, sauf, sans
malheureusement, heureusement
De temps en temps, parfois, quelquefois, jamais, souvent, tous les jours, tous les jeudis, tous les soirs, fréquemment, tous les quinze jours....
Maintenant, aujourd'hui, demain, l'année prochaine, l'année dernière, il ya deux ans, autrefois...
Etc...

---

10) Les pronoms intérrogatifs :

Qui ?	Who ?
Que / qu'est-ce que... ?	What ?
Quand ?	When ?
Où ?	Where ?
Comment ?	How ?
Combien ?	How many ?
Pourquoi ?	Why ?
Quel /quelle / quels / quelles ?	Which ?

11) Ce / cet / cette / ces *(this / these)*

Ce / **cet** / **cette** / **ces** are *demonstrative adjectives* and as adjectives, they vary according to the noun they "describe".

Ce guide *(noun masculine)* de révision est très utile.
Cet homme *(noun masculine starting with a silent «h »)* est un homme politique célèbre.
Cette solution *(noun feminine)* me convient parfaitement.
Ces questions *(noun plural)* ne sont pas faciles.

Let's practise !

.... verre	.... fille	.... gens
.... stylo	.... histoires	à .... heure là
.... image	.... homme	.... jour-là
.... enfant	.... hasard	.... pantalon
.... fleur	.... historien	.... messieurs

---

12) **Mon / ma / ton/ ta etc.....** *(my / your / their…)*

Mon / **ma** / **mes** / **ton** / **ta** / **tes** and Co are *possessive adjectives*. Again, as adjectives, they vary according to the gender and number of the ***possessed object*** (*and **not** to whom it belongs*!).

	Masculine singular	Feminine singular	In front of vowel	plural
my	**mon**	ma	**mon**	**mes**
your	**ton**	ta	**ton**	**tes**
His / her / its	**son**	sa	**son**	**ses**
our	**notre**	notre	**notre**	**nos**
your	**votre**	votre	**votre**	**vos**
their	**leur**	leur	**leur**	**leurs**

Je range toujours ***ma*** chambre *(feminine singular)* avant d'aller me coucher.
Elle a téléphoné à ***ses*** parents*(masculine plural)* dès ***son*** arrivée *(feminine singular + start with vowel)* à l'hôtel.
Les enfants ont passé le week-end chez ***leurs*** grands-parents *(masculine plural).*

Let's practise !

1) Pourriez-vous me prêter .... téléphone s'il vous plaît ? J'ai oublié le mien dans .... voiture.
2) Comment vont ..... parents ? Tu les a vus récemment ?
3) …… alimentation laisse à désirer ! Il ne mange que des produits surgelés.
4) Ils ont le sens des affaires. …….. initiative a remporté un franc succès.
5) ……. horloge avance de 10 minutes. Il faudrait que tu la remettes à l'heure.

13) <u>Le mien / la mienne / le tien / les siens…..</u> *(mine / yours / his …)*

Like all pronouns, the possessive pronouns replaced nouns. They replace nouns which are originally accompanied by a possessive adjective.

C'est ***mon*** guide. C'est ***le mien***.

possessive adjective *possessive pronoun*

As pronouns, they take the ***number*** and ***gender*** of the noun that they are replacing.

→ Regarde, voilà tes parents. ***<u>Les miens</u>*** ne sont pas encore arrivés. De toute façon ils sont toujours en retard. /*(« **<u>Les miens</u>** » replaces « **mes parents** »)*
*Look, here are your parents. **<u>Mine</u>** have not arrived yet. In any case, they are always late!*

- « A qui appartient cette voiture ? C'est celle de ta sœur ?
- Oui, c'est ***<u>la sienne</u>***. » / *(« **<u>la sienne</u>** » replaces my sister's car)*

	Masculine singular	**Feminine singular**	**Masculine plural**	**Feminine plural**
mine	**le mien**	la mienne	**les miens**	les miennes
yours	**le tien**	la tienne	**les tiens**	les tiennes
His / hers / its	**le sien**	la sienne	**les siens**	les siennes
ours	**le nôtre**	la nôtre	**les nôtres**	les nôtres
yours	**le vôtre**	la vôtre	**les vôtres**	les vôtres
theirs	**le leur**	la leur	**les leurs**	les leurs

---

14) <u>Tout / Toute / Tous / Toutes</u>

« **Tout** / **toute** / **tous** / **toutes** » means « all / every ». It varies according to the gender and number of the noun it describes...when it is used as an **<u>ADJECTIVE</u>**!

*Je me lève **<u>tous</u>** les jours à 7h.*
(Here it is used as an adjective as it gives us information about the days...it is <u>every</u> day.)

Be careful, "**tout**" can also be used as an **<u>ADVERB</u>** and as you know adverbs do not change in gender or number.

C'est facile. J'ai **<u>tout</u>** compris!
(here, "tout" gives us additional information about the verb- you have understood <u>everything</u>)

<u>Let's practise</u> !

1) …………. mes amis et ………… mes amies sont venus.
2) Avez-vous fini ………. les exercices de grammaire ?
3) Il est …….. le temps en retard.
4) Il a dormi ……….. la journée.
5) ……… travail mérite salaire.
6) Tu trouveras .... les réponses dans le chapitre 6.

15) Prepositions :

Prepositions are little words used mainly in front of words to give indication of place / time / material / manner / direction....Below is a list of the essential ones.

- **à**......................*to, at*
- **à côté de**.........*next to*
- **après**..............*after*
- **au dessus de**...*above*
- **avant**............. *before*
- **avec**...............*with*
- **chez**...............*at*
- **dans**..............*in*

- **de**...............*from*
- **depuis**........*since, for*
- **en**...............*in,on*
- **en dessous de**...*under*
- **en face de**.....opposite
- **entre**........*in between*
- **jusque**........*until, up to*
- **loin de**........*far from*

- **par**........... *by*
- **parmi**........*amongst*
- **pendant**.......*during*
- **pour**.............*for*
- **près de**..... *near*
- **sans**..........*without*
- **sous**..........*under*
- **sur**.............*on*
- **vers**..........*toward*

Remember as well that "**à**" should be used in front of a town "**à** Paris".
As far as countries are concened it depends on the grammatical gender of the country:

Masculin:	**au**	**- au Maroc / au Canada**
Féminin : *(+ l')*	**en**	**- en Norvège / en Angleterre**
Pluriel:	**aux**	**- aux Etats-Unis**

Let's practise !

Fill in the blanks with the appropriate prepositions.

FAITS DIVERS :

1) Les pompiers ont dû intervenir hier après-midi ...... Caluire, une petite ville .... de Lyon .... France, ... effectuer le sauvetage du chat de Madame Lafaille, 69 ans, domiciliée ..... Caluire. Coincé .... l'arbre, le chat de Madame Lafaille miaulait de peur. Heureusement, les pompiers sont arrivés ...... place très rapidement et Madame Lafaille a récupéré son chat sain et sauf !

2) Un cambriolage a eu lieu ..... une station service, hier matin .... Toulouse. Une fourgonnette blanche s'est arrêtée .... l'entrée de la station et 3 hommes armés ont fait irruption dans le magasin. Les trois cambrioleurs étaient cagoulés et portaient un pull noir ..... laine. Ils ont menacé les clients .... leurs armes et les ont obligés à s'allonger par terre .... la durée du cambriolage. Heureusement, personne n'a été blessé et tous les clients ont pu rentrer ..... eux dans la soirée.

3) Accident de la route mortel hier ...... l'autoroute du soleil .... Lyon et Grenoble. Un camion et une voiture sont entrés en collision. Le conducteur de la voiture est mort sur le coup. Le chauffeur de camion est resté coincé .... la roue de son véhicule. Les pompiers ont mis 3 heures à le dégager. Le chauffeur a été emmené ...... l'hôpital de Lyon mais ses jours ne sont pas en danger.

- To kick start your revisions, why don't you try and fill in the table below with form of the verbs in the present?
- Then check those verbs with a grammar book and add some more.

The present is essential and useful to form many other tenses so it is really a good place to start.

Au travail!

être	**avoir**	**aller**	**chanter**
Je **suis** Tu Il / elle / on Nous Vous Ils / elles	J' Tu Il / elle / on **a** Nous Vous Ils / elles	Je Tu Il / elle / on Nous Vous **allez** Ils / elles	Je **chante** Tu Il / elle / on Nous Vous Ils / elles
nager	**finir**	**partir**	**venir**
Je Tu Il / elle / on **nage** Nous Vous Ils / elles	Je Tu Il / elle / on Nous Vous Ils / elles **finissent**	Je Tu Il / elle / on Nous **partons** Vous **partez** Ils / elles **partent**	Je **viens** Tu Il / elle / on Nous Vous Ils / elles ***(tenir)***
faire	**lire**	**écrire**	**conduire**
Je Tu Il / elle / on Nous Vous Ils / elles	Je Tu Il / elle / on **lit** Nous Vous Ils / elles	J' **écris** Tu **écris** Il / elle / on **écrit** Nous Vous Ils / elles	Je **conduis** Tu Il / elle / on Nous Vous Ils / elles
boire	**voir**	**savoir**	**pouvoir**
Je Tu Il / elle / on **boit** Nous Vous Ils / elles	Je Tu Il / elle / on Nous **voyons** Vous Ils / elles	Je Tu Il / elle / on Nous **savons** Vous **savez** Ils / elles **savent**	Je **peux** Tu **peux** Il / elle / on **peut** Nous Vous Ils / elles
devoir	**vouloir**	**croire**	**apprendre**
Je Tu Il / elle / on Nous Vous Ils / elles	Je Tu Il / elle / on Nous Vous Ils / elles	Je Tu Il / elle / on Nous **croyons** Vous **croyez** Ils / elles **croient**	Je Tu Il / elle / on Nous **appre*n*ons** Vous **appre*nez*** Ils / elles **appre*nnent***

vendre Je vends Tu Il / elle / on Nous Vous Ils / elles	**ouvrir** J' ouvre Tu Il / elle / on ouvre Nous Vous Ils / elles *(offrir)*	**mettre** Je Tu Il / elle / on Nous Vous mettez Ils / elles *(permettre- soumettre)*	**rire** Je ris Tu Il / elle / on Nous Vous Ils / elles
courir Je cours Tu Il / elle / on Nous Vous Ils / elles	Je Tu Il / elle / on Nous Vous Ils / elles	Je Tu Il / elle / on Nous Vous Ils / elles	Je Tu Il / elle / on Nous Vous Ils / elles
Je Tu Il / elle / on Nous Vous Ils / elles	Je Tu Il / elle / on Nous Vous Ils / elles	J' Tu Il / elle / on Nous Vous Ils / elles	Je Tu Il / elle / on Nous Vous Ils / elles
Je Tu Il / elle / on Nous Vous Ils / elles	Je Tu Il / elle / on Nous Vous Ils / elles	Je Tu Il / elle / on Nous Vous Ils / elles	Je Tu Il / elle / on Nous Vous Ils / elles
Je Tu Il / elle / on Nous Vous Ils / elles	Je Tu Il / elle / on Nous Vous Ils / elles	Je Tu Il / elle / on Nous Vous Ils / elles	Je Tu Il / elle / on Nous Vous Ils / elles

As mentioned at the beginning of this unit, this guide is not a grammar book and its purpose is not to re-explain all the grammar to you. This is why only some essential grammar points have been covered in some detail but some others are missing.
Grammar is important at both level, SL and HL, even if a greater degree of both variety and accuracy is expected of HL students; if you want your message to be clear and your work to have a touch of fluency, you can't ignore grammar!

Good news!! It is never too late to practise and get better so don't panic.
If you have realised that you need to go back in more details and / or do more practice on some of the grammar points mentioned in the previous pages of this guide, just go and have a look at the reference section at the back as a few grammar reference books are listed there...and get started!

Always bear in mind that grammar is best revised in context so keep on reading too!

In addition...Make sure you keep some time at the end of your written exam in order to check your work thoroughly. Do the same for the *Written Task*.

And don't forget to.....

- **Use different verb tenses :** *présent, passé-composé, imparfait, futur, subjonctif, conditionnel…*
- **Vary your vocabulary and your structures**
- **Use link words to structure your work**
- **Check on your adjectives and past participle agreements**
- **Use comparisons**
- **Use adverbs**
- **Use pronouns**
- **Use relative clauses**
- **Use "si" clauses**
- **Check your prepositions**

And....**check your spelling too, for it does matter. Don't forget the accents!**

L'année dernière avant les examens j'étais stressée. La grammaire n'était pas mon point fort.
Il a fallu que je révise tous les temps et en particulier le subjonctif. Mais j'ai eu une bonne note alors crois-moi, réviser la grammaire, ça en vaut la peine !

Chapter 6

Vocabulary

In the same way as it is impossible to know all French vocabulary, it would be impossible to give you a list of all the words you might need to know for the exam. The aim of this guide is not to provide you with all of the answers but to point you in the right direction. It is also worth pointing out that acquiring a language is a "building" process and, hopefully, you have been meticulously listing all the new words that you have seen over the course of the past two years and learnt them!! So, it is just a question of revising them all, isn't it?

Below are some examples of topics that you can come across in the exam either in Paper 1 (based on the Core), or Paper 2 (based on the Options) or both as many topics are interrelated and can be studied in both the Core or the Options!

- La famille / les amis
- L'éducation
- La violence
- Les discriminations
- Les medias
- La faim dans le monde
- L'environnement
- Les loisirs et le sport
- La santé
- La technologie
- Les coutumes et traditions
- L'immigration
- La guerre
- Le terrorisme

Etc.

If you are desperately in need of specific vocabulary lists to help you revise and feel more confident, here is a suggestion of a useful vocabulary guide you might want to get hold of:

- ***Mot à Mot*** - Humberstone, P

However, you will undoubtedly encounter words that you have never seen before in the text handling paper. Don't panic, it is sometimes possible to guess the meaning of a word. When you encounter a word for the first time, it is essential to:

- look at the context as it might help you understand the word.
- have a close look at the word itself for it might be close to its English translation (eg. *une aventure = an adventure*) **BUT** again, don't neglect the context in order to avoid falling into the *faux-amis* trap (*eg: une journée = a day but a journey = un voyage*).
- the word might be close to another French word you know.

If all else fails, remember that it is not always essential to understand every single word in order to understand a text. As far as paper 2 is concerned, if you can't say it, say something else or say it differently! Don't get stuck on words and don't try and second guess; in paper 2 avoid using *franglais*!
In paper 1, **NEVER** neglect the context as a word can have a different meaning in different context. Don't just assume, **check** it!

As far as paper 2 is concerned, make sure that all the key words that appear in the question are used appropriately in your work. It really does not give a good impression to your examiner when you make a gender or a spelling mistake in your work when re-using one of the question's key words!! Start by making sure you know the French equivalent and their gender for each one of the type of texts.

- **un** journal intime – **Cher** journal,
- **un** article - dans **cet** article....
- **un** discours – le but de **ce** discours est de......
- **un** guide de recommandations – dans **ce** guide..... ***mais*** **une** brochure
- **un** rapport / **un** compte-rendu ***mais*** **une** déclaration
- **une** interview – dans **cette** interview....
- **une** lettre - Je me permets de vous écrire **cette** lettre pour vous exprimer .....
- **un** éditorial
- **une** dissertation

une revue de film

As you know, and as I have said before, trying to give you a complete vocabulary list is mission impossible. However, below are a few expressions / words / verbs etc... related to each one of the types of texts that you need to master for paper 2 purposes. These words and expressions are in no particular order and can be used and adapted to different topics. They complement the vocabulary that has already been covered in part 2 of this guide. I hope that they come in handy. But remember to be cautious when using colloquial or set expressions as, if they are inappropriately used (wrong context etc...), the impression of authenticity that the use of one might have given you will just serve to show that you have learnt them by heart and re-used them without really understanding what they mean and the cultural context within which they work. Remember that you can also make changes to these expressions to adapt them to what you want to say. They are not all set in stone.

NB: the abbreviation (*fam*) that you can see in brackets after certain words or expressions means that these words or expressions belong to the familiar register and are to be used in informal context only.

le journal intime

- **J'en ai marre!** (fam) / **j'en ai ras-le bol** (fam)– *I have had enough!*
- **Ça suffit!** – *It's enough!*
- **Pourquoi ça tombe toujours sur moi?** – *Why does it always have to be me/ happen to me ?!*
- **Il / elle m'énerve / ça m'énerve!** - *He / she / it gets on my nerves!*
- **Il me tape sur les nerfs !** – *He is getting on my nerves !*
- **Mes parents sont toujours sur mon dos** – *My parents are always on my back*
- **Ils ne peuvent pas me lâcher les baskets ?** (fam) – *Can't they leave me alone ?*
- **Mais qu'est-ce qu'ils ont tous à vouloir que je....** ! – *Why to they all want me to..... !*
- **Ils ne peuvent pas me ficher la paix ?!** – Can't they leave me alone ?!
- **Mes parents me prennent la tête / ça me prend la tête** – *My parents are doing my head in !/ It is doing my head in.*
- **Ils m'agacent**- *They annoy me*
- **Je n'en peux plus!** – *I can't bear it anymore ! / I have had enough !*
- **Je n'en reviens toujours pas!** – *I still can't believe it !*
- **Je suis trop content** – *I am extremely happy !*
- **Quelle galère** ! – *What a mess !*
- **Elle ne peut pas s'occuper de ses affaires / se mêler de ses oignons (fam) ?** – *Can't she mind her own business ?*
- **C'est l'enfer !** – *It is hell !*
- **C'est toujours la même histoire / la même chose (avec elle / lui / eux)!** – *It is always the same story / the same thing (with her / him / them)!*

L'article

- **les statistiques montrent que ....** – *the statistics show that............*
- **prouver** – *to prove*
- **d'après le reportage de** ..... – *according to X's report....*
- **Témoignages / propos recueillis par** – *statement taken by*
- **Selon** – *according to*
- **Des chiffres stables** – *stable figures*
- **Des chiffres fiables** – *reliable figures*
- **De source fiable** - *from a reliable source*
- **15% des personnes intérrogées se disent choquées par ....**- *15% of people interviewed say that they find it shoking that....*
- **un (recent) sondage** – *a (recent) survey*
- **Il va sans dire que**.....- *it goes without saying that....*

La lettre / le courriel

Lettre formelle :

To start a letter :

- **Je me permets de vous écrire pour** – *I am taking the liberty of writing to you in order to...*
- **Suite à l'annonce parue dans votre journal** – *following the announcement published in your newspaper*
- **Je vous écris pour postuler au poste de** ... - *I am writing to apply to the job of....*
- **Je vous écris pour vous remercier** – *I am writing to you to say thank you*
- **Je vous écris pour vous féliciter** – *I am writing to you to congratulate you*
- **Je vous écris pour vous exprimer mon mécontentement** - *...to express my dissatisfaction*
- **Je vous écris pour protester contre** - *........ to protest against*
- **Je vous écris pour vous informer que / de** - *........ to inform you that / of*
- **J'ai à me plaindre de** – *I have to complain about*

To end a letter : (to be used ***before / in conjunction*** with the "***formule de politesse***" ***NOT instead*** of)

- **J'espère que vous tiendrez compte de mes remarques pour la prochaine fois** – *I hope that you will consider my suggestions / comments for next time*
- **Dans l'attente de vous lire** – *in anticipation of your letter*
- **J'attends votre réponse avec impatience** – I am looking forward to your reply
- **Si vous avez besoin de renseignements complémentaires, n'hésitez pas à me contacter** – *if you need more information, do not hesitate to contact me.*

Others :

- **Comment osez-vous suggérer que...?** - *How can you dare suggesting that...?*
- **Comment pouvez-vous oser insinuer que ...?** – *How can you dare insinuating that... ?*

Lettre informelle :

To start a letter :

- **Comment ça va depuis la dernière fois ?** – *How have you been since last time?*
- **Alors quoi de neuf depuis la dernière fois ?** (fam) – *So what's new / up since last time ?*
- **Je m'excuse de ne pas t'avoir écrit plutôt...** - *I apologise for not writing to you sooner*

To end a letter :

- **J'attends de tes nouvelles avec impatience** – *I am looking forward to receiving your news*
- **J'attends ta lettre avec impatience**- *I am looking forward to receiving your letter*
- **Écris / réponds-moi vite!** – *write back soon!*
- **A bientôt** – *See you soon*
- **J'espère te lire bientôt** – *I hope to read you soon*
- **Gros bisous / je t'embrasse** – *Kiss kiss (XXX)*
- **Amitiés** –

PS: *There is no need to finish your letters with XX in French as it does not mean anything to a French person.*

Le discours

- **Chers / chères collègues** – *Dear colleagues*
- **Chers amis / camarades** – *Dear friends / comrades*
- **Je suis ici aujourd'hui pour** – *I am here today to*
- **Je vais vous parler de** – *I am going to talk to you about*
- **Je vais vous présenter** - *I am going to present / introduce to you*
- **Le sujet dont je vais vous parler aujourd'hui...**- *The topic that I am going to talk to you about today….*
- **J'aimerais maintenant aborder la question du racisme dans notre société**- *I would now like to talk about racism in our society*
- **Laissez-moi vous décrire la situation…**- Let me describe to you the situation…
- **Imaginez…..**- *Imagine…*
- **Considérons maintenant la question du racisme** – *Let's now take into consideration the problem of racism*
- **C'est la raison pour laquelle nous ne pouvons rester passif face à une telle menace**- *It is the reason why we cannot remain passive when confronted by such a threat*
- **C'est en connaissance de cause que je.......** - *It is in full knowledge that I ….*
- **En tant que délégué des élèves…..** - *as the students' representative….*
- **Je vous remercie pour votre attention**- *Thank you for your attention*
- **Je voudrais vous remercier pour l'intérêt que vous portez à ce problème** – *I would like to thank you for your interest regarding this problem.*

Le guide de recommandation / la brochure

- **Il vaut mieux que + subjonctif** – *It is better if*
  → *Il vaut mieux que ne vous contredisiez pas vos parents lorsqu'ils sont fatigués même si vous pensez qu'ils ont tort !*
- **Il vaudrait mieux que + subjonctif** – *It would be better if*
- **Sache que … / Sachez que….**- *Know that…..*
  → *Sachez que 30 minutes d'activité physique par jour suffisent à réduire vos risques de maladies cardio-vasculaires de 30%.*
- **Il est indispensable / essentiel / primordial / utile / inutile de + infinitif** – *It is indispensable / essential / useful / useless*
  → *Il est essentiel de dormir au moins 8 heures par nuit.*
- **Il est urgent / nécessaire / utile etc… que + subjonctif** – *It is urgent necessary / useful that...*
  → *Il est urgent que le gouvernement prenne des mesures concrètes pour résoudre la crise des banlieues.*
- **Les chiffres le prouvent** – *statistics prove it.*
- **D'après un sondage réalisé par…**- *According to a survey led by…*
- **L'enquête menée par des diététiciens a montré que 30% des adolescents interrogés se nourrissaient mal** – *the survey led by dieteticians has shown that 30% of teenagers questioned had bad eating habits.*
- **Démonstration en dix points** –*Demonstration in ten steps! (can be used as a title or sub-title before giving a list of actions to take for example)*
- **Par exemple** – *for example*
- **Le saviez-vous? / Le savais-tu?** – *Did you know? (can be useful as a sub-heading)*
- **Pour le savoir, réponds / répondez aux questions suivantes** – *to know the answer, just answer the following questions*
- **Faites / fais le sondage ci-dessous** – *Take part in the survey below*
- **Ne pas + infinitif mais + infinitif** – *Not……. but…..(can be used as effective sub-headings for pargraphs)*
  Ne pas interdire mais limiter. (not forbidding but restricting)
- **Pour plus d'informations / pour en savoir plus rendez-vous sur le site www.jeréussismonBI.fr** – *for more information consult the site…..*

La revue / critique de film

Most of the expressions of opinion given below (*in the book critic section*) can also be used and adapted to the film review. However, some of the specific film vocabulary will have to be used. Here are some of the most useful ones.

un acteur / une actrice	*an actor / an actress*
jouer / interpréter un rôle	*to play a role / a part*
le jeu des acteurs	*the portrayal of a role*
le metteur en scène	*the producer*
le réalisateur	*the director*
le scénario	*the script*
le décor	*the set*
les dialogues	*the dialogues*
l'intrigue	*the plot*
les cascades	*the stunts*
un cascadeur / une cascadeuse	*Stuntman /stuntwoman*
une star de cinéma	*a film star*
une personne célèbre / une vedette	*A celebrity*
la renommée	*fame / celebrity*
l'adaptation cinématographique d'un roman	*the screen adaptation of a novel*

If you are referring to a television programme, below are just a few more key words.

une émission (télévisée)	*a TV programme*
l'heure de grande écoute	*prime time*
une chaîne de télévision	*a TV channel*
un feuilleton	*A soap*
un épisode	*an episode*

<u>+ Get it right.... :</u>
Hier j'ai regardé un dessin animé (a *cartoon*) **<u>à la</u>** télévision.

L'interview

- **Pourriez-vous nous parler de ...**-*Could you talk to us about*
- **interrompre quelqu'un-** *to interrupt someone*
- **une rumeur-** *a rumour*
- **Qu'en pensent vos proches ? –** *What does your family think of...?*
- **contredire quelqu'un-** *to contradict someone*
- **Quels conseils donneriez-vous à nos lecteurs? –** *What advice would you give to our readers ?*
- **Quel a été le moment fort de votre carrière ?-** *What has been the highlight of your career ?*
- **une entrevue exclusive / un entretien exclusif-** *an exclusive interview*

La brochure / le tract / l'appel

Again, for these types of text, refer back to the "*guide de recommandations*" and speech sections for some of the essential items and vocabulary and structures that you may need have already been provided in these sections.

La dissertation

A "dissertation" can be on any given topic, therefore it is impossible to give you all the specific vocabulary that you may need. However, you will need some essential link words to structure your argumentation. Although most of those link / transition words have already been given to you in another section, below is a short list of the main ones.

- **en effet-** *indeed*
- **premièrement / d'abord-** *firstly*
- **deuxièmement / troisièmement...-** *secondly / thirdly ...*
- **cependant / toutefois-** *however*
- **par ailleurs / en outre-** *moreover*
- **bien que** + subjonctif- *although*
- **par exemple-** *for example*
- **en conclusion / pour conclure-** *in conclusion*
- **c'est la raison pour laquelle-** *this is the reason why*
- **ce phénomène peut être expliqué par-** *this phenomenon can be explained by...*
- **dans ce livre, il s'agit de-** *this book is about...*
- **le thème / l'argument principal est... -** *the main theme / topic / argument is*
- **une preuve / prouver-** *a proof / to prove*
- **cet argument peut facilement être réfuté-** *this argument can easily be dismissed*
- **cet argument n'est pas valide / ne tient pas la route-** *this argument is not valid*

La proposition raisonnée

For this type of text refer back to both the speech and essay sections.

A few more in order to give you more choice for the Written Assignment

Le récit d'imagination / d'invention / suite d'un chapitre (HL)

As this is an invented story, the vocabulary that you are going to need will depend on the creative task you are trying to come up with for your Written Assignment. . It is therefore virtually impossible to give you any particular item of vocabulary. Just remember that you will need to use lots of **link words** to create a sense of chronology / fear / suspense etc... Refer back to Section 2F of this guide as all of these tools have been given to you there. Remember to use as varied a vocabulary as possible.

Le compte rendu

Same comment as above as it will mainly depend on the context. However, below is a list of a few context-specific words or expressions, but it is certainly not an exhaustive list...far from it!

- **une activité** – *an activity*
- **participer à** - *to take part in*
- **un projet** - *a project*
- **mener un projet à bien** – *to realise / complete a project*
- **collecter de l'argent / des fonds** – *to collect money / funds*
- **une association caritative** – *a charity*
- **faire du bénévolat / être bénévole** - *to work for a charity / a charity worker*
- **organiser un événement** - *to organise an event*
- **assister à un concert** – *to attend a concert*
- **faire de la publicité pour un événement**- *to publicise an event*
- **faire / mener une enquête** – *to lead a survey*
- **se joindre à / rejoindre un groupe / une organisation etc.** ...- *to join a group...*
- **s'inscrire à** – *to enrol*
- **être responsable de** – *to be responsible for*

La déclaration à la police

Again, not a lot of specific vocabulary can be provided here (same for the "anecdocte"). However, below are just a few words which may prove useful.

- **être victime de / une victime** – *to be the victim of / a victim*
- **un témoin** - *a witness*
- **un témoignage / une déclaration** – *a witness statement*
- **un accident** - *an accident*
- **un incident** – *an incident*
- **un meurtre** - *a murder*
- **un vol** – *a theft*
- **une aggression** – *an attack on someone*

Top 15 useful vocabulary items per topic !

As you know, it is impossible to give you all the vocabulary that you may need for the final exam. Equally, as this guide is only a revision guide, your bank of vocabulary should be quite substantial by now at this stage of the revision process....The next few pages are intending to remind you of some essential vocabulary items per topics like *family, education* and so on.
Again, it is impossible to cover all the potential topics and remember that this list is far from being exhaustive. I have made some suggestions of more comprehensive vocabulary books that you may want to use (*refer to resources pages*) and don't forget either that vocabulary only really comes to life in context so keep on reading and refer back to the examples of texts provided in section 1 and 2 of this guide too!
This list may also prompt you about some of the issues you can go and read article about before the exam!
Note that when a word / verb etc....belongs to the familiar register, it will be followed by the following (fam).

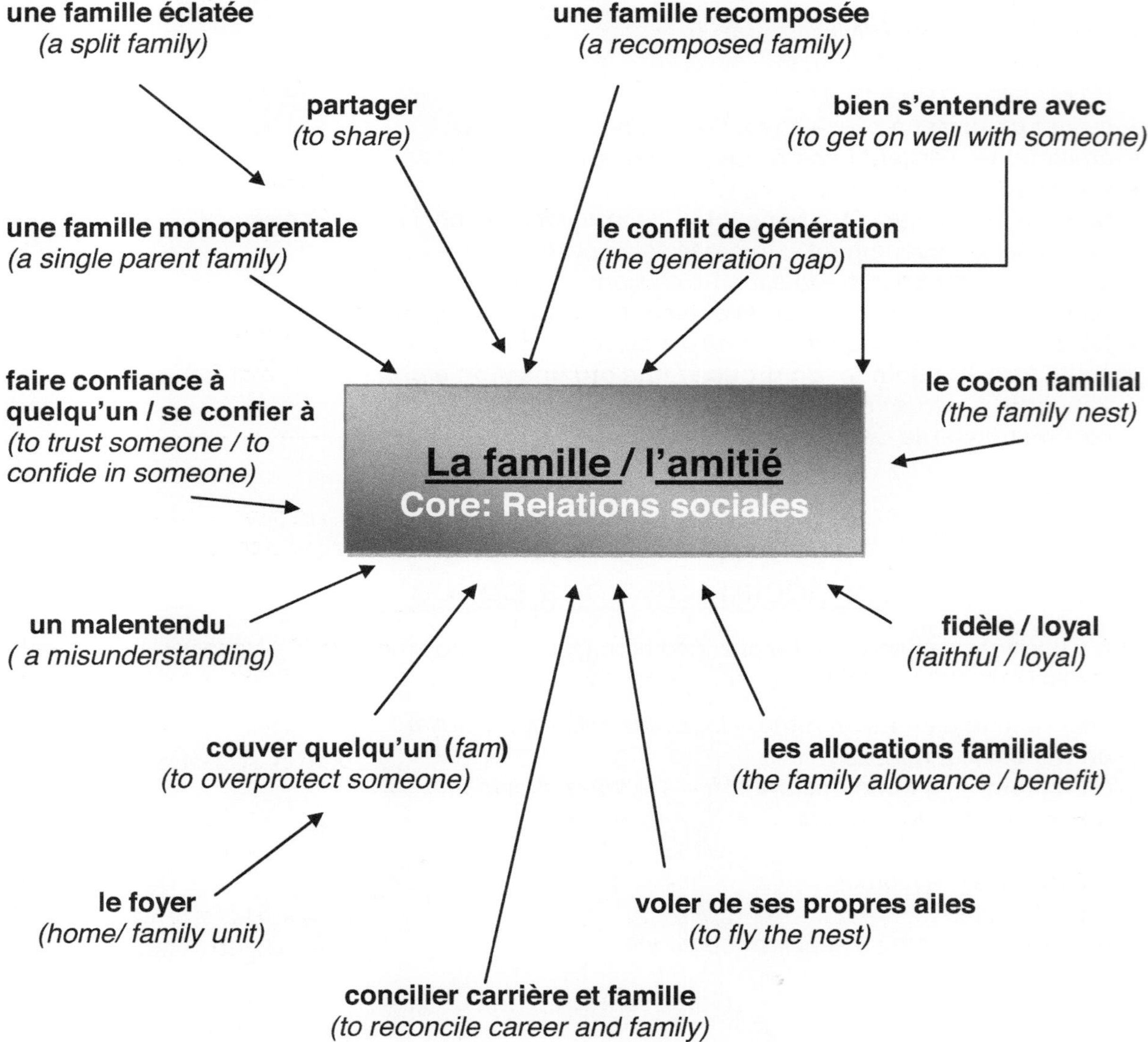

Sports et loisirs
Options: loisirs

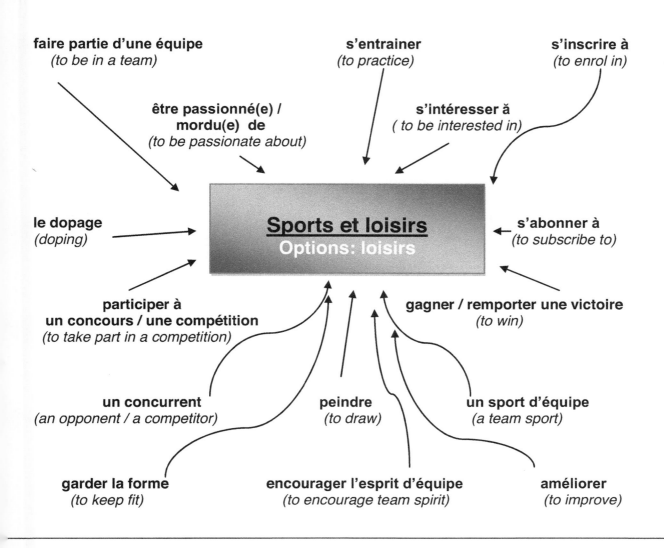

- **faire partie d'une équipe** *(to be in a team)*
- **s'entrainer** *(to practice)*
- **s'inscrire à** *(to enrol in)*
- **être passionné(e) / mordu(e) de** *(to be passionate about)*
- **s'intéresser ă** *(to be interested in)*
- **le dopage** *(doping)*
- **s'abonner à** *(to subscribe to)*
- **participer à un concours / une compétition** *(to take part in a competition)*
- **gagner / remporter une victoire** *(to win)*
- **un concurrent** *(an opponent / a competitor)*
- **peindre** *(to draw)*
- **un sport d'équipe** *(a team sport)*
- **garder la forme** *(to keep fit)*
- **encourager l'esprit d'équipe** *(to encourage team spirit)*
- **améliorer** *(to improve)*

L'éducation
Core: relations sociales

- **Le lycée / le bahut** (*fam*) *(secondary school)*
- **le taux d'absentéisme** *(number of students absent)*
- **un pion** (*fam*) *(a supervisor)*
- **être renvoyé** *(to be expelled)*
- **redoubler** *(to repeat a class)*
- **sécher les cours** *(to skive)*
- **un emploi du temps** *(a timetable)*
- **le bulletin de notes** *(report)*
- **la réunion de parents** *(parents evening)*
- **le conseiller d'orientation** *(the career advisor)*
- **l'égalité des chances** *(equality of opportunities)*
- **l'internat (être interne)** *(the boarding house / to be a boarder)*
- **être en retenue / en colle** (*fam*) *(to be in detention)*
- **les examen blancs** *(mock exams)*
- **la scolarité** *(schooling)*

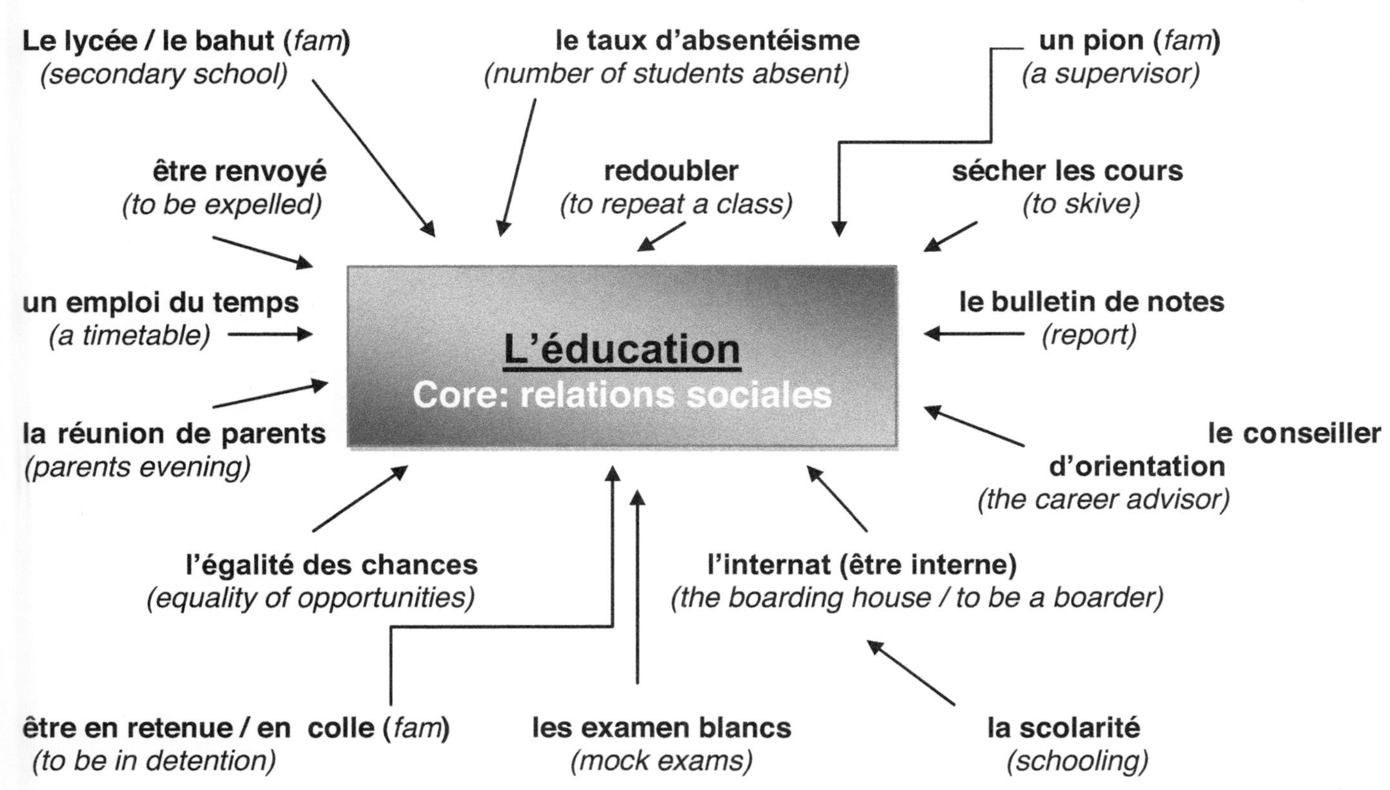

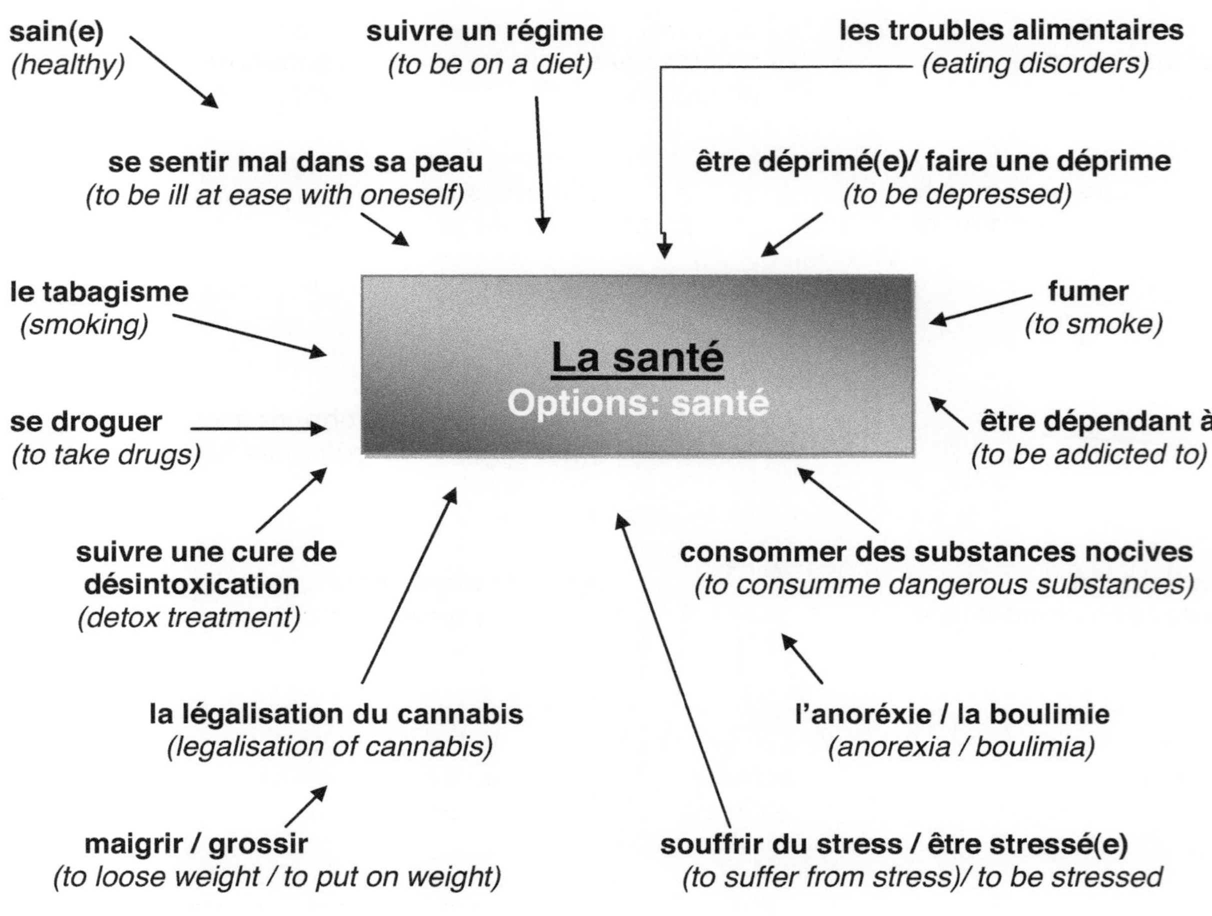
sain(e)
(healthy)
suivre un régime
(to be on a diet)
les troubles alimentaires
(eating disorders)
se sentir mal dans sa peau
(to be ill at ease with oneself)
être déprimé(e)/ faire une déprime
(to be depressed)
le tabagisme
(smoking)
La santé
Options: santé
fumer
(to smoke)
se droguer
(to take drugs)
être dépendant à
(to be addicted to)
suivre une cure de
désintoxication
(detox treatment)
consommer des substances nocives
(to consumme dangerous substances)
la légalisation du cannabis
(legalisation of cannabis)
l'anoréxie / la boulimie
(anorexia / boulimia)
maigrir / grossir
(to loose weight / to put on weight)
souffrir du stress / être stressé(e)
(to suffer from stress)/ to be stressed

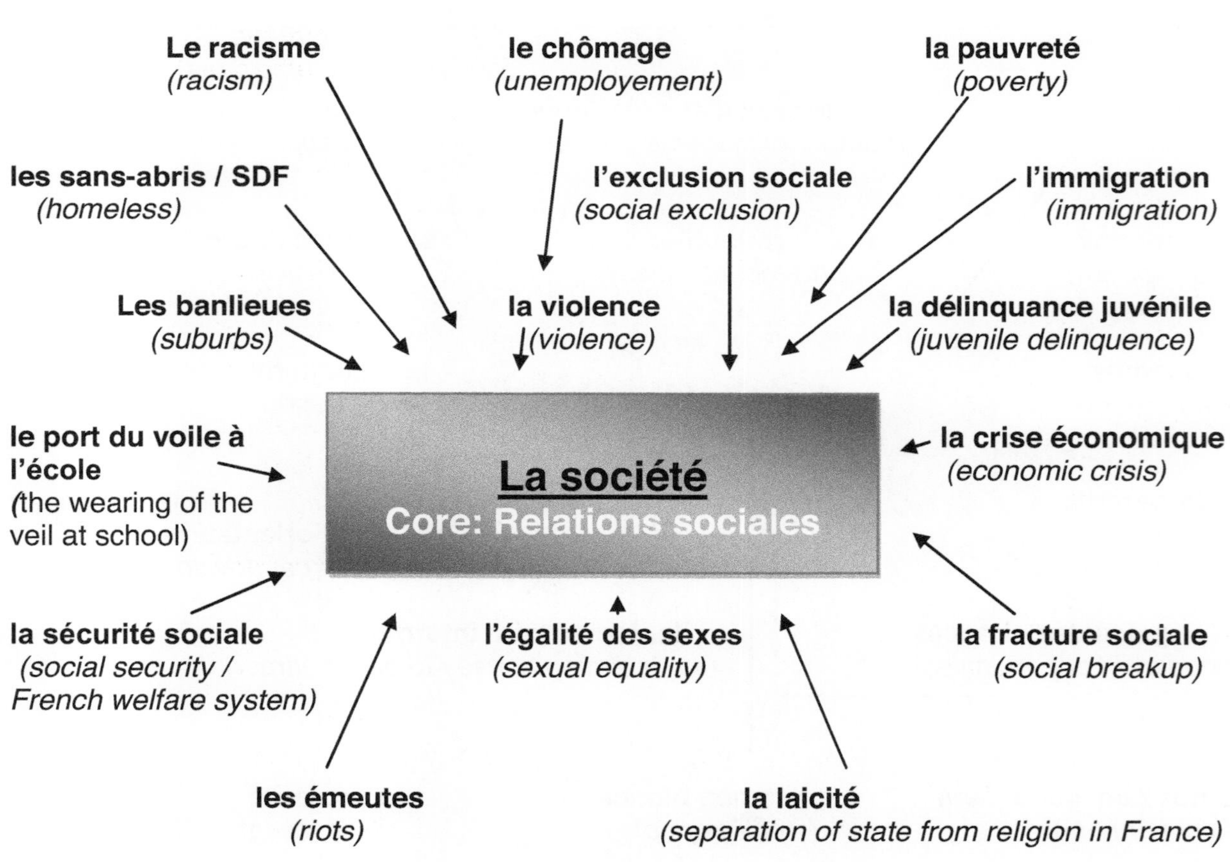
Le racisme
(racism)
le chômage
(unemployement)
la pauvreté
(poverty)
les sans-abris / SDF
(homeless)
l'exclusion sociale
(social exclusion)
l'immigration
(immigration)
Les banlieues
(suburbs)
la violence
(violence)
la délinquance juvénile
(juvenile delinquence)
le port du voile à
l'école
(the wearing of the
veil at school)
La société
Core: Relations sociales
la crise économique
(economic crisis)
la sécurité sociale
(social security /
French welfare system)
l'égalité des sexes
(sexual equality)
la fracture sociale
(social breakup)
les émeutes
(riots)
la laicité
(separation of state from religion in France)

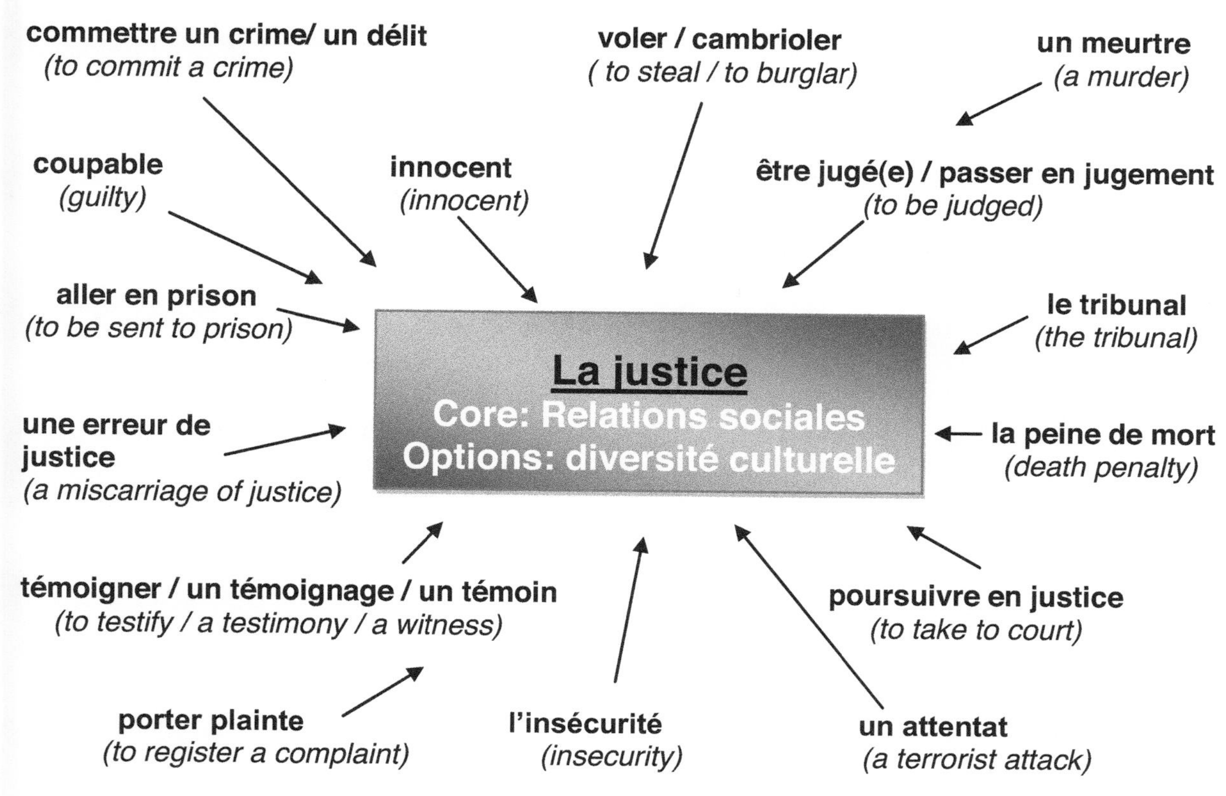
commettre un crime/ un délit
(to commit a crime)
voler / cambrioler
(to steal / to burglar)
un meurtre
(a murder)
coupable
(guilty)
innocent
(innocent)
être jugé(e) / passer en jugement
(to be judged)
aller en prison
(to be sent to prison)
le tribunal
(the tribunal)
La justice
Core: Relations sociales
Options: diversité culturelle
une erreur de justice
(a miscarriage of justice)
la peine de mort
(death penalty)
témoigner / un témoignage / un témoin
(to testify / a testimony / a witness)
poursuivre en justice
(to take to court)
porter plainte
(to register a complaint)
l'insécurité
(insecurity)
un attentat
(a terrorist attack)

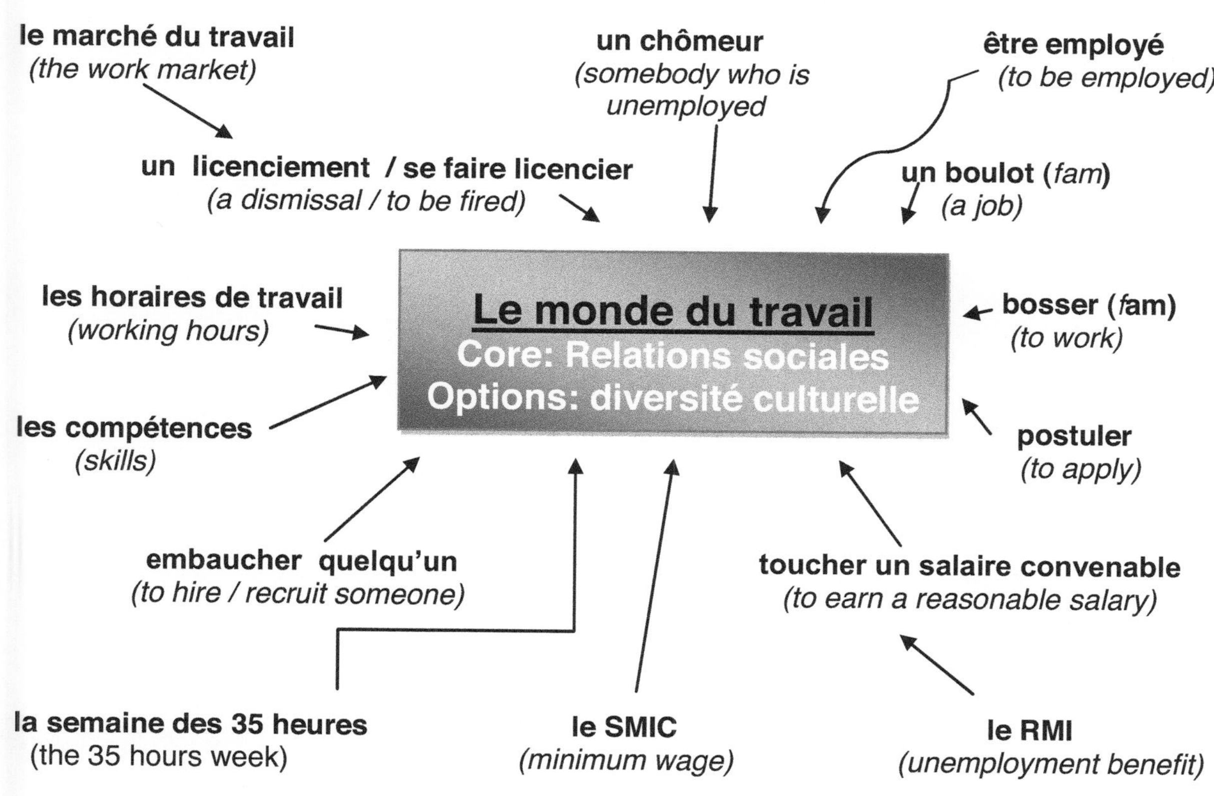
le marché du travail
(the work market)
un chômeur
(somebody who is unemployed
être employé
(to be employed)
un licenciement / se faire licencier
(a dismissal / to be fired)
un boulot (fam)
(a job)
les horaires de travail
(working hours)
Le monde du travail
Core: Relations sociales
Options: diversité culturelle
bosser (fam)
(to work)
les compétences
(skills)
postuler
(to apply)
embaucher quelqu'un
(to hire / recruit someone)
toucher un salaire convenable
(to earn a reasonable salary)
la semaine des 35 heures
(the 35 hours week)
le SMIC
(minimum wage)
le RMI
(unemployment benefit)

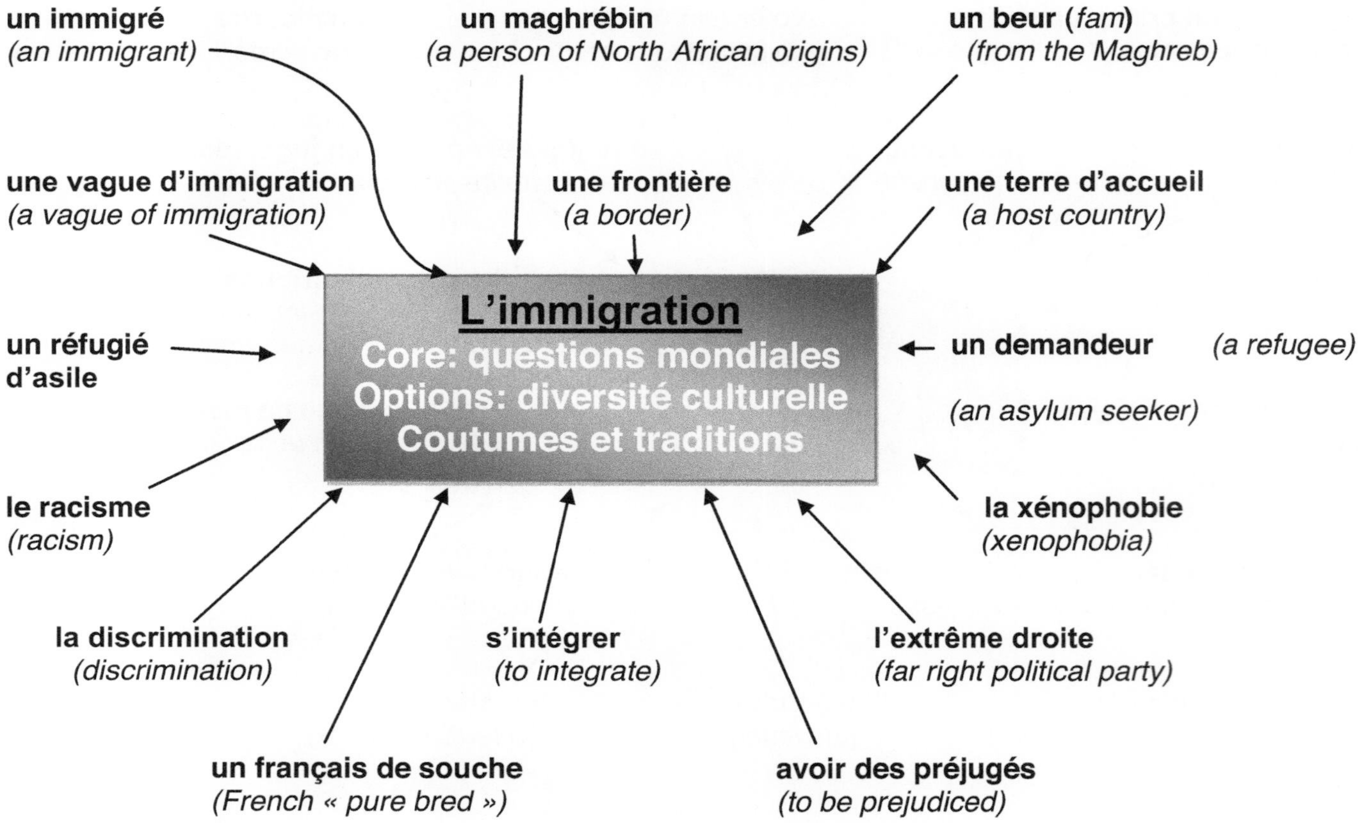

un immigré
(an immigrant)

un maghrébin
(a person of North African origins)

un beur (*fam*)
(from the Maghreb)

une vague d'immigration
(a vague of immigration)

une frontière
(a border)

une terre d'accueil
(a host country)

L'immigration

Core: questions mondiales
Options: diversité culturelle
Coutumes et traditions

un réfugié *(a refugee)*

un demandeur d'asile
(an asylum seeker)

le racisme
(racism)

la xénophobie
(xenophobia)

la discrimination
(discrimination)

s'intégrer
(to integrate)

l'extrême droite
(far right political party)

un français de souche
(French « pure bred »)

avoir des préjugés
(to be prejudiced)

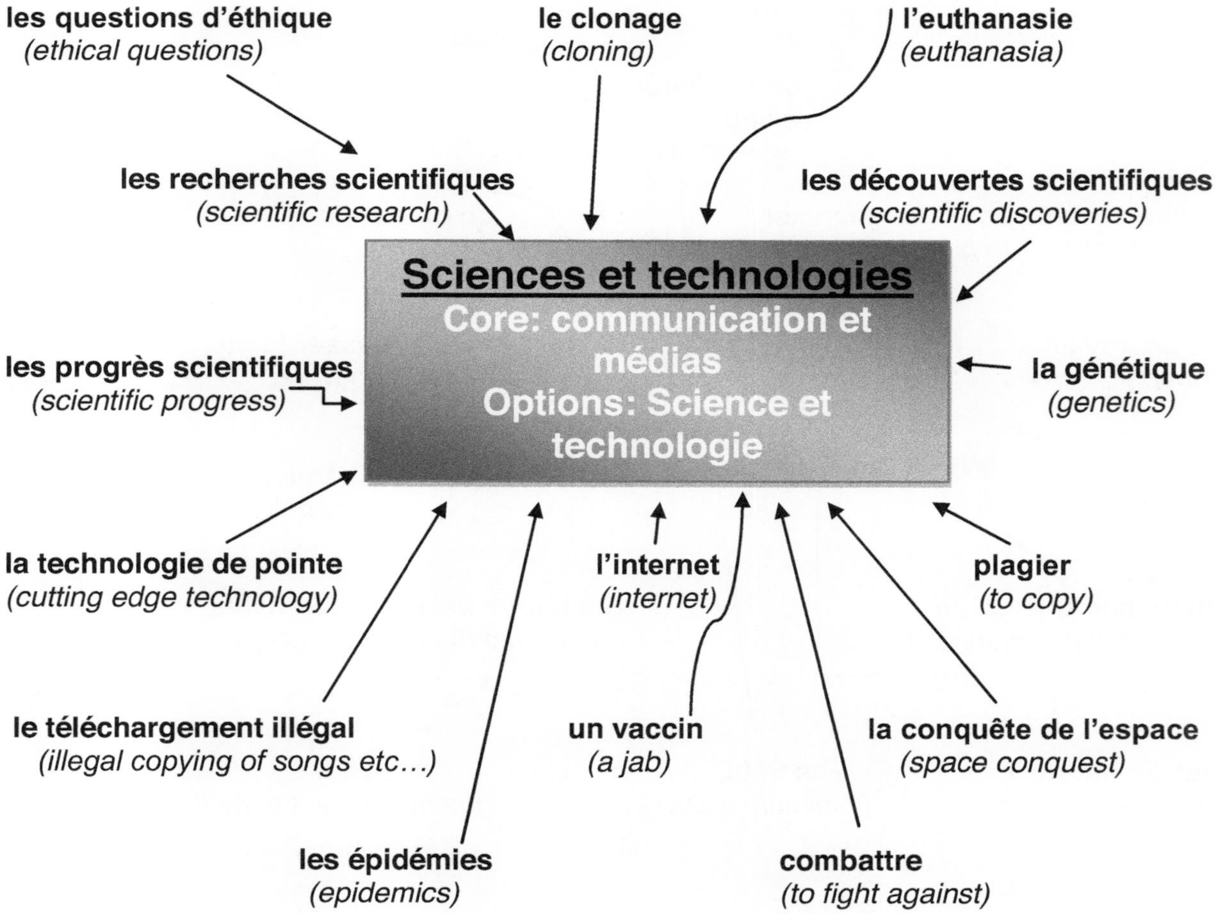

---

les questions d'éthique
(ethical questions)

le clonage
(cloning)

l'euthanasie
(euthanasia)

les recherches scientifiques
(scientific research)

les découvertes scientifiques
(scientific discoveries)

Sciences et technologies

Core: communication et médias
Options: Science et technologie

les progrès scientifiques
(scientific progress)

la génétique
(genetics)

la technologie de pointe
(cutting edge technology)

l'internet
(internet)

plagier
(to copy)

le téléchargement illégal
(illegal copying of songs etc…)

un vaccin
(a jab)

la conquête de l'espace
(space conquest)

les épidémies
(epidemics)

combattre
(to fight against)

*As I said previously, it is impossible to cover all the potential topics that might come up in the exam (*be it at SL or HL levels*) but these mini-lists should have given you pointers and ideas of what to revise. They should at the very least be a starting point. Remember also that spelling does matter and that it is important to learn the gender of nouns too.*
I am now going to finish with one more topic: L'environnement*; and as there are so many topics that can be covered within this notion, I will give you 25 words instead of 15. Again, it is only a starting point and the rest is for you to do! So let's get cracking!*

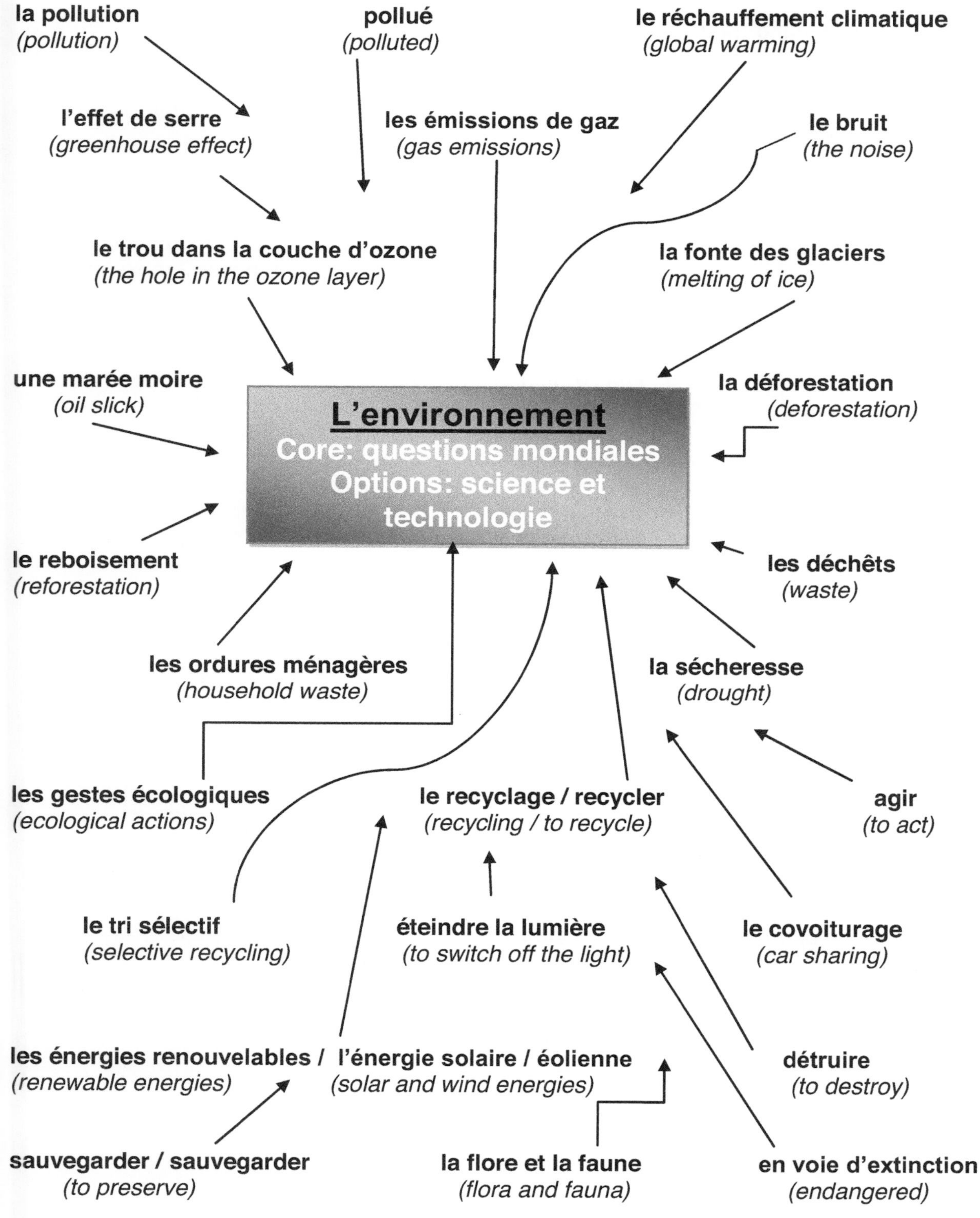

Some useful tips to improve the quality of your written work

- **avoid repetition**

Avoid using the same words and expressions all of the time. Try and impress your examiner by varying your language. Use synonyms when possible. When you learn new words, you should aim to learn one or two synonyms at the same time wherever possible.

- **make sure you are using the right register**

Remember that you must always make sure that you identify your targeted audience (*paper 2*) and use the appropriate vocabulary (*see page on registers*). Remember that using the right register not only means paying attention to your use of the "je" and "vous" but it also means choosing the right register of vocabulary (formal / informal and familiar).

- **Pay attention to the meaning of words in context**

Remember that words can have different meanings. Make sure that you check the word in the context in which it is used in paper 1. Equally, ensures that the words that you are using in paper 2 make sense in the context.

- **avoid overusing the verbs "*avoir*" / "*être*" / "*faire*" or "dire"**

In your written work, it is always tempting to use the verbs *avoir* / *être* / *faire* or *dire* and sometimes, they are indeed the only option. However, they tend to be overused and often a better and more precise verb or expression could be used. It is important that you show off your vocabulary knowledge in the exam. After all, you have been studying French for a while now and you should be able to use a wide range of vocabulary. If you are a HL candidate, again, even more will be expected of you in this area.
Below are a few random examples of expressions using verbs other than the 4 commonly used ones.

faire quelque chose pour sauver la planète	***agir*** pour la sauvegarde de la planète
faire un métier	***exercer*** un métier
avoir une mauvaise influence sur quelqu'un	***exercer*** une mauvaise influence
avoir une lettre/ un cadeau de quelqu'un	***recevoir*** une lettre / un cadeau de quelqu'un
avoir l'argent nécessaire	**disposer** de l'argent nécessaire
essayer d'*avoir* quelque chose	essayer de ***se procurer*** ou d'***obtenir*** quelque chose
être dans un club de rugby	***appartenir à / faire partie d'***un club de rugby
avoir une bonne note	***obtenir*** une bonne note
dire son avis / opinion	***donner / exprimer*** son avis / son opinion
faire un trou dans le sol	***creuser*** un trou dans le sol

Let's practise !

In each sentence, replace the verb « *passe-partout* » for a better, more precise one. All the verbs are provided in the circle underneath the sentences. You may need to adjust the sentence slightly in some cases (*sentences marked with an asterisk*)

1) C'est moi qui ***fais*** le repas ce soir. ________________

2) Ma meilleure amie m'***a dit*** un secret. ________________

3) Il ***a fait*** une erreur en l'invitant à cette soirée ! ________________

4) Les résultats du concours ***seront dits*** à la radio. ____________

5) Je ne ***suis*** pas du tout de votre avis ! ________________

6) Je crois qu'il ***est*** bien dans sa peau. Il n'a aucun complexe. En plus, je crois qu'il est amoureux en ce moment. Il ***a*** des sentiments pour ta sœur. ____________ / ____________

7) Pendant la Seconde Guerre Mondiale, il était difficile d'***avoir*** des denrées de base comme le sucre. ________________

8) Je ne sais pas pourquoi, journal, mais mes parents me ***font*** toujours la vie dure ! ________________

9) Ça n'a pas été facile mais il s'***est*** enfin ***fait*** à son nouveau lycée. ________________

10) Puis-je ***faire quelque chose*** pour vous ?* ________________

11) Le tremblement de terre ***a fait*** beaucoup de dégâts. __________

12) Je suis collé vendredi soir. Il va maintenant falloir que je ***dise*** la mauvaise nouvelle à mes parents. Je vais sûrement ne pas ***avoir le droit*** de sortir samedi* ____________ / ____________

- aider - partager - mener - révéler -
- causer - éprouver - s'habituer - annoncer -
- commettre - priver - préparer - se sentir -
- annoncer / avouer - se procurer -

- **colloquial / set expressions / idioms**

As we have seen before, colloquial expressions can be useful and you now have a few up your sleeves if needs be. However, although using colloquial expressions can demonstrate a good knowledge and understanding of the language and demonstrate a certain fluency in the use and mastery of that language, it is important to make sure that you understand them well before you use them. You should always learn them in context for it might not always be possible to use them in all situations. Furthermore, some will be for use in a familiar context only while others will be to be used in a formal context. Before you use them inappropriately, you must be sure of what they mean and how to use them. If you are unsure, then don't use them…and whatever you do, avoid overusing them!
***NB**: Below are a few idiomatic / set expressions. Ideally, it would be better to look at them in context but this is not the purpose of this guide, and, again, if you feel that you need more, go and have a look at the pointers given in the reference section.*

Let's practise!

Match each expression to its English translation. *(again, they are in no particular order and the list is far from being exhaustive!)- **NB**: (fam) indicates that the expression is best only used in a familiar context.*

1) **passer un savon à quelqu'un** *(fam)* ☐
2) **casser du sucre sur le dos de quelqu'un** *(fam)* ☐
3) **jeter l'argent par les fenêtres** ☐
4) **c'est la goutte qui fait déborder le vase** *(fam)* ☐
5) **couper l'herbe sous le pied de quelqu'un** ☐
6) **avoir mangé du lion** ☐
7) **poser un lapin à quelqu'un** *(fam)* ☐
8) **manger sur le pouce** ☐
9) **avoir un poil dans la main** *(fam)* ☐
10) **se mettre le doigt dans l'œil** *(fam)* ☐
11) **brûler les étapes** ☐
12) **avoir le cafard** *(fam)* ☐
13) **(c'est) une histoire à dormir debout** ☐
14) **passer au peigne fin** ☐
15) **payer les pots cassés** ☐

a) to be full of energy
b) to have a quick snack
c) a tell tale
d) to pull the rug from under someone's feet
e) to rush into something
f) It is the last straw
g) to tell someone off
h) to be depressed / down
i) to search thoroughly
j) to suffer the consequences
k) to talk about someone behind their back
l) to be lazy
m) to waste money
n) to be mistaken / wrong
o) to stand someone up

Le français, *c'est le pied*!

Mais si tu penses que tu vas réussir sans réviser…tu ***te mets le doigt dans l'œil*** !

- **Faux amis**

Be aware of words that we commonly called "*faux amis*" in French. They are those words that sound like an English word (*and sometimes they are also spelt the same way!*) but have a different meaning altogether. A good knowledge of these subtleties of the language will demonstrate your degree of mastery of the language. You will also have to be wary of them in paper 1 for a misinterpretation of such a "*faux ami*" could result in you missing the point in one of the passages. Again, remember to double check the meaning of the words in context.

français	*anglais*		**français**	*anglais*
achever = to finish / to end		**vs**	**réussir** = to achieve	
actuellement = currently		**vs**	**en fait / en réalité** = actually	
un agenda = a diary		**vs**	**un ordre du jour** = un agenda	
attendre = to wait		**vs**	**assister à** = to attend + aider quelqu'un = to assist someone	
une attente = an expectation		**vs**	**un essai** = an attempt	
un avertissement = a warning		**vs**	**une publicité**= an advertisement	
un bonnet = a woolly hat		**vs**	**un capot** = a bonnet	
un caractère = a personality		**vs**	**un personnage** = a character	
un chandelier= a candle stick		**vs**	**un lustre** = a chandelier	
consistant = of substance		**vs**	**coherent**= consistent	
un coin= a corner		**vs**	**une pièce de monnaie** = a coin	
décevoir = to disappoint		**vs**	**tromper** = to deceive	
une journée = a day		**vs**	**un voyage / un trajet** = a journey	
une librairie = a bookshop		**vs**	**une bibliothèque** = a library	
une location = a hire		**vs**	**un endroit / une place** = a location	
marcher = to walk		**vs**	**défiler** = to march / to demonstrate	
une occasion = an opportunity		**vs**	**un événement** = an occasion	
onéreux = expensive		**vs**	**pénible / lourd** = onerous	
un préjudice = damage		**vs**	**un préjugé** = a prejudice	
sensible = sensitive		**vs**	**sensé** = sensible	

The A to Z of some of the most useful verbs

A

- **abimer**: *to damage*
- **abriter**: *to shelter*
- **aggraver**: *to make worse*
- **améliorer**: *to improve*
- **appréhender**: *to arrest*
- **atteindre**: *to reach*

B

- **bannir**: *to ban*
- **bouger**: *to move*
- **bricoler**: *to DIY*

C

- **cacher**: *to hide*
- **craindre**: *to fear*
- **corrompre**: *to corrupt*

D

- **déménager**: *to move house*
- **diffuser**: *to broadcast*
- **dramatiser**: *to make a fuss*

E

- **emprunter**: *to borrow*
- **éviter**: *to avoid*
- **exprimer**: *to express*

F

- **frimer** (*fam*) : *to show off*
- **freiner**: *to slow down or brake*

G

- **gagner** :*to win*
- **garder**: *to keep*
- **grandir**: *to grow up*
- **grignoter**: *to nibble / to snack*
- **gronder**: *to tell a child off*

H

- **heurter**; *to hit*
- **hospitaliser**: *to send / admit to hospital*

I

- **ignorer**: *to ignore*
- **inventer**: *to invent*

J

- **jardiner**: *to do the gardening*
- **jeter**: *to throw (away)*

K

- **kidnapper**: *to kidnap*

L

- **lier**: *to link*
- **louer:** *to rent or praise*

M

- **mentir**: *to lie*
- **menacer**: *to threaten*

N

- **nier**: *to deny*
- **nourrir**: *to feed*

O

- **obliger**: *to force*
- **offenser**: *to offend*
- **oublier**: *to forget*

P

- **pleurer**: *to cry*
- **prévenir**: *to warn*

Q

- **questionner**: *to question*

R

- **réagir:** *to react*
- **réchauffer**: *to warm up*
- **reconnaitre**: to recognise
- **redouter**: *to fear*

S

- **sécher les cours** : *to skive*
- **soumettre**: *to submit*
- **soutenir** : *to support*
- **suivre**: *to follow*
- **surveiller**: *to watch / observe*

T

- **terminer**: *to end*
- **terroriser** : *to terrorise*
- **trouver** : *to find*

U

- **unir**: *to unit*
- **utiliser** : *to use*

V

- **vaincre**: *to overcome*
- **varier**: *to vary*
- **venir** : *to come*
- **vomir**: *to throw up*

W

n/a

X

n/a

Y

n/a

Z

- **zapper**: *to change channels*

The top 10 common mistakes... that *you* won't make!!

1) the word ***problème*** is masculine - ***un problème*** → Hier, j'ai eu ***un problème*** avec mon ordinateur.
2) s'habiller *means to get dressed BUT* **habiter** *means to live* → Elle ***s'habille*** toujours en noir; c'est triste. → Elle ***habite*** dans un petit appartement avec sa famille.
3) entendre means *to hear* BUT **écouter** means *to listen* → ***J'ai entendu*** dire qu'un nouvel hôtel allait bientôt être construit près de la plage. *I heard that a new hotel was soon to be built near the beach.* → Il ***écoute*** toujours de la musique classique quand il travaille. *He always listens to classical music when he works.*
4) connaître and **savoir** both mean *to know*. However, you can't use one for the other. • ***Connaître*** *is used with a place and / or a person* → Est-ce que tu ***connais*** un bon restaurant où on peut aller manger ce soir ? Je ***connais*** quelqu'un qui pourrait vous renseigner. • ***Savoir*** *- is often used on its own when you are giving an answer to a question* (I know !) → A quelle heure est-elle rentrée hier soir ? – Je ne ***sais*** pas. J'étais sorti aussi. - *It is also used in conjonction with* ***qui, que, quand, où, comment, pourquoi.*** → Je ne ***sais*** pas pourquoi ils n'ont pas voulu venir à la soirée. (*I don't know why she did not want to come last night)* Vous ***saviez*** que le cannabis pouvait avoir un effet nocif sur la santé ? *(Did you know that cannabis could be harmful to your health ?)* *- Savoir is also used with an infinitive to say that one can do something / is able to* → Il ne sait pas parler français. Quel dommage !
5) rapide and **vite** are also often misused. They both mean *quick / fast.* ***Rapide*** is an adjective and is therefore used in conjunction with nouns. As it is an adjective, it agrees with the noun that it describes. → Dans ce restaurant, le service est toujours *rapide.* Les Ferrari sont des voitures très ***rapides***. ***Vite,*** however, is an adverb. It is therefore used in conjunction with a verb and it never changes form. → Mon cousin court ***vite***. *("vite" is describing the action of running).* Il est ***rapide***. *("rapide" is describing my cousin).*
6) « ma famille » (like « ***tout le monde)*** is grammatically SINGULAR even though it has a plural meaning as more than one person makes up a family. → ***Ma famille*** est allée à un concert hier soir. ***Tout le monde*** a applaudi le chanteur.
7) La raison pour laquelle *means the reason why (it can be used in the plural too)* → **La raison pour laquelle** il a séché les cours aujourd'hui est qu'il n'avait pas fait ses devoirs. *(the reason why he skived school today is that he had not done his homework)*
8) ***un avertissement*** is *a warning BUT* ***une publicité*** is *an advert.*
9) ***épouser*** means *to wed or to marry someone.* ***Se marier*** *means to get married.* → Ma mère ***a épousé*** mon père. Ils ***se sont mariés*** à l'église de leur village.
10) Even though the word **le *temps*** always has a « s », it is SINGULAR. It means the *weather* or the *time* depending on the context.

Chapter 7

Answers to practice questions

Chapter 1:
PAPER 1

Page 10: C

Page 11 : 1- FAUX – L'augmentation du nombre de voitures
2. FAUX – le problème de circulation déjà existant
3. VRAI – souvent mortels
4. FAUX – malheureusement, le concept de covoiturage ne semble pas très populaire.
5. FAUX- Beaucoup d'entre vous n'en sont toujours pas satisfaits.

Page 12: 1D / 2F / 3A / 4E / 5C / 6B

Page 13: 1D / 2H / 3C / 4A / 5G / 6F / 7E / 8B

Page 14: 1E / 2D / 3G / 4B / 5H / 6F / 7A / 8C

Page 16: 1) vieux jeu / 2. je me trompe / 3C / 4. (mes) parents / 5. (ma) mère

Page 17: 1. en effet / 2. grâce à / 3. voire / 4. ainsi / 5. afin de (pour) / 6. par ailleurs
7. notamment / 8. bien que

Page 18: A) 1. mais / 2. plutôt que / 3. lorsque / 4. pour
B) 1. sous prétexte que / 2. aussi / 3. à force d' / 4. en effet / 5. mais
6. pourtant / 7 en plus / 8. bien que

Page 20 a 33:

TEXTE A
1.C
2. pallier à la misère quotidienne
3. la pauvreté et la précarité grandissantes / l'augmentation de la pauvreté et de la précarité
4. pour faire face à l'augmentation des prix pour l'aide alimentaire
5. A et D
6. afin de
7. mais
8. en dépit de
9. auxquelles

TEXTE B
10. le coût des services vétérinaires / l'emplacement des cliniques animales
11. (leurs) chiens
12. qu'il n'y a pas d'accès aux vétérinaires / pas d'accès à l'éducation à la propriété animale
13. G
14. E
15. A
16. F
17. pour éviter les naissances non voulues
18. élaborer une stratégie nationales pour les chiens

TEXTE C

19. B
20. FAUX - Préparer la fête en collaboration avec ses voisins
21. FAUX – (obtenir les autorisations nécessaires auprès de la municipalité) au moins un mois en avance
22. G
23. A
24. E
25. F

TEXTE D

26. Ils ont émigré en occident
27. D
28. Difficulté pour obtenir un visa de tourisme
29. FAUX- poussées par la famille
30. FAUX – Certaines quittent même leurs petits copains pour un modou-modou qu'elles connaissent à peine
31. FAUX- Les émigrés sont loin d'être majoritaires
32. Son union est un mariage d'amour
33. D
34. F
35. A
36. H
37. G
38. Parce qu'ils sont le fruit / ils sont nés de grossesses extra-conjugales
39. C
40. Les femmes
41. Ma tante
42. L'adolescente
43. Son mari
44. Leurs nouveau-nés

TEXTE E

45. D
46. B
47. – vivre une expérience concrète de solidarité internationale
- Faire l'acquisition d'un bagage de connaissances sur la réalité des pays en développement
48. Arides
49. Hostile
50. Zones arides
51. (leurs) terres
52. Production locale insuffisante pour combler les besoins alimentaires / manque de nourriture
53. C
54. D
55. B
56. F
57. Les outils pédagogiques
58. Les profs / les professeurs

Chapter 2 :
PAPER 2

Page 43: a) 1 / 8 / 12 - b) 1 / 11 / 12 / 14 - c) 4 / 16 - d) 3 / 19 - e) 9 - f) 15
g) 10 / 12 / 16 / 20 - h) 6 - i) 7 - j) 2 / 5 / 11 / 12 / 14 / 17 / 18

Page 47: 1d / 2h / 3b / 4g / 5a / 6e / 7c / 8f

Page 55: 1e – assurez-vous / vérifiez
2b – ne laissez jamais / assurez-vous
3h – faites / arrêtez-vous
4a – pensez / n'oubliez pas
5d – emportez
6g – prévoyez / préparez / emportez
7c – prenez / demandez
8f – soyez / chargez-vous / facilitez-vous

Page 68: 1d / 2o / 3s / 4k / 5a / 6p / 7b / 8j / 9q / 10r / 11t / 12h / 13e / 14n
15l / 16s / 17c / 18g

Page 69: 1. tout à coup / 2. après quelques minutes / 3. d'abord / 4. puis / 5. mais
6. quand / 7. de plus / 8. c'est alors qu'

Page 71:

1. guide de recommandations ou article
2. lettre officielle
3. journal intime
4. discours
5. lettre officielle
6. lettre informelle
7. lettre / compte rendu / rapport / déclaration à la police / article / éditorial
8. lettre à un ami / guide de recommandations
9. article
10. discours
11. dissertation / discours
12. lettre à un ami / guide de recommandations / discours
13. journal intime
14. discours / tract / appel
15. lettre / discours

Page 73: 1e / 2g / 3c / 4i / 5k / 6f / 7a / 8l / 9h / 10j / 11b / 12 d
1e / 2c / 3b / 4f / 5a / 6d

Page 77: 1. village / 2. perdu (isolé) / 3. a plu / 4. vêtements / 5. chaussures
6. parents / 7. prêter / 8. voiture / 9. amis / 10. a faim / 11. manger
12. difficiles / 13. travail / 14. travaillé / 15. l'argent / 16. livre
17. être embarrassé / 18. lycée / 19. nul / 20. rates / 21. pleurer
22. grasse matinée

Page 79: 1c / 2h / 3i / 4g / 5f / 6a / 7d / 8b or e / 9b or e

1. tout à coup / soudain
2. cependant / pourtant
3. bien que
4. quand
5. puis / ensuite
6. quand
7. d'ailleurs
8. cependant

Page 80: 1. comme / 2. grâce à / 3. sous le coup de / 4. à force de / 5. en réponse à
6. comme / 7. sous l'emprise de / 8. sous prétexte que / 9. à défaut de
10. dès l'instant où

Chapter 5:
GRAMMAR

Page 114: 1. ont / 2. veulent – énervent / 3. choisis / 4. comprends – met – a
5. produisons – polluent / mangeons – grossissons / 7. faites / 8. a – peut
9. continue / 10. fait / 11. réussit / 12. partons / 13. sait – échoue
14. écris / 15. mentez / 16. interdisons

Page 118: 1. ont fait / 2. n'a pas voté – a perdu / 3. a appelé / 4. ont eu / 5. a conduit
6. a remporté / 7. sommes allés - sommes restés / 8. s'est produit – a heurté
9. me suis disputée / 10. as lu

Page 120: 1. s'est réunies / 2. avons offert / 3. a ouverts / 4. a eu / 5. a mises
6. ont joué / 7. se sont bien amusés / 8. n'ont pas voulu / 9. a sorti
10. a regardés / 11. sommes allés / 12. suis tombé(e) / 13. je me suis cassé
14. a prêté / 15. ai oubliées

Page 122: 1. était – habitait / 2. rangeait / 3. buvait – semblait / 4. neigeait – faisait
5. preniez / 6. s'apprêtaient

Page 123: 1. sommes allés – faisait / 2. n'ai jamais compris – étaient partis
3. ne pouvaient pas – n'existait pas
4. s'est produit – a fait – traversaient – a heurtés
5. s'est rassemblée – étaient installés – sommes arrivés – avons joué – avons battus – sont restés – ont regardé – a sorties *ou* avaient sorties – discutaient
6. ont-ils cru / 7. avais révisé – ai obtenu
8. avez-vous remarqué – êtes rentré(e / s / es) / 9. avait bu – a pris
10. était – était monté – avait refusé – étaient – se trouvaient

Page 125: 1. annoncera / 2. iront / 3. viendrez / 4. finiront / 5. se lèvera
6. saurai – écrirai – enverrai

Page 126: 1. feriez / 2. passerais / 3. lirions / 4. enverrais / 5. n'auraient plus
6. augmenterait

Page 127: 1. irons / 2. regarderai / 3. ferais / 4. pourriez / 5. voudrais / 6. viendront
7. auras / 8. dirais / 9. serait / 10. n'acceptera jamais / 11. boirait
12. pleuvra

Page 130: 1. comportez-vous / 2. fais / 3. rends / 4. allons / 5. écrivons / 6. évite
8. abonnons-nous / 8. prenez / 9. range / 10. mettons-nous / 11. pars
12. n'aie pas / 13. dépêchez-vous / 14. choisis / 15. battez-vous

Page 131: 1. Si j'avais le temps, j'irais en France.
2. Si je gagne au loto, j'arrêterai de travailler.
3. Si je te vois, je te donnerai l'argent.
4. Si j'avais fini plus tôt , je serais venu(e) te voir.
5. Si j'étais allé(e) aux toilettes avant l'examen, je n'aurais pas été obligé(e) de quitter la salle.
6. Si j'étais un homme politique, j'interdirais l'école le samedi matin.

Page 133: 1. prenions / 2. rentre / 3. lisiez / 4. réservions / 5. écrives / 6. connaisse
7. aide / 8. se mette

Page 137: 1. subj / 2. ind – présent / 3. subj / 4. subj (subj passé) / 5. ind – futur
6. subj

1. obtiennent / 2. réussissiez / 3. soit / 4. quitte / 5. connaisse / 6. dormes

Page 141: 1. Cet appartement ***a été loué*** par l'agence immobilière.
2. Cette émission ***était suivie*** par des milliers de téléspectateurs tous les mois.
3. Il faut que les enfants défavorisés ***soient*** mieux ***protégés*** par la loi.
4. Des mesures efficaces pour lutter contre l'inflation ***seront prises*** par le gouvernement.
5. La caissière du magasin ***aurait été menacée*** par des hommes cagoulés.
6. Les paroles de cette nouvelle chanson ***ont été écrites*** par Sébastien Lirique.
7. J'***ai été opéré*** de l'appendicite par le plus grand chirurgien de Paris.
8. Des ossements humains ***ont été retrouvés*** par des chercheurs sur ce site archéologique.

Page 144: 1. Ce discours s'adresse aux adolescents.
2. Les hommes politiques commencent à se rendre compte de l'importance de la protection de la planète.
3. Les médecins vont essayer de cloner de plus en plus d'humains et d'animaux.
4. Si le centre sportif était ouvert, nous bénéficierions d'une gamme d'activités.
5. Il est difficile de comprendre pourquoi les terroristes tuent des femmes et des enfants.
6. Il est essentiel d'empêcher les enfants de regarder des émissions violentes à la télé.
7. Il a besoin de persuader ses parents de le laisser partir en vacances avec ses amis.
2. Les élèves doivent s'habituer à travailler avec des ordinateurs.
3. La publicité encourage les gens à acheter des choses inutiles.
4. Elle s'obstine à choisir des vêtements qui sont chers et qui ne lui vont jamais.

Page 146: 1. équilibrée – saine / 2. monoparentales / 3. douces – nocives - dures
4. gentille - mignonne / 5. sélectifs / 6. injuste – quotidienne - difficile
7. mauvaise – prochaines / 8. sympathique

Page 150: 1. **Nous y** sommes allés. / 2. Le prof **leur** a demandé de se taire.
3. Il faudrait que je **lui en** achète <u>une</u>. / 4. Ils **l'**ont regardé<u>e</u> tard hier soir.
5. Il s'**en** ai acheté <u>trois</u>. / 6. Tu **la lui** as revendu<u>e</u> ?
7. Le conseil d'orientation **leur** donne toujours de bons conseils.
8. Demande **lui** de t'**en** prêter ! / 9. Il **y** croit. / 10. Je **les** connais.

Page 154: 1. dont / 2. ce qu' / 3. que – avec lesquelles / 4. ce qu' / 5. qui
6. avec qui *ou* à côté de qui / 7. qui / 8. que
9. où *ou* avec laquelle *ou* pour laquelle / 10. ce qui / 11. dont
12. dont / 13. ce qui / 14. où / 15. auquel / 16. dont / 17. ce qui
18. grâce à qui / 19. auquel / 20. que

Page 157: ce verre – ce stylo – cette image – cet enfant – cette fleur
cette fille – ces histoires – cet homme – ce hasard – cet historien
ces gens – cette heure – ce jour-là – ce pantalon – ces messieurs

1. votre / 2. tes / 3. son / 4. leur / 5. ton

Page 158: 1. tous – toutes / 2. tous / 3. tout / 4. toute / 5. tout / 6. toutes

Page 159: 1. à – près – en – pour – à – dans – sur
2. dans – à – devant – en – avec – pendant – chez
3. sur – entre – sous - à

Chapter 6:

VOCABULARY

Page 177: 1. préparer / 2. révéler / 3. commettre / 4. annoncer / 5. partager
6. se sentir – éprouver / 7. se procurer / 8. mener / 9. s'habituer
10. Puis-je vous aider? / 11. causer / 12. annoncer ou avouer – je vais être privé de sortie.

Page 178: 1G / 2k / 3m / 4f / 5d/ 6a / 7o / 8b / 9l / 10n / 11e / 12 h / 13c / 14i / 15j

List of useful websites

Newspapers and magazines

Reading the News regularly will help you improve your vocabulary and reading skills as well as keeping you informed.

www.lemonde.fr
www.liberation.fr
www.leprogres.fr
www.lavoixdunord.fr
www.leparisien.fr
www.l'express.fr
www.lefigaro.fr

www.lesoir.be
www.tdg.ch
www.lactualite.com
www.lexpress.to
www.phosphore.com
www.courrierinternational.com
www.parismatch.com

News programmes on the net

Following the news regularly will also help you develop your vocabulary and keep you up-to date with what is happening in the francophone world. Moreover, even though your listening skill is not formally assessed in the exam, it is an integral part of language learning,

www.tf1.fr
www.france2.fr
www.m6.fr

www.rfi.fr
www.tv5.org

Grammar websites

www.polarfle.fr
http//french.about.com
www.bbc.co.uk

Topical websites

You will find a lot of vocabulary related to specific topics on these websites. The good thing is as well that this vocabulary is used in context.

www.sijefume.com
www.pubstv.com
www.developpement-durable.gouv.fr
www.defipourlaterre.org/
www.evene.fr

www.sante-jeunesse-sports.gouv.fr
www.justice.gouv.fr
www.phosphore.com
www.sos-racisme.org
www.jukebo.fr *(to listen to French Music)*

NB: *This list is not exhaustive- it only gives you a few examples of useful sites. I am sure that you know other useful websites too.*

List of useful resources
References

A) VOCABULARY:

- ***Mot à Mot*** – *Humberstone*
- ***Vocabulaire progressif du français*** – *published by Clé Internationale*

B) GRAMMAR:

- ***Conjugaison française*** **–** éditions Librio
- ***Reprise*** **–** *Mcgraw-Hill*
- **Schaum's French Grammar** – *published by Schaum*
- ***Practice in French Grammar*** – M. Gross – Nelson Thornes publisher
- ***Grammaire progressive du français*** – *published by Clé Internationale*
- ***Conjugaison progressive du français*** – *published by Clé Internationale*
- ***L'exercisier*** – *published by PUG*

C) AUTRES RESSOURCES DIVERSES:

- **Les Dossiers de l'actualité** (*journal pour les lycéens*)
- **Phosphore** (*magazine pour les lycéens*)
- **Okapi** (*magazine- SL students)*
- **Le Monde**
- **L'express**
- **Science et vie junior**

Recommended reading list

Whether you are studying the language at Higher or Standard level (*although it is essential if you are doing HL*), I would recommend (*if it is not too late!!*) that you read as much as possible and as often as possible in the target language. Reading some francophone newspapers regularly would be a good start as not only will it help widen your range of vocabulary, it will also keep you up-to date with what's is happening in the world and in the francophone world. However, it is also important *(and this not just for the purpose of the exam preparation!)* to read books written in French as much as you can. They can be French/ francophone classics or contemporary francophone books. If you are tempted, but don't know what books to look for, below are a few suggestions.

Alors….**Bonne lecture**!

- **Anouilh**: *Antigone*
- **Bâ:** *Une si longue lettre*
- **Balzac :** *Le père Goriot / Le colonel Chabert / La peau de chagrin*
- **Bazin :** *Vipère au poing*
- **Camus :** *L'étranger / La Peste / Les Justes*
- **Cardinale:** *La clé sur la porte*
- **Chédid :** *Le message / La maison sans racine*
- **Colette :** *Le bé en herbe*
- **Delerm :** *La première gorgée de bière et autre plaisirs minuscules*
- **De Vigan :** *NO et moi*
- **Duras :** *L'Amant / Hiroshima mon amour / Moderato Cantabile*
- **Flaubert** : *Madame Bovary / 3 Contes*
- **Fournier :** *Le Grand Meaulnes*
- **Gary :** *La vie devant soi*
- **Grimbert :** *Un secret*
- **Hugo :** *Le dernier jour d'un condamné*
- **Ionesco** : La Cantatrice chauve / La leçon
- **Laye** : *L'enfant noir*
- **Le Clézio** *: Désert / l'Africain*
- **Maupassant :** *Une vie / Boule de Suif et autres contes / nouvelles*
- **Modiano :** *Place de l'étoile / Dora Bruder*
- **Molière :** pièces
- **Nothomb** : *Stupeur et tremblement*
- **Orsenna :** *La grammaire est une chanson douce / Madame Ba*
- **Oyono :** *Une vie de boy*
- **Quint :** *Effroyables jardins*
- **Rochefort :** *Les petits enfants du siècle*
- **Sagan :** *Bonjour tristesse*
- **Saint Exupéry :** *Le Petit Prince*
- **Sarraute :** *Enfance*
- **Sartre :** *Le mur / les mots*
- **Schmitt :** *Oscar et la dame rose / Monsieur Ibrahim et les Fleurs du Coran / L'enfant de Noé / Le sumo qui ne voulait pas grossir*
- **Simenon :** la série des Maigret
- **Siji :** *Balzac et la Petite tailleuse Chinoise*
- **Stendhal :** *Le rouge et le noir*
- **Troyat :** *La neige en deuil / Aliocha*
- **Voltaire :** *Candide*
- **Zola :** *Thèrèse Raquin / Au bonheur des dames / l'Assommoir*

+ a few suggestions of poems from the following :

- Baudelaire
- Verlaine
- Prévert
- Césaire
- Apollinaire
- Senghor
- Rimbaud

NOTES

Acknowledgements

Most of the texts in this guide are the author's own, with the exception of:

1. Les restos du cœur en difficulté - *Reproduit avec l'aimable autorisation de: http://www.zurbains.com*
2. Animaux de Compagnie au Canada - Article adapté du site : http://fr.wspa.ca – avec l'aimable autorisation de la WSPA.
3. Étapes d'organisation d'une fête - Texte reproduit avec autorisation - http://www.fetedesvoisins.qc.ca
4. Au Sénégal, la solitude des femmes d'immigrés - *Adapté (avec l'aimable permission de l'auteure) de l'article d'Aurélie Fontaine sur le site : http://www.rue89.com*
5. Au-delà des mots, il y a les gestes - Texte reproduit et adapté avec l'aimable autorisation du réseau in-Terre- Actif – www.in-terre-actif.com
6. Le discours du Général de Gaulle (*Paper 2 section*)
7. *Conseils pour voyager avec de jeunes enfants* – p.55 (adapted from the brochure « *Bon voyage mais…* » from the Canadian Tourist Office.
8. The texts on page 59 and 60 were inspired by the article published in *Les Clés de l'Actualité* of December 2002.
9. L'esclavage domestique en France - *Extrait reproduit avec l'aimable autorisation du Comité contre l'esclavage (http://www.esclavagemoderne.org)*
10. Premier procès pour esclavage domestique en France - Catherine Lagrange, édité par Clément Guillou - http://www.rmc.fr/editorial/131561/premier-proces-pour-esclavage-domestique-en-france/ - toutes les démarches ont été faites pour obtenir la permission.
11. Moi Rania, esclave en France de mes 10 ans à mes 20 ans - http://www.bladi.net/esclavage-moderne-maroc-france.html - reproduit avec permission –
12. Les photos du chapitre 4 ont été reproduites avec permission. Merci notamment à Christphoto et Benoit et Christine Delesalle.
13. Any pictures come from *Microsoft Word Clip Art*

This Guide could not have been written without the support and encouragement of many people.

The re-edition of this guide took much longer than originally anticipated mainly due to a series of major technical difficulties. I would like to thank Simon Watts (from Tula / OSC) for his support and continued patience and for helping me carry on and not give up when adversity kept striking.

Thanks to Kim Polgreen, David Russell and the OSC team for entrusting me to come up with the original version of this guide (5 years ago or so now), the first Language B guide, which then became the template and framework for both the old and revised versions of the OSC Spanish Revision guides.

Special thanks to Benoit Delesalle for being a brilliantly supportive friend and keeping me going when I needed it most.

Thanks to all of my 6th Form students who have once again been guinea pigs. This guide is for students, primarily, so their feedback and advice has been invaluable.

À mes parents, who would have loved to have seen this new version.

À mon petit Romain, for keeping me smiling.

À Benco, I miss you so much !

*This book was designed with students in mind i.e. with **you** in mind. So if you have any comments or suggestions that could be useful for a revised edition in the future, please send these comments or suggestions to Marie-Laure Delvallée care of osc@osc-ib.com*

CPI Antony Rowe
Chippenham, UK
2016-09-16 13:17